DAN CHAUCER

GEOFFREY CHAUCER

From a copy of Thomas Occleve, *De Regimine Principum,*
executed in England, early fifteenth century.

DAN CHAUCER

An Introduction to the Poet, His Poetry and His Times

By

HENRY DWIGHT SEDGWICK

"Thorgh me men gon into that blysful place
Of hertes hele and dedly woundes cure;
Thorgh me men gon unto the welle of grace,
There grene and lusty May shal evere endure.
This is the wey to al good aventure.
Be glad, thow redere, and thy sorwe of-caste;
Al open am I—passe in, and sped thee faste!"

THE BOBBS-MERRILL COMPANY

Indianapolis   *Publishers*   New York

COPYRIGHT, 1934
BY THE BOBBS-MERRILL COMPANY

FIRST EDITION

Printed in the United States of America

PRINTED AND BOUND BY
BRAUNWORTH & CO., INC.
BOOK MANUFACTURERS
BROOKLYN, NEW YORK

DEDICATED

to

M.M.S., H.D.S. II, F.H.S., A.S., R.M.S. II

Poetry is the breath and finer spirit of all knowledge.

WORDSWORTH.

CONTENTS

INTRODUCTION

For some poets, poetry constitutes an ideal realm, builded by the imagination; and this actual world is but the quarry, the emporium, the junk shop, in which the creative imagination finds its materials. For them, poetry is a kingdom of the spirit, tenanted by spirits, and at its threshold, unable to pass over, the dull of soul stumble and stop. As these poets, however unwilling, were created out of the dust of the earth, they can not wholly ignore this world of forces and resistances, of two-legged, four-pawed and winged creatures, of elementary appetites and satieties, but they find it far less interesting, and, as best they can, turn their backs upon it; they have no pride in animal life. Such poets are primarily poets, and but in a secondary degree human beings.

Of such Edmund Spenser was one. He is primarily a poet. His muse is angelical, and as she strikes her lyre, moral ideas, didactic precepts, holy thoughts, shape themselves into the forms of fair ladies and lovely knights, and go their beatific ways. Spenser lives in the world of fancy, and seldom puts foot to the ground. As for Shakespeare, I think that he, too, is primarily a poet, more concerned with the world of his invention than with Stratford and London, more interested in his own handiwork, and perhaps for cause, than in that of the Lord God. And there is many another English poet, Coleridge, Shelley, Tennyson, Swinburne, for example, who are poets first and human beings secondly.

Geoffrey Chaucer, on the other hand, is primarily a human being, one that found *nil humanum alienum,* and but secondly a poet. His muse is not winged. She walks upon this earth and loves it; she jogs upon our muddy footpath

way and merrily hents the style, she clambers over the fences
of joy and sorrow, holding on her head with shapely hand
her pail, full of the milk of human kindness, and never
spills a drop. She is an earth-born and earth-loving creature.
Chaucer, I assert, was a man before he was a poet, and
among men essentially an Englishman, more so perhaps than
any English poet since; Shakespeare is too universal, Milton
too moral, Wordsworth too philosophic, Keats too sensuous,
Byron too unreasonable, Shelley too divine. And in point
of chronology, Chaucer was the first real Englishman, for
up to his time there had been no perfect blending of races,
no true English breed; the famous men that we call English,
Alfred the Great, William the Conqueror, Richard Cœur de
Lion, were Saxon, or Norman, or Plantagenet. The Black
Prince, Chaucer's senior by some dozen years, was to all in-
tents and purposes a Frenchman, and Wycliffe had but a
portion and not the most characteristic portion of the English essence, whereas Dan Chaucer was English all English,
athwart the diaphragm from skin to skin, and proud of England. You will find that pride of his in England all through
The Canterbury Tales, in verse, in thought, in the personages, the Knight, the Squire, the Host, the Poor Parson,
and so on. That pride in England has been expressed by
Shakespeare, and as he has put his immortal praises into
the mouth of Chaucer's patron and friend, John of Gaunt,
I will quote them here, partly because beginners in Chaucer
should start from a high standard in poetry, and also because, if you will bear it in mind, you will find that same
English pride that Shakespeare has beating in Chaucer's
heart:

    This royal throne of kings, this scepter'd isle,
    This earth of majesty, this seat of Mars,
    This other Eden, demi-paradise;

This fortress built by Nature for herself
Against infection and the hand of war;
This happy breed of men, this little world,
This precious stone set in the silver sea,
Which serves it in the office of a wall,
Or as a moat defensive to a house,
Against the envy of less happier lands;
This blessed plot, this earth, this realm, this England,
This nurse, this teeming womb of royal kings,
Fear'd for their breed, and famous by their birth,
Renowned for their deeds as far from home,
For Christian service and true chivalry,
As is the sepulchre in stubborn Jewry
Of the world's ransom, blessed Mary's Son;
This land of such dear souls, this dear dear land.

As I say, this same love and pride, expressed to be sure in
quite a different way, pervades the atmosphere of the Pilgrimage to Canterbury, and makes it the first great English
epic. And because Chaucer was primarily a man and an
Englishman, before he was a poet, I shall tell what I can of
his life, so far as the meager records allow, of his goings
and comings, of his reading, his studies, his admired authors,
of his business in the employ of the state, of his foreign
journeys, and of his friends; and, in order to give substance
to the scattered items concerning him that we possess, I
shall introduce such history of the times as shall seem befitting, for, even a scanty knowledge of the world in which he
moved and of the events among which he found himself,
gives to light-minded readers a greater interest in him and in
his poetry.

This is not a scholar's book, Reader, and if you are too
serious-minded to find content in my amateurish, epicurean
approach to a great poet, why, do not read this book, but
go direct to the Gates of Scholarship, where, indeed, by a

leisurely circuitous way it is my ambition to lead those that shall have the patience to read me. But if you are very serious, or impatient, knock at once upon the Scholars' door.

To a humbler hospitality I invite you. I write for boys and girls at school or college, who feel that some information about Chaucer is the necessary part of an academic education; for women who think that Chaucer should have his niche in every proper discipline of culture; for bachelors, who in adolescent moods are drawn to poetry and, finding Keats's verse too sugared and Shelley's veins too full of ichor, ask whether there is not some man, more like other men, who has written poetry; and for everybody, who has but little leisure, lawyers, bankers, doctors, merchants, clergymen, women with children and household cares, who can spare but an hour or two at most every other evening, and wish to become acquainted with the great palace of English literature, and before deciding upon a favorite haunt, think it best to peregrinate through all the chief halls and corridors, and see what most suits their taste. And how vast the palace of English literature is, with epic and drama, with novel and essay, with ballads, odes and sonnets, with stories, sermons, biographies, histories, with works that utter forth all passions, moods, tastes, whims, fancies, from the spiritual to the bestial!

What a glorious sanctuary of refuge after *swinking* in this workaday world of actuality! The range is so vast and the reader's leisure so brief, *the lyf so short, the craft so long to lerne,* that I am hoping that the moderation, the humility, as well as the limited knowledge, of the dilettante, may be more serviceable to such persons as I have described in their decision of how much time to give to Chaucer, than the insistence, the copiousness and the justifiable assurance of the Scholar.

I shall try to set forth for ordinary people an ordinary

man's admiration for a most excellent artist, his enthusiasm for the English qualities that radiate through Chaucer's poetry, his pleasure in an extraordinarily skilful story-teller, his liking for a jolly good fellow, his gratitude for poetry, often tender, often pathetic, often shining with the illumination of genius, and always, or almost always, charged with common sense, as indeed a typical English book must be. And I shall follow the scholars obediently, according to my lights, in their less recondite expositions, but in offering any opinion other than my own upon Chaucer's poetical qualities I shall leave the scholars, in case there should be a divergence between them and the poets, and follow the poets, for many poets have expressed themselves about Chaucer, and poets are the best judges of poetry. Samuel Taylor Coleridge says: "I take unceasing delight in Chaucer. His manly cheerfulness is especially delicious to me in my old age. How exquisitely tender he is, and yet how perfectly free from the least touch of sickly melancholy or morbid drooping! The sympathy of the poet with the subjects of his poetry is particularly remarkable.—[this] Chaucer—does without any effort, merely by the inborn kindly joyousness of his nature." And my ambition would be to help the reader to take "unceasing delight" in Chaucer's "manly cheerfulness" and in the "inborn kindly joyousness of his nature." These two delightful qualities are nobly conspicuous all through English literature, in the greatest and in the less great, in Shakespeare, in Isaac Walton, in Henry Fielding, Oliver Goldsmith, in Robbie Burns, in Charles Lamb, in Walter Scott, Dickens and Stevenson; they strengthen and vivify the human spirit, they comfort and console, and one can not do better than make their acquaintance at the very source and fountain where they first show themselves.

It fills us with wonder, and some of us with awe, to plant a seed in the ground, and after the sun and the rain have blessed the spot, watch the little shoot rise from its winter bed, and then the stalk, the flower, the fruit; but the study of poetry is still more wonderful, a verse swells and expands in the human heart, it fortifies the soul, it raises a higher roof, it fans a freer air, it may open a window on the deep blue serenity that overarches us and reveal to us what men mean by *God,* or, perchance, it may open on this variegated world to show us how beautiful, how gay, how comic, how pathetic, how tragic, a world it is. I am not sure that the first window is open in Chaucer, but the second is, and open wide.

It is not for me to praise Professor Robinson's edition of Chaucer—that, the scholars are doing and have done— but I may thank him for permission to use his text, and I do thank him heartily. Also I thank Miss C. F. E. Spurgeon for permission to quote from her admirable collection of criticisms on Chaucer; it is most interesting and enter- taining to learn what poets and men of letters have said of him during these five hundred years. I have also borrowed from Gilchrist's *Life of William Blake,* that poet's descrip- tion of the Canterbury pilgrims in his explanation of his painting. In short, I have taken from other men's labors— from Professors Kittredge, Lowes, French and many more—all that I could.

DAN CHAUCER

DAN CHAUCER

CHAPTER I

On Chaucerian Scholars

CHAUCERIAN scholars are enviable men; their lives, their interests, their values, are different from those of ordinary people. They spend their days and nights in patient, laborious, triumphant travail to extend their knowledge, and ours, concerning the Master. They dig among the wastes of time to discover in what year he was born; what his duties were as *vallectus dilectus* in the household of Prince Lionel and of King Edward III; whether he loved his wife; which he read first, Ovid, or the *Roman de la Rose;* whether such a verse he borrowed from Guillaume de Machaut or hit upon it for himself; whether an allusion to Cicero comes direct or through Macrobius; and such other similar matters as occupy scholars and justify their ways—all interesting, but more so to serious-minded students than to such readers as I have in mind. Do not for a moment think that I would deter any one from taking the steep and narrow road to scholarship, I merely suggest that those who may be indisposed to climb to the summit, whence they shall see all that there is to be seen, should take the sinuous by-path that I offer them, which, it is my hope, will lead them to a noble prospect, much less wide-spread but I think scarcely less beautiful.

And, on the way, let me point out some of the famous scholars: There is Thomas Tyrwhitt, a contemporary of Doctor Johnson; you shall not have read four or three pages, but you will see how pleasant, how sensible, how intelligent a guide he is. There is William Godwin, into whose *Life of Chaucer* you will look, not to see the vagaries and waywardness of statement for which scholars chide him, but because he was Mary Shelley's father. There is Doctor Furnivall, founder of the Chaucer Society, Professor F. J. Child of revered memory, the Dutch ten Brink, Thomas R. Lounsbury, the Reverend W. W. Skeat, and Ward, Pollard, Kittredge, Manly, Lowes, Robinson, a shining company of studious men who have gained honor in service of the Master, and many another less well known. If you become a very serious student, I dare say that you will have to see with your own eyes the eighty odd Chaucerian manuscripts, housed in London, Cambridge, Oxford, or wherever they may be, and the editions by old Caxton, by Wynkyn de Worde, by Thynne, chief clerk of the kitchen to King Henry VIII, and perhaps you will touch with your own hands the Royal Wardrobe Rolls, the Issue Rolls of the Exchequer, the Customs Rolls, and other wonderful far-off things. In any event, you will read what the critics, what Dryden, what Matthew Arnold, what James Russell Lowell, have said of Chaucer.

Of all these high matters you will find but little here; it would be forthputting if I were to mix myself in them. My purpose is quite other than that of the scholars. My justification, if I have one, is that sometimes an outsider, a dilettante if you will, sees a great poet, such as Chaucer, in a more detached manner than the scholar does, sees him with more dispassionate eyes, and so can better help his readers to give Chaucer his proper place in English literature, that is, he is better able impartially to judge Chaucer's deserts and Chaucer's inadequacies, for we do wrong to a poet, I think, and certainly to the poet's readers, if we extol him for qualities that he does not possess, or slur over his faults;

[18]

mispraise, quite as much as unjust depreciation, distorts our values and muddies the clear delight of our pleasure in poetry.

The great Chaucerian scholars, some of whose names I have mentioned, have studied Chaucer because they loved him, or else they have come to love him because they have studied him, they are partisans, they proceed from general knowledge to niceties, from niceties to enthusiasm, and from enthusiasm sometimes to extravagance. At least I have read of scholars busied with some great personage in literature, such as Montaigne, or Cervantes, who have given rein unduly to an extravagant admiration. So it may be with respect to Chaucer. Some of these scholars may have been carried away by their great learning, and by their enthusiasm, to praise and magnify Chaucer, I will not say more than he deserves, for I am not qualified to pronounce such a judgment, but to a point where the commonplace reader, who reads poetry for the mere pleasure of it, will hardly go along with them. Scholars are lovers and, like lovers, perceive beauties and delights and wonders that the fancy-free do not see. And, quite apart from the question whether the scholar or the dilettante is the more impartial judge, Chaucerian scholars discuss abstruse matters that belong only to scholars and to students who entertain an ambition to become scholars. On the slightest provocation they run back to Anglo-Saxon grammar for an inflection, to Norman-French for a pronunciation; they will thread any labyrinth of medieval romance to track a simile, and study rent rolls and epitaphs in order to discover the original reeve or shipman, from whom, as they surmise, Chaucer may have drawn his portraits. Oblivious, or possibly disdainful, of the outside world, scholars constitute themselves into a sort of club where they play games with one another concerning the scansion of a verse or the origin of a phrase;

[19]

and an exceedingly pleasant club it must be, because all the members worship their honored Master, and the Master is such a good fellow, his humanity so broad and generous, his irony so delicious, his verse so melodious, and many of his *dramatis personæ* such rantipoling characters, that he attracts persons of like disposition as himself, kindly, gentle, well-mannered men. But when they come to publish their dissertations, comments, criticisms and suggestions, they often fail to remember that persons outside this club do not understand what they are talking about.

It is my ambition, then, not merely to narrate Chaucer's life, and give such a background of historical events as may be pertinent, but also to suggest such an estimate of the poet's work as will seem to a dispassionate reader, who is neither a partisan nor a detractor, reasonable and just.

CHAPTER II

The Triumph of English

GEOFFREY CHAUCER, it is my belief as I have said, was the first true Englishman, for before his time the governing class was French, while burghers, yeomen, serfs, were what we call Anglo-Saxon; the two parts had not yet been welded into one, there was no definite national unity, there were no real Englishmen; the most you can say is that there were French-speaking islanders and English-speaking islanders. We often complain of the inevitableness of fate, of an inexorable determinism, but that is only when we look back, for if we look forward we behold uncertainty facing a hundred ways. If an envoy from Genoa, Prague or Seville had gone to England at the time of Chaucer's birth, he would have written home that it lay in the toss of a penny whether the infant genius would write English poetry or French, and that in his judgment it would be French.

King Edward III was a Frenchman. You may run up the list of his crowned ancestors to William the Conqueror and you will find that every king married a Frenchwoman, except one who married a Castilian lady, and her mother was French. The court, the aristocracy, the great officers of state, spoke French; proceedings in Parliament, in the courts of law, were in French; boys of the higher classes were taught French at home and in the schools; burghers, with the social bee in their bonnets, learned French. The upper clergy and scholars, when busy with serious affairs, wrote and spoke Latin, the international language, otherwise they employed French. The speech of fashionable society

[21]

was purely French. For a hundred and fifty years after the conquest the Kings of England had held Normandy, and now for near two hundred years they had held and were holding the Duchy of Aquitaine; England never thought of these lands as foreign provinces, she strode the Channel like a Colossus. The barons and feudal lords, who owned castles and broad acres in England, had much more in common with the barons and feudal lords of Normandy or Aquitaine, than they had with the common people beneath them; their culture was French, their feudal system was French, they thought their thoughts in French. There was, indeed, a difference between the French language as spoken in Paris and as spoken in England, but not so great as that between the dialects of Essex and Wessex, of Surrey and Lancaster.

And only a few years before Chaucer's birth, Edward III claimed the crown of France, not as a foreigner but as the French heir, and he assumed the title of King of France. He was a grandson of Philippe le Bel, and nearer of kin to the last deceased monarch of the Capetian dynasty than the other claimant, Philippe of Valois. Suppose that the French lawyers had not interposed the Salic Law, had not hauled it in for the nonce, or that King Edward had conquered the Kingdom of France and set his throne in Paris, as head of an empire that extended from the Pyrenees to the Orkney Islands; it is not hard to imagine that he might well have succeeded. Flanders, controlled by its weavers, would have been glad to come into an empire which grew the English wool, and the Channel would have become a mere waterway between the insular and continental ports of one country. Merchant ships, "swift shuttles of an empire's loom," from Havre, Rouen, Boulogne, Calais, La Rochelle and Bordeaux, would have anchored in home ports at Dartmouth, Pevensey, Dover, Sandwich and London.

The Channel and the Bay of Biscay would have been home waters, safe from pirates, and trade would have brought such prosperity in its wake, that townsmen in every city, and country folk in every shire in England, and in every province of France, would have found it to their advantage to uphold and maintain such an empire.

Chaucer's fate, as one light-mindedly speculates on possibilities, seems to tremble in the balance. Shall he be the first true Englishman, and a great English poet, or a valet in attendance at the Louvre and a French versifier? But this imaginary empire was not to be. Fate gave an emphatic no. Instead of union between the lands on either side of the Channel, there was violent disruption. War divided the two nations, and threw the French-speaking nobility of England into the arms of its English-speaking burghers and yeomanry; the burghers supplied money and the yeomanry archers. The great victories, of Sluys at sea (1340), of Crécy on land (1346), did more for the unity of England than a hundred years of domestic statesmanship. The English language plucked its opportunity; it had been crushed down and kept among the lower classes, but it was living and vigorous. Lords and ladies, great merchants, might speak French among themselves, but masons, weavers, dyers, carpenters, haberdashers, millers, reeves, mariners, and "uplandish" men, who digged, plowed, reaped in the fields, knocked down acorns from the oak trees for the pigs, who bred sheep and cattle, who ditched, dyked, and squandered their earnings at the ale-stake, they spoke English even when they spoke to their landlords and masters. And, after the English yeomanry, who since boyhood had practised shooting at the butts, their bows made from yew grown in English churchyards, arrows tipped with gray goose feathers from English fens, had put to rout the nobility of France, the spirit of triumph, of enmity and hate, stirred the country to patriotic self-consciousness and self-admiration.

Laurence Minot, a north countryman, who, I dare say, could not speak French, burst into patriotic English verse over the victories; he asserts that King Edward is the Boar, foretold by Merlin, that shall ravage the fields of France, and he shouts aloud about Franche-men fers (fierce) and fell, and the fels (false) folk of Normandy, and how Inglismen had delt great knokkes on their pates, had burned their towns, harried their lands, and, in short, given them a good lesson. His readers cheered. Of other literature in English there was not much, homilies, sermons in prose and verse, lives of saints, translations from the Bible; there was Richard Rolle, the mystic; there was Layamon's translation of Wace's *Brut* into English verse, and other translations from the French, some songs of which the form and inspiration are purely French, and not much else. I am speaking from the Philistine's point of view. But such as there was, served as foundation stones for Chaucer to build upon. Had England become a dependency of a French Empire, it is likely that this rude beginning—I refer to the English literature before Crécy—would have been swept into a provincial limbo, interesting only to patriotic persons who upheld local traditions, but as it is these poets and prose-writers are entitled to the credit of upholding the English language and of laying the foundation of English literature.

CHAPTER III

BOYHOOD

GEOFFREY CHAUCER was a lucky fellow. The first bit of good fortune that fate bestowed upon him was to cast his boyhood and youth in a time when the tide of England's national self-consciousness was sweeping away alien domination from its language and literature. His second bit of good fortune was to be born in London, and to receive as his native speech the dialect of the East Midlands which, thanks to London and Westminster, was destined to outdistance its rivals, the dialects of Wessex, Northumbria and the West Midlands, and to become the King's English. The third was to be born with a silver spoon in his mouth, and of a social rank that on the one hand enabled him to push open the door of the royal palace, and on the other to hobnob on equal terms with such men as Harry Bailly, Host of the Tabard Inn at Southwark.

In the middle of the fourteenth century London town within its gated walls lodged some forty thousand inhabitants upon a plot of land about a mile long and a half-mile wide, and yet even then she possessed the power and prestige of a capital. Jean Froissart, a quick-eyed Fleming, who came over from Flanders in the train of Queen Isabella and was familiar with the proud cities of Ghent, Bruges and Ypres, says that when the men of London are in accord and fully agreed, no man dare gainsay them, for they outweigh all the rest of England and are most mighty in soldiery and in wealth. As far back as a hundred years before, when King Henry III, in grievous need of money, was advised by his counselors to sell all his royal vessels of gold and silver, he asked scornfully, "Who could buy them?" His counselors answered, "The Londoners." "I know, I know," the King remarked, "that if the treasure of Octavian [a magical treasure] were for sale, the City of London would buy it all, for those churlish Londoners, who call themselves lords, are nauseously rich, the city is an inexhaustible well of opulence." And during the intervening years the city had grown and prospered. In spite of wars with France, of wars with the Scots, of depredations by pirates on the high seas, trade had thriven, wool merchants had grown rich trading with Flanders and wine merchants from trading with Gascony. Wool was the great staple of commerce, but the importation of wines from Bordeaux and La Rochelle was a matter of high consequence; wines, which in the twelfth century cost from three farthings to twopence a gallon, and in the fifteenth, sixpence, wrought the political bonds that held Gascony and England together, and wine merchants were people of importance.

As I say, the town physically was small. A man might walk the circuit of the walls within an hour. Let him start from the north end of London Bridge, go eastward along the bank of the Thames, he would pass Billingsgate, where in the reign of Edward I oysters were sold 2d a gallon, and a dozen eels for a penny, until, continuing on, he would reach the Tower of London, not having walked five hundred yards. From the Tower, following the wall, he would go northerly to Aldgate. Thence, inclining northwesterly, he would arrive at Bishopsgate; traveling westward, he would cross Wall Brook to a postern subsequently to Moorgate, pass Cripplegate, Aldersgate and Newgate, and there turning southerly very near to the entrance of Saint Paul's Cathedral, proceed to Ludgate, and thence, by the side of Fleet River, past the Black Friars, back to the north bank of the Thames, at a point about three-quarters of a mile west of London Bridge, and then again easterly to his starting-point. These limits were already too narrow for the inhabitants, and suburbs were reaching out. Fleet Street leaving the city at Ludgate ran past the Temple, then occupied by students of law, past Saint Clement Danes, and on a couple of miles to the town of Westminster where the King's palace was and the Abbey. Within the city walls there were castles, monasteries, nunneries, hospitals, six score churches and so forth; but I suppose that the sights most interesting to a visitor, such as Jean Froissart, would be the Tower, built by William the Conqueror, Saint Paul's Cathedral, which from its place of vantage on Ludgate Hill, lifted its great bulk, longer and taller than Sir Christopher Wrenn's Cathedral, and far more beautiful (I read), and dominated the town, and third, London Bridge. This was the only bridge then across the river, and rested on twenty arches; toward its southern end, beyond the drawbridge, stood a chapel to Saint Thomas of Canterbury, and perhaps, people were already beginning to build houses and shops along the sides, but there was still space left for two knights to joust on horseback with people looking on.

Wine merchants, as I stated, were important people, for the trade with Gascony was prosperous; frequent ships, laden with white wine and red, made the voyage, when not intercepted by pirates, from Bordeaux to London, and the *Merchant Vintners of Gascoyne* held their heads high. One of their members, John Gisers, became mayor of London, so did another, Henry Picard, who was a friend of John Chaucer, Geoffrey's father, and this Henry Picard, some years after his mayoralty, entertained at dinner at his house in the Vintry, the wine merchants' quarter, a company of Kings, Edward of England, John of France, David of Scotland and Pierre de Lusignan of Cyprus. John Chaucer was not so distinguished, and not so rich, as Henry Picard, but the two seem to have been of the same social rank. Picard was at one time King's butler at Lynn, and John Chaucer was deputy to the King's butler at Southampton.

John Chaucer was the son of Robert Chaucer, who had been a wine merchant and at one time collector of customs on wines from Gascony. Robert had married a widow, Mrs. Mary Heyroun, and on Robert's death she married one Richard Chaucer, who likely enough was a kinsman. This lady's three husbands were all wine merchants. John, in due time, became a wine merchant and married Agnes, a resident of London apparently, niece and heiress to a rich man, Hamo de Copton. Their son, Geoffrey, was born about 1342, and there may have been one or two daughters, neither of whom come into our story. The family lived in a house on Thames Street, next Wall Brook, and near the river. John Chaucer prospered. In 1338 King Edward, at the beginning of the Hundred Years' War, made a journey to Coblenz in order to meet the Emperor, Louis of Bavaria, and in his train went John Chaucer as far as Cologne. Possibly John Chaucer had gone merely on his own business for the purchase of Rhenish wines or some such matter, and had taken advantage of the King's going for the sake of escort; possibly he had some business for the King, such as stocking the royal cellar at Windsor; at any rate, John Chaucer is mentioned once or twice, again, in matters that show him to have been a person of consideration.

John's son, Geoffrey, our poet, first appears in history in a record of 1357. Up to that time we know nothing of him. He was too young to take part in the rejoicings over the famous victory of Crécy (1346), and the capture of Calais (1347), or in the sorrow over the terrible visitations of the Black Death (1348-1349). From this record of 1357 we learn that he was a page in the household of

Prince Lionel, a younger brother of the Black Prince, or, at least, of the Prince's wife, Elizabeth, Countess of Ulster. This record, together with sundry items of the Countess's household accounts, was accidently found on a parchment, which had been used to line the cover of an old volume of manuscript. The item states that on April 4, 1357, four shillings were paid *cuidam paltokmakere Londonie,* to a certain London tailor, for a short cloak, *paltok,* delivered to Geoffrey Chaucer, at her ladyship's expense, and three shillings for a pair of red and black breeches and a pair of shoes, bought in London, and also delivered to the said Geoffrey Chaucer. As the Countess was to attend the celebration of the Feast of Saint George (April) at Windsor, perhaps she wished her pages to look smart and fresh. But there were also other festivities soon to come, for it was the year after the great victory at Poitiers and the Black Prince, having made a truce for two years with the French, was bringing his illustrious prisoner, King John, and a long train of captive knights, in triumph to England. Victor and vanquished landed at Sandwich on May fourth, and after a two days' stay in order to give London time to prepare a suitable reception, proceeded to Canterbury, and then by the road that Chaucer was to make familiar to all the world to Rochester, to Dartford and to Greenwich, and having passed through Southwark, near the Tabard Inn, where perhaps an independent urchin, little Harry Bailly, ran after the procession, shouting himself hoarse, and on, across London Bridge, into the city. Crowds had lined the road all the way from Canterbury, but here triumph appeared in all its finery. The city went wild with pride and delight. The guilds were out in their liveries, and nobles and commons, gentlemen, ladies, men servants and maid servants, old and young, rich and poor, mothers with their babies, boys and girls, crowded the streets, cheering and shouting, or stared from doorway and window. Never had London seen the like of this day. David, King of Scotland, was there a prisoner, also the French Charles of Blois, the deposed Count of Brittany. The procession crossed London Bridge and turning westward passed very near the Chaucer house, and on by Blackfriars and Whitefriars, and along Fleet Street, and so to the Savoy Palace. It was a gallant sight. First came a thousand citizens on horseback, then troops of men-at-arms and archers, next the Gascon nobles and their retinues, then the captive King of France on a great white charger, richly caparisoned, with the Black Prince riding at his side on a little black hackney, as became the lieutenant of the Duchy of Guienne attending his superior lord, and after them a company of French knights, prisoners waiting for ransom, and so on. It can hardly be doubted that Prince Lionel and his wife, the Countess Elizabeth, were there, and that young Chaucer in his new shoes and particolored breeches beheld the procession. It is likely that his heart beat high with English pride. And, even if the grown man may see many similar sights, none stir him to the quick as does the first heart-bursting show of national glory. A little after this, on May twentieth, Geoffrey received a gift of two shillings, and in December, two shillings and sixpence, for necessaries against the feast of the Nativity (Christmas). The scale of money then was one-fifteenth, one-twentieth, or one-thirtieth, or some such fraction of what it is to-day, there are varying computations—I adopt the one-thirtieth—nevertheless a couple of shillings was not very much, and these gifts seem to imply that Chaucer could not have been more than fifteen years old.

It is reasonable to assume that, as a page, Geoffrey accompanied the Countess Elizabeth wherever she went, and in that case he visited the castles at Windsor, Woodstock, Doncaster and Hatfield (in Yorkshire), where the Countess spent Christmas, and here Chaucer must have made the acquaintance of Prince Lionel's younger brother, John of Gaunt, a lad of even age with Chaucer, or perhaps a couple of years older, and this acquaintance seems to have ripened into friendship, which was finally tightened by a closer connection. In 1359 John of Gaunt married Blanche, daughter to the Duke of Lancaster, at Reading, and it seems likely that Prince Lionel and his wife would be present and that Chaucer went in attendance to them. At any rate, Chaucer probably remained a page in the Countess's household until 1359, when he became a soldier.

CHAPTER IV

CHAUCER'S FIRST CAMPAIGN

KING EDWARD showed every courtesy to his royal prisoner except in the conditions imposed for the prisoner's release; he demanded the surrender of half of France, as well as vast sums of money. King John, who wished to go home, was ready to subscribe to any conditions, but his son Charles, the Dauphin, and the French council refused; they declared that they had much rather endure the distress in which they lay than suffer the Kingdom of France to be diminished. King Edward replied that in that case he would invade France with great puissance and stay until they did consent to a satisfactory peace, made according to his honor and good pleasure. And forthwith he made preparations suitable to the renown of Crécy and Poitiers. All the manhood of England was on fire; there was not a knight, squire or man of honor from the age of twenty to sixty that did not go. The Black Prince was there, and his brothers, Lionel, and Edmund though a mere boy. There was Henry, Duke of Lancaster, Gaunt's father-in-law, the Earls of March, Warwick, Suffolk, Hereford, Northampton, Salisbury, Stamford and Oxford, the Bishops of Lincoln and Durham, Lords Percy, Neville, Despenser, Roos, Manny, Cobham, Mowbray and Delaware, Sir John Chandos, Sir James Audeley, Sir Bartholemew de Burghersh, Sir Nigel Loring, and whoever else was of gentle blood in the kingdom. Chaucer undoubtedly was there in the train of Prince Lionel. The host assembled at Dover, and there the King harangued it; he said that he would die sooner than not accomplish his object, and that if any there did not approve of his resolution, he desired them to go home. All shouted their approval, with loud cries of "God and Saint George!"

The army disembarked at Calais on October 28, 1359. Never had so large, or well equipped, an army left England. It is said that there were upward of six thousand carts and wagons, carrying stores and provisions of all sorts, utensils for preparing food, such as handmills to grind corn, ovens to bake bread and so forth, the like of which had never been seen before. The King divided his army into three divisions, and all marched, by different and indirect routes, toward Rheims, where, in the great cathedral, the King intended to be anointed and crowned King of France. The Black Prince commanded one division, and as Prince Lionel accompanied the Black Prince it is highly probable that Chaucer would have been with him, too. This division marched southwesterly to Montreuil, which lies near the sea a little south of Boulogne, and then southeast to Hesdin. There is always a temptation in the path of the unscholarly to guess at what might be, especially in a great dearth of other details. In this town Chaucer might have made his first acquaintance with one aspect of that French culture, which in its literary aspect he afterward admired so greatly, as Hesdin had been and still was a center of art for painters and craftsmen of various sorts; and it is likely enough that young Jacquemart de Hesdin, who subsequently became famous as a miniature painter, then a boy of ten, was gazing out of a window at the horrible but fascinating spectacle of English knights, men-at-arms and archers tramping through the town, and at their long baggage train. Chaucer probably went into some church there out of curiosity, or perchance to pray for the success of the campaign, and may have seen the handiwork of these local artists in among Gothic sculpture and Gothic glass. After Hesdin, the Black

[33]

Prince's division crossed the River Somme at the towns of Nesle and Ham, and, passing near Saint-Quentin, crossed the Oise near Ribemont or Séry, then, heading southeast, crossed the Aisne at Château-Porcein a little west of Rhétel, and joined the King's division before Rheims. There are two references in Chaucer to this route. In *The House of Fame* he says,

> And therout com so gret a noyse
> That, had hyt [the House] stonden upon Oyse,
> Men myghte hyt han herd esely
> To Rome, y trowe sikerly.

And again, long afterward, he speaks of having been at Rhétel. He calls the place Retters, but as Froissart writes Reters, Retiers, Rhetiers, it is safe to identify the town as Rhétel. This reference is in the testimony that he gave in a lawsuit between Richard, Lord Scrope, and Sir Robert Grosvenor, as to which had the right to bear a certain heraldic device, *armez dazure ove en bende dor;* Chaucer testified that he had seen Sir Richard Scrope display this device "before the town of Retters, and so, during the whole expedition until the said Geoffrey was taken prisoner."

Taken prisoner he was, but just how or where we do not know for sure. The three converging divisions of the English army had arrived before Rheims about the beginning of December. The walls were too strong to admit of capture by assault, and the English army settled down for a siege. The King had brought hawks, thirty falconers, sixty couple of greyhounds, and sixty couple of other hounds, to cheer heavy hours; but luck was against him, it rained and rained. The rain not only interfered with hawking and hunting, but with the conduct of the siege and the health of the soldiers. The country had been so devastated in earlier raids that it was difficult to find food for the men or forage for the horses. Expeditions had to go farther and farther to obtain supplies. Sir Eustace D'Aubréchicourt in raiding the little town of Attigny was so fortunate as to find seven hundred casks of wine, and great foison of provisions, but most raiders had gone farther and fared worse. It was probably on one of these raids that Chaucer was captured, perhaps shortly before Christmas. He was held a prisoner for about two months, and it is most likely that he was taken into Rheims, and here again the unscholarly sciolist likes to indulge his fancy. Chaucer spoke French as well as he spoke English, perhaps better, he was a squire in an English Prince's retinue, and a charming person, and he had even then, one may guess, a taste for French poetry. He had, as I believe, become acquainted in the royal palace with the young Flemish poet, Jean Froissart, and was eager to make the acquaintance of other French poets. Now, at this very time the most distinguished French poet living, Guillaume de Machaut, was one of the canons attached to the Cathedral of Rheims, and was very likely within the city walls during the siege. Chaucer certainly knew Machaut's poems when he himself began to write poetry, and he may well have read the *Jugement dou Roy de Behaigne* or some other of Machaut's poems before this. He was probably taken into the city after the English army had withdrawn and he must, if he was granted any liberty at all, have visited the glorious cathedral, and if he had learned that Machaut was a canon there he may well have asked for the privilege of seeing him. But such guesses are reprehensible things, and I dare say that no serious student would be foolish enough to entertain them.

By January 11, 1360, it was clear that the city of Rheims could not be taken; the King broke up the siege, and marched south into the Duke of Burgundy's dominion, and there bargained with the Duke over the price to be paid him for turning round and going back into the French King's provinces. These pourparleys lasted nearly a month, and during the course of them, on March first, the Keeper of the Wardrobe of the King's household paid sixteen pounds toward Chaucer's ransom, a sum calculated to be worth twenty-four hundred dollars to-day. After his release Chaucer must have rejoined the army at Guillon, and continued with it during the rest of the campaign. King Edward marched to Paris, where Chaucer could see the towers of Notre-Dame and the spire of the Sainte Chapelle rise above the city walls. Here, as at Rheims, the fortifications were too strong to admit of assault, and as the Dauphin prudently refused to go out into the open and fight, Edward was forced to march on toward Brittany in search of food. The task of the commissariat was growing daily more difficult, nevertheless the King was obstinate and proposed to wander about, living on the country, and return to attack Paris or Rheims in the next summer and make himself *de facto* King of France. The French were suffering cruelly, and the Dauphin made very liberal offers. Some of the English generals approved of making peace; but it seems that they were not listened to until a portent shook the King's spirit, and inclined him also to peace. The English were encamped at Brétigny near Chartres, when a storm such as never happened in the memory of man burst upon them; wind, rain, hail, snow, thunder and lightning caused such a pother over their heads that it seemed as if earth and sky would be destroyed. The chronicler Knighton declares that more than six thousand horses and unnumbered men perished. The worst day, April thirteenth, engraved itself in men's minds as Black Monday. A treaty was signed at Brétigny, on May 8, 1360, by which the French agreed to cede all the southwestern third of France, nearly from the Loire to the Pyrenees, and to pay a great sum, while Edward, on his part, was to renounce his claim to the French crown and to the northern provinces, always excepting Calais. Chaucer seems to have gone back to England in May.

There is one more item of history during this year that concerns Chaucer; he went back to France a little later, for a note in Prince Lionel's expense account states that Geoffrey Chaucer was paid three royals, that is the value of nine shillings, by the Prince's orders for going with letters to England. So ended Chaucer's first military campaign.

CHAPTER V

1360-1369

THESE scraps of information that I have quoted shine but as candles out-of-doors on a dark night, feebly illuminating certain stages on the poet's way, and then leaving him to darkness again, or to the twilight of conjecture. After his return to England from the French campaign there is not a word for seven years, then one word, and again for two years not another, not a rush-light, not a farthing-dip; nevertheless we know something from circumstantial evidence.

The royal family, on which Chaucer was in attendance, seems to have been at this time a very happy, kindly, friendly family. Queen Philippa, according to report, was a charming person, "tall, stately, wise, cheerful, humble, devout, generous, courtly, decked and adorned with all noble virtues and beloved by God and man," a lady of boundless charity toward everybody, who all her life long helped knight, lady or damsel, that went to her in need. The Black Prince was a *preux chevalier,* "the perfect root of all honor and nobleness, of wisdom, valor and bounty" who (I am quoting the Herald of Sir John Chandos) "from the day of his birth cherished no thought but loyalty, gallantry, courage and goodness." His wife was very handsome, and they appear to have been devoted to each other, but they were only married in 1361, and very soon afterward went to live at Bordeaux. Of Prince Lionel's wife little or nothing, I think, is known. John of Gaunt's wife, Blanche of Lancaster, was according to Chaucer's description a most charming person.

[38]

In the elegy written to commemorate her death, he makes her husband mourn his

>   . . . lady swete,
> That was so fair, so fresh, so fre,
> So good, that men may wel se
> Of al goodnesse she had no mete [equal]!

And, long after her death, when there could be no suspicion of self-interest on his part, Froissart said that if he should live a thousand years he would never see a lady like Queen Philippa or Duchess Blanche. John of Gaunt was always, it seems, friendly to Chaucer, and in his younger days not a bad fellow at all, and the King, until the sad degenerate last years of his life, was a very gallant, courteous gentleman. Lionel's wife died in 1363, and it is possible that there was an interruption here of Chaucer's connection with the royal family, and that he went for a time to the inns of Court to study law. He was then about twenty-one, an age at which our young men nowadays begin the study of jurisprudence.

For some years the old buildings of the suppressed order of the Knights Templars had been handed over to students of law and were frequented by young men, who expected to be called to the bar, or thought that they would find a knowledge of law serviceable for rising in the world. Law was offering new opportunities; the common law was often in conflict with the civil law, and royalty had need of trained lawyers in its disputes with the Papacy as well as with ecclesiastical powers within the realm. These buildings lay on the south side of the road from Ludgate to Westminster, near to where the Temple Church still stands. The usual procedure was for a student to begin by entering one of the inns of Chancery, and then to advance into one of the inns of Court. If he was bound for the Inner Temple, he would matriculate at Clifford's Inn or Clement's Inn or Lyon's; if for the Middle Temple, or Lincoln's Inn, or Gray's Inn, then at one of the chancery inns that were preparatory to them. And, connected in some manner with these legal institutions, there was also a sort of academy where various courses of instruction were given, in music, singing, dancing, and in sacred and profane history, as well as in the law. The inns of Court were not merely places to form lawyers, but a kind of fashionable college where knights, barons, and even the great nobility, put their sons, partly to acquire some knowledge of law, partly to form their manners, or merely to keep them out of mischief during the effervescent years of adolescence.

You remember that Mr. Justice Silence intended to send his son, William, to the inns of Court after the lad had finished at Oxford, and how Mr. Justice Shallow in his lusty youth had been of Clement's Inn, and had sown a jolly crop of wild oats. Shallow, little John Doit of Staffordshire, black George Barnes, Francis Pickbone, and Will Squele, a Cotswold man, had been the nonpareil swingebucklers of all the inns of Court, about the time when Sir John Falstaff was page to the Duke of Norfolk. Shallow remembered well how Falstaff broke the pate of a fellow named Skogan at the Court Gate and how he himself, that very same day, fought with one Sampson Stockfish, a fruiterer, behind Gray's Inn. Clement's Inn lay across Fleet Street from the Temple, and Shallow and Silence were but little younger than Geoffrey Chaucer, and student life there in his time must have been a great deal such as it was in theirs. The historical link that connects Chaucer's life with the Inner Temple is a statement, which once existed in that society's records, that Chaucer was fined two shillings for beating a Franciscan friar in Fleet Street; at least Master Buckley, Keeper of the Records, told Thomas Speght (who wrote a life of Chaucer in 1598), that he had seen such a record.   One would like to think that, while Jack Falstaff, then not an eagle's talon round the waist, was breaking Skogan's crown, Geoffrey Chaucer was thwacking a Franciscan friar in Fleet Street, such a friar, that is, as he describes in *The Canterbury Tales*.

If Chaucer was not at the Inner Temple, he probably remained attached to the household of Prince Lionel.   Senti-mental biographers have ascribed to that period a great passion of love that lasted for eight years, a theory based upon some lines in *The Book of the Duchess,* written about Christmas time in 1369, and on some verses in his short poems.   The poet says that he can not sleep,

> But men myghte axe me why soo
> I may not sleepe, and what me is.
> But natheles, who aske this
> Leseth [loses] his asking trewely.
> Myselven can not telle why
> The sothe; but trewly, as I gesse,
> I holde hit be a sicknesse
> That I have suffred this eight yeer,
> And yet my boote [cure] is never the ner [nearer];
> For there is phisicien but oon,
> That may me hele . . .

It is highly probable, and wholly commendable, that he was madly in love in his youth.   But men in older, calmer years, with grizzling hair, who dip their noses in Gascon wine, are inclined to heighten the color of their youthful emotions. Montaigne says: *"Je m'y eschauday en mon enfance, et y souffris toutes les rages que les poètes disent advenir à ceux qui s'y laissent aller sans ordre et sans jugement."*   And Polonius says, in commenting upon his hypothesis that Hamlet had lost his wits for love of Ophelia, "And, truly,

[41]

in my youth I suffered much extremity for love; very near this." And, if Chaucer was very love-sick, and he says

> . . . in this world was never wight so woo
> Withoute deth,

he probably recovered from it, as Polonius and Montaigne did. At any rate, he and the other young squires in the King's household were in familiar company with the young ladies in attendance upon the Queen or her daughter-in-law, the Duchess of Lancaster, and among these were the two daughters, Philippa and Katharine, of Sir Payne Roet, a Flemish knight who had come with the Queen to England, as the celebrated Sir Walter Manny and others had done.

In default of any other information concerning Chaucer's life at this period, we can get some idea of what that was by Jean Froissart's account of his own boyhood and youth, for the two young men had a number of things in common. Both were born in the middle class, both were placed as pages or squires in the royal household, both were curious of life, of their fellow men, of the human comedy, though Froissart never cared much except for the outward show, both were healthy-minded and enjoyed life, and both were interested in poetry and wrote verses. Froissart was by three or four years the elder of the two; he was born in Valenciennes, a more civilized city, I presume, from the point of view of intellectual interests, than London. From the first he was a jolly boy and went whistling through life. He made mud-pies and tied thread to butterflies' legs. He admired the girls at school, and gave them presents of apples and pears, of glass rings and brooches; he fell to fisticuffs with other boys, and incidentally learned Latin. At twelve he was fond of dancing and singing; a little later he took to reading amorous novels and began to dream of love.

One May morning, when the hawthorne blossoms were blithe, he saw before his bewildered eyes the three goddesses, Juno, Pallas and Venus, and they asked him what he thought of Paris's award of the apple. He answered that Paris was right; and Venus in her gratitude promised him a lady, more exquisite than Helen. Soon afterward he met a maiden reading a romance; her face was fresh and fair, her eyes bright as stars, her hair like summer flax, her hands, her voice, her lips, beyond compare. Enough. He wrote ballades and virelays in her honor and fell desperately in love with her. Alas! The girl loved another. For three months, he says, he lay at death's door and expected to die. This sad experience of Froissart's is the best comment upon the old theory, to which I have referred, that Chaucer suffered the pangs of unrequited love and expressed his own grief in the *Compleynt to Pite,* the earliest of his poems (so Doctor Furnivall thought) that has come down to us.

Froissart went to England with letters to the Queen in 1356, the year of Poitiers, and was cordially received but before a year was out he was homesick for his lady-love, and went back, as I have said, in vain. He returned to England in 1361, after the Treaty of Brétigny, going from Calais to Dover. Chaucer had made that same crossing but a little while earlier. On board Froissart's ship were some French hostages who were to take King John's place, on his return to France, until full payment of his ransom; and Froissart must have become well acquainted with many of these gentlemen. On this crossing, he brought with him a book of rhymed chronicles of the wars of his time, and presented it to the Queen, who thereupon made him one of her secretaries. He and Chaucer, the only two poets at court, must have known each other and discussed romance and versification.

When John of Gaunt's wife, Lady Blanche, died, Chaucer,

as we shall see, wrote an elegy and Froissart, too, mourned her in verse:

> *Elle mourut jeune et jolie,*
> *Environ de vingt et deux ans*
> *Gay, lie, friche, esbatans.*

After Froissart had abandoned poetry for history, he must have buttonholed, in his eagerness to learn the details of every battle and skirmish, all the famous soldiers who came to the King's court; he was agreeable, quick-witted, gay and well-bred, and probably encountered neither snub nor reserve. Among those who made much of him were Sir Walter Manny, Sir Edward Despenser, the Earl of Pembroke and the Duke of Hereford. He was always ready "to sing, dance, talk or laugh," and he had a jolly good time; he never missed a joust or fête. If this was so with Froissart, it is fair to surmise that young Chaucer, well-graced, cultivated and well-bred, also made many friends among the important people who visited the court. In later life, he must have had powerful friends to suggest and procure his appointment to important positions; the King could not have relied solely on his own impressions. To be sure in *The Canterbury Tales,* the Host, Harry Bailly, when he calls on Chaucer (himself one of the pilgrims) for his story, says:

> . . . "What man artow? . . .

> "Thou lookest as thou woldest fynde an hare,
> For evere upon the ground I se thee stare.

> "Approche neer, and looke up murily.
>
>   *   *   *   *   *
>
> He semeth elvyssh by his contenaunce,
> For unto no wight dooth he daliaunce [gossip]."

A reader, ignorant of Middle English, would guess that elvyssh meant "roguish, like an elf"; but Skeat says it means "absent in demeanor." The word reappears in *The Canon's Yeoman's Tale,* where Chaucer speaks of *elvyssh craft* and *elvyssh nyce lore* to designate alchemy, and here Skeat says it means "foolish"; but Skeat renders *nyce* also by "foolish," and so under his interpretation the second phrase would mean *foolish, foolish lore.* Kittredge says that *elvish* means "shy"; Robinson gives "Elvish, mysterious, elf-like, absent in demeanor, not of this world." Tyrwhitt translates *elvish* by "mischievous," and that seems more reasonable. I should suppose that Chaucer by this adjective meant what he says, elfish, Puck-like, inclined to roguishness, and in applying it to himself, meant to refer to his ironical, quizzical expression, which suggested that under a quiet outside lurked something that was ready to make fun of other people. It can hardly imply any unsocial trait, for at the opening of the *Prologue,* Chaucer says that while he was at the Tabard, a company of pilgrims, twenty-nine in number, entered the hostelry, and that within a short time he had spoken to every one of them. That was just what you would expect of Chaucer. And I feel sure that in his youth, this same natural, simple sociability showed itself while he was attached to the Countess's or the King's household, modestly, without forthputting, but friendly and inquisitive. Everything about him bears testimony that he was, when not bent on study, a very companionable person, and when he had arrived at maturity he must have been an accomplished man of the world.

Apart from such speculations, we know that his father died in 1366, that his mother soon afterward married again, and apparently went out of his life, and that he himself at about that time married Philippa Roet, and Sir Hugh Swynford married her sister, Katharine. Chaucer's marriage to

[45]

Philippa Roet was evidently looked upon with approbation in high places, and very likely the Queen had a kindly feeling for her namesake, for the King granted the bride an annuity of ten marks, perhaps one thousand dollars in our money to-day, and the next year he granted to the groom, "dilectus vallectus noster Geoffrey Chaucer," an annuity of twice that amount. In 1368, in July, he received a passport from Dover, and ten pounds for his traveling expenses; and that is all we know about that. He was probably about the King's business. At all events it shows that his character and talents were recognized.

CHAPTER VI

LITERARY EDUCATION

DURING this decade between Chaucer's first campaign in France (1359-1360) and his second (1369), there were sundry important political happenings; King John died in captivity (1364), and his far more intelligent son, Charles V, reigned in his stead, the Black Prince invaded Spain and won a great victory (1367), and Prince Lionel went to Milan (1368) to marry money in the person of Violante Visconti, daughter of the Lord of Milan, and shortly afterward died, not without suspicion of poison. Froissart was a member of Prince Lionel's retinue, and in Milan saw Petrarch, who was hobnobbing as usual with princes. But these matters did not affect Chaucer, who was now spending his energies in the study of literature and of prosody.

At court, as I have said, French was the only language. Chaucer and Philippa spoke French, so did the Queen, so did Sir Payne Roet, and Katharine Swynford, and all the ladies and gentlemen of the royal household; it is said that the King knew but little English. All these people however, except the King and perhaps the Flemings, also spoke English and did so habitually with servants, grooms, shopkeepers, and people of lower social position.

Chaucer, no doubt, spoke English in his infancy and learned French a little later as a second language, but he certainly regarded French as the language of culture. He knew Latin pretty well, and read Ovid, the *Metamorphoses,* the *Heroides,* the *Ars Amatoria,* and the *Fasti,* the *Æneid,*

Lucan's *Pharsalia,* Statius's *Thebais,* something of Claudian, scraps of Horace and Juvenal, Boethius, and perhaps some other authors. As to English literature, whatever there was of it, legend or history, lives of saints, homilies, poems to the Virgin, to the cuckoo, to the rose, whether he knew its poetry or its prose, whether he had come upon Laurence Minot, *Sir Gawayn and the Grene-Knyght, Piers Plowman,* or not, it does not appear that he gave such literature much attention till considerably later in life. This was natural. The society, among which he lived, as far as it took any notice of literature, read French authors, and was probably extremely snobbish about any English poetry or prose; and Chaucer naturally adopted the same attitude.

His contemporary, John Gower, a somewhat older man, who afterward became his friend, wrote his first long poem in French, his second in Latin, and only his third in English, and that not till 1390, and even after that he wrote little poems in French. Of course, Chaucer may have read English poems during these years and certainly tried his hand at writing some, but it is clear from his earlier works, that he fixed his attention upon French literature; for, in addition to the fact that French was the language of cultured people, French literature was far richer, far more developed, and far more interesting in form and matter than English literature then existing.

Of French books, the chief that he read appear to be poetry, that of Froissart, of Guillaume de Machaut, Eustache Deschamps, and, more than all else, the *Roman de la Rose.* Froissart I have told about; I can not doubt that they knew each other, that Froissart showed Chaucer his poems, and by his lively enthusiasm encouraged Chaucer to write verses himself. *The Paradys d'Amour,* for instance, is one of Froissart's poems from which Chaucer borrows; like other adolescent poems of the time it deals lightly with young love,

Mieuls ne poet employer le tems
Homs, ce m'est vis, qu'au bien amer;

Man can not better use his time,
Me thinks, than in true love.

But Guillaume de Machaut, beside being much older than
Froissart, was a more experienced, a more artful poet, more
careful with meter and rhythm. He is said to have written
over eighty thousand lines. God rest his soul! He wove
his rhymes very subtly in and out, he arranged them in
unexpected and bewildering positions, *rimes serpentines,*
équivoques, léonines, rétrogrades, sonnantes, and composed
a rondeau, a ballade, a virelay, a chant royal, a lay, empty
trifles, with excellent dexterity. It sounds tedious, but M.
Lanson adds that at times there is in Machaut *quelque*
chose de fin, de vif, de charmant, une fantaisie discrète et
une forme sobre. What was chiefly lacking was common
sense, and that Chaucer possessed abundantly. Now, the
town of Machaut, where Guillaume was born, lies a little
to the northeast of Chalons in Champagne, and Champagne,
centuries before the happy days of Pommery et Greno, Moët
et Chandon, Mumm, and la Veuve Clicquot, was famous as
a land of poetry. Marie de France, daughter of Louis VII
and Eleanor of Aquitaine, who married Henri, Count of
Champagne, lived at Troyes and created the "literature of
courteous love." She was patron of Chrétien de Troyes;
and it was at her bidding that Chrétien wrote *Le Roman de*
la Charette, in which he expounds the code of love and
chivalry. Her grandson, Thibaut-le-Grand, also wrote
poems about courteous love. Henry Adams says that his
poetry has "the simplicity of thirteenth century glass—so
refined and complicated that sensible people are mostly satisfied to feel, and not to understand," and he adds that the

verses are as perfect as the colors in the windows of Notre-Dame de Chartres, and the versification as elaborate as the blending and contrast of those colors. Guillaume de Machaut was following, and perhaps refining upon, a well-established poetic tradition. His life, too, had been passed at courts, for he had been almoner, notary and secretary to King John of Bohemia for a dozen years prior to the fatal battle of Crécy, where the gallant blind old King had been killed. Since then, as I have said, he had been a canon of the cathedral at Rheims, and now, in his old age, though a canon and feeble and gouty, he lost his heart to the lovely Péronnelle d'Armentières and was wooing her with verses, until that young lady slammed the door in his face, by marrying another. Chaucer evidently studied Machaut with great admiration for he borrows ideas and phrases both from the *Jugement dou Roy de Behaigne* (Bohemia), and from *La Fonteinne Amoureuse*.

As to ourselves, I think that we may learn from Henry Adams' hint concerning Thibaut-le-Grand's verses, and include Machaut's among those that "sensible people are mostly satisfied to feel and not to understand," or we may even refrain more than that.

Eustache Deschamps was also a Champenois. He was born in Vertus, now celebrated for champagne, a year or two after Chaucer probably; between 1340 and 1346, the commentators say. He was brought up with great kindness by Machaut who may have been his uncle; he himself says that Machaut *"M'a nourry et fait maintes douceurs."* He was in Rheims during the siege by the English, and he says

bien m'en remembre.

Afterward he studied in the University of Orléans, obtained service under King Charles V, and traveled far and wide.

Numbers must have come to him early, and they continued to come all his life, torrentially, like the waters at Lodore—

> And glittering and frittering,
> And gathering and feathering,
> And whitening and brightening,
> And quivering and shivering,
> And hurrying and skurrying,
> And thundering and floundering—

especially, it seems to me, floundering. They fill eleven volumes. Moral ballades against vices, against the rich, the envious, against military life, avarice, Flanders, against the English, against old husbands of young wives, against borrowers of books, against women, in short, against almost all categories of sinners. This was rather because the ills of life fretted him; but he also had a noble discontent:

> *Fay ce que doiz, et aviengne que puet.*

He loves to give advice, how a man should live after fifty, how dangerous it is to travel in Germany, to marry an old woman, to believe all you hear, and so forth. But his interest to us is that he certainly knew about Chaucer, even if he did not know him personally. Mr. Lowes has discovered what frequent use Chaucer makes of Deschamps' poems—in *The Merchant's Tale,* in *The Wife of Bath's Prologue,* in *The Prologue to the Legend of Good Women* and so on. And what is still more interesting, Deschamps sent Chaucer his works with a ballade in his honor:

> *O Socrates plains de philosophie,*
> *Seneque en meurs et Anglux en pratique,*
> *Ovides grans en ta poeteries*
> *Bries en parler, saiges en rethorique*

[51]

Aigles treshaulz, qui par ta theorique
Enlumines le regne d'Eneas
L'Isle aux Geans, ceuls de Bruth, et qui as
Semés les fleurs et planté le rosier,
Aux ignorans de la langue pandras,
Grant translateur, noble Geoffrey Chaucier.

Tu es d'amours mondains Dieux en Albie.

It is pleasant to see how highly he appreciated Chaucer's poetry and learning. He hails him as a new Socrates, a Seneca, an Ovid, who has illuminated England *(le regne d'Eneas),* planted and transplanted flowers from the French *(la langue pandras),* and in especial as the Great Translator, by which I should suppose Deschamps means not merely the translator of the *Roman de la Rose,* but the poet who had transferred the flowers of French poetry to England. One would like to think that the two poets met as young men, during the time that Chaucer was a prisoner, as is quite possible, for Chaucer was probably taken into Rheims at the retirement of the English army on January 11, 1360.

But no French poem interested Chaucer one-half so much as the *Roman de la Rose;* he read and reread it, he studied it, he translated it, or part of it, he incorporated hundreds of lines into his poems with little or no change, no more than enough to run them in among his own verses, he imbued himself with the spirit of it. A translation of about one-third of the French poem has come down to us, and scholars usually, but by no means invariably, for the life of scholarship is contradiction, agree that Chaucer wrote the first seventeen hundred and five lines, whether or no any of the rest of the translation is from his pen, as to which they also disagree. If it seems strange to you that Chaucer should find the first part of the *Roman de la Rose* so full

of beauty, of sympathy, of delicate sentiment, of amorous
charm, remember that that poem was to him, what Keats's
is to romantic young poets of to-day. If you wish to understand what Guillaume de Lorris was to Chaucer, you must
read Keats. For instance, I open *The Eve of Saint Agnes,*
and I find what Chaucer found in the *Roman de la Rose:*

"Ah, Porphyro!" said she, "but even now
Thy voice was at sweet tremble in mine ear,
Made tunable with every sweetest vow;
And those sad eyes were spiritual and clear.
How chang'd thou art! how pallid, chill, and drear!
Give me that voice again, my Porphyro,
Those looks immortal, those complainings dear!
Oh, leave me not in this eternal woe,
For if thou diest, my love, I know not where to go."

Beyond a mortal man impassion'd far
At these voluptuous accents, he arose,
Ethereal, flush'd, and like a throbbing star
Seen mid the sapphire heaven's deep repose;
Into her dream he melted, as the rose
Blendeth its odour with the violet.

When you have read this you understand what Chaucer
felt when he read pages of courtly love about the Lover and
the Rose. Of all the difference between Chaucer's generation and ours the greatest is that between the meager sum
of poetry of love that they had and the vast opulence of
noble amorous verse, in which English poets have outdone
the world, that we possess. Run over the names of the
poets who have written of love, Shakespeare, Spenser, Milton, Herrick, Lovelace, Burns, Coleridge, Byron, Shelley,
Keats and the rest, builders of the great palace of English
poetry, and write a *Compleynt to Pite* for the young poet

[53]

who was born when the *Roman de la Rose* was the chief
pleasure dome of poetry then builded. Imagine the gifted
lad in love for the first time, his eyes fresh from Philippa's
face, his ears melodious with the music of her mocking
laugh, his heart beating to the rhythm of her dancing steps,
back in his room with the *Roman* (which perhaps Froissart
had lent him) in his hands for the first time, reading, and
that, while dreaming of her, it flashed through his mind that
he would translate the poem, and snatching his tablets, on
the instant wrote,

> Many men sayn that in sweveninges [dreams]
> Ther nys but fables and lesynges [falsehoods].

The *Roman de la Rose* consists of two parts: the first, a
very pretty tapestried picture of adolescent love and wooing,
with love's attendant helps and hindrances personified in conventional allegory, written by Guillaume de Lorris, a native
of the Orléanais, who lived in the beginning of the thirteenth
century. The town, or village, of Lorris is not sixty miles
from Chartres as the crow flies, and during Guillaume's life
the cathedral was building. It can hardly be a mere guess
that the young poet visited the Virgin's shrine there, gazed
at the stately, long-drawn-out Kings and Queens upon the
western portal, gazed at the great rose window above, the
lancet windows below, and their wondrous blue glass beyond
the art of modern glaziers, at the window of Notre-Dame
de la Belle-Verrière, and all the storied glory of color, until
he was obsessed by theories of reds and blues, of purples and
greens, rendered in pictured verse. At any rate, some such
theory he put into execution in this poem,

> *Ou l'art d'amours est toute enclose.*

[54]

The poem begins with the account of a dream that the poet dreamt in the month of May when he was twenty. The heroine is a high born lady

> *Et tant digne d'être amée,*
> *Qu'elle doit Rose etre clamée*

> She
> So worthy is biloved to be,
> That she wel ought, of pris and ryght,
> Be cleped Rose of every wight.

Young Geoffrey certainly felt that these verses prefigured the lady who occupied his thoughts; so the story began propitiously. Besides, the month of May is England's glory—

> *temp amoureux plein de joye,*
> *Qu'il n'y a ne buissons ne haye*
> *Qui en celluy temps ne s'esgaye*

> . . . it was May, thus dremed me,
> In tyme of love and jolite,
> That al thing gynneth waxen gay,
> For ther is neither busk nor hay
> In May, that it nyl [will not] shrouded ben,
> And it with newe leves wren [clothed].

Even Ralph Waldo Emerson says, "What potent blood hath modest May!"—and Geoffrey Chaucer was at the most susceptible age, when the not-impossible She is Nature's masterpiece. The description of the month of May is charming and none the less so that other trouvères and troubadours had sung its delightfulness, for all young lovers are much alike and pass the same thoughts and words from one to another; moreover, Chaucer had seen this flora and this verdure in the meadows and gardens about Hatfield, and had heard the sweet woodland notes of mating birds in coppice and dingle near Windsor and Woodstock. No reader was ever more ready to squeeze all the sweetness from a book than this young amorous adolescent. If we had a record of when Keats first read Shakespeare's sonnets we should find the same excited receptivity. Well, to the story. The Dreamer leapt from his bed, washed and dressed and hurried out of town to hear the birds and see the flowers. He came upon a garden girdled in by a great wall. The adventure had begun. On the outside of the walls hideous figures were painted in gold and blue, Hate, Felony, Villainy, Covetousness, Avarice, Envy, Sorrow, Old Age, Hypocrisy and Poverty. Their very ugliness made him the more sure that the garden within the walls must be most delectable; he was ready to give a hundred pounds to get in, and then he came upon a little, narrow, wicket gate, which was opened for him by

> *une pucellette* [a maiden]
> *Qui assez estoit cointe et nette.*

This rarely charming young lady is described as Chaucer would have liked to describe the lady of his thoughts; perhaps it seemed to him as if the poet must have known her. This damsel introduced herself as *Oyseuse,* Ydlenesse, and said that the entrancing garden before him belonged to *Deduyt,* Sir Myrthe, a fine youth who was sitting there in the midst of a handsome group. The describing of these radiant scenes is like going from one stained-glass window, through which the hot sun pours, to another. Milton's *L'Allegro,* will give you the idea. A girl, *Lyesse,* Gladnesse, was singing, and then others sang and danced, while musi-

cians played on harps and flutes; one of the girls, *Courtoisie,*
Curtesie, came forward and invited the Dreamer to join
them. He did so and looked about him. A little apart
from Mirth and Gladness he saw *le Dieu d'Amours* all
dressed in flowers, looking like an angel that had come direct from heaven.

> His garnement [adornment] was everydell [every bit]
> Yportreied and ywrought with floures,
> By dyvers medlyng of coloures.
>
> * * * * *
>
> . . . all in floures and in flourettes,
> Ypaynted al with amorettes,
> And with losenges, and scochouns [escutcheons],
> With briddes [birds], lybardes [leopards], and lyouns,
> And other beestis wrought ful well.

The plot is developing; the Dreamer has come into the
presence of the God of Love, and every sight that meets his
eye and every sound that greets his ear is ravishing. All
this might not be so thrilling to persons well acquainted with
such literature, and certainly not to those not in love. But
Chaucer never forgot the scenes and episodes that he read
there; in every poem, or nearly, that he wrote you will
find references, borrowings or memories of this *Romaunt.*
Cupid, the God of Love, carried a bow and arrows, and, as
was apparent, he was greatly taken by *Dame Beaulté* who
stood beside him. Next her stood *Richesse,* a lady greatly
admired, to whom both high and low paid court. She was
holding by the hand a young man, *Joliveté,* Jollity, a great
swell, very smartly dressed, who wore elegant boots, and
was so proud of his stables that he would rather have been
accused of theft or murder than of having a poor horse,
and because of his fondness for prodigality he sought the

[57]

friendship of *Richesse*. But I need not run through the allegory. The Dreamer is pierced by Cupid's arrows, becomes the Lover, and swears fealty to Cupid, and wandering off sees the rose-bush, on which hangs the Rose, hedged about by thorns. The Rose is not only protected by thorns but by a horrid churl Daunger and his attendants, Wikkid Tunge, Shame and Fear. The story tells how the Lover, aided by his friends, and hindered by his foes, advances and finally attains his object so far as to kiss the Rose. This is far from plucking it; fearful adventures still lie across the path, and here suddenly Guillaume de Lorris stops.

Chaucer's part of the translation has ended a great deal sooner. The translation is extremely accurate, as nearly word for word as the two languages permit. And I think that if you are curious to get near the young Chaucer during these years, of which we know so little, you will do much better to read the *Roman de la Rose* than waste your time in building conjectures upon the life records published by the Chaucer Society.

CHAPTER VII

Jean de Meung

It is usual for the purposes of convenience, and accurate enough, to divide Chaucer's poetical career into three periods, and to designate these periods as his French period, his Italian period and his self-taught, English period. In his third period he had not forgotten his Italian and French masters, nor in his second had he discarded the artifice and the art which he had learned from these French poets. The style, the imagery, the clarity, the refinement and delicacy of his verse, acquired in this period of beginnings, stayed with him always. He dropped the allegory, and various medieval conventions of thirteenth- and fourteenth-century French poetry, he sifted and sifted, keeping the grain and casting away husks and shucks, though I do not think he cast away as much as he should have done. So, both to explain the grain and also that portion of the husks and shucks that he kept, I must say something more of his French studies, the preparation for his first productive period.

A strange adventure happened to Guillaume de Lorris's poem some fifty years after he died; a young fellow from the town of Meung, which lies about fifty miles west of Lorris, who had finished his studies at the University of Paris, or of Orléans, or wherever it was that he studied, felt the bourgeoning of poetry in his breast, and coming upon the courtly poem of Guillaume de Lorris, decided to continue it. It almost seems as if he did this as a lark, for he was a very different person from his predecessor, had had a very different education, and was interested in a wholly different set of ideas. Fifty years had gone by; the age that looked to Saint Louis as all that is admirable in man, had given way to an age that was ready to admire the shrewd, skeptical audacity of Philippe le Bel. A new kind of literature had come in; fabliaux had pushed the romances from public favor. The old generation that had enjoyed the delicate perfume of courtly love, that had delighted in pictures of sweet gardens, of maidenhood, of a Preraphaelite paradise, had gone, and had been succeeded by what we call to-day a *realistic* generation. There was as great a change during those fifty years in the aspects of literature, as that which we see now between the present and the days of Queen Victoria. This delicate Preraphaelite quality, though it forsook literature, did not wholly pass away, but snuggled in miniatures by Jacquemart, by Beauneveu, by Pol de Limbourg and others such, and afterward proceeded to early Flemish tapestry, but that does not concern us. The fabliaux were little *genre* pictures of bourgeois life, tracing their origin, it is thought, to the Far East, where there were no Ten Commandments, and no dominant fashion of decency. The plot, I am told, usually concerns three persons, one of them a woman, and one a priest, but there is no hard-and-fast usage. M. Lanson says: "The morality, or, if that word seems out of place, the conception of life, found in the *fabliaux,* is the coarsest, the most brutal, and the most sordid that one can imagine." We shall find traces of this, and more than traces, in a number of *The Canterbury Tales.* Jean de Meung is not like that, but the breath of such a social atmosphere has breathed upon him, and he wanders far outside the pale that Guillaume de Lorris had set about his garden. Mr. F. R. Ellis, I notice, thought it best in his translation of the poem to omit the last episode.

Jean de Meung may have found Guillaume's poem unfinished, as we have it, or he may have lopped off the conclusion in order to be able to continue it according to his own satisfaction. Once started, he added more than eighteen thousand lines to Guillaume's four thousand and fifty-eight. I need not narrate the plot; there is not any, other than that in the end the Lover gathers the Rose. A series of persons, L'Amis, Faux-Semblant La Vieille, Nature and Genius, utter long homilies, satirical, rationalistic, concerning all sorts of subjects, ethics, religion, life, the contents of the universe, rainbows, mirrors, visions, hallucinations, witchcraft, pauperism, justice, instinct, priests, monks and so forth. In particular La Vieille expresses the satirical views of the monkish Middle Ages upon women, and reveals where Chaucer got the stimulus for his portrait of the Wife of Bath, and Faux-Semblant does for friars much the same thing that La Vieille does for women, and gave Chaucer sundry suggestions for his rascally Friar. Jean was very clever, and likes to make parade of his learning; he cites Aristotle, Cicero, Virgil, Lucan, Saint Augustine, Claudian, Macrobius, André le Chapelain, and borrows freely, especially from Ovid, Boethius, Guillaume de Saint-Amour, and Alain de Lille (Alanus de Insulis). No doubt Jean started Chaucer on his course of study. Besides, he was a philosopher in his way, a stirrer-up of ideas, and has been compared to Voltaire. Naturally he was intensely interesting to an intellectual young man like Chaucer, brought up and educated in a society of limited and conventional notions. Jean's part of the *Roman de la Rose* reads a little as if a medieval Montaigne had taken to writing in verse, and though the modern unscholarly reader finds it intolerably tedious, there are witty sayings as, for instance, in a long arraignment of adolescent love,

> *C'est la soif qui tousieurs est yvre*
> *Yvresse qui de soif s'enyvre,*

[61]

which is much better than the English translation,

A thrust [thirst] drowned in dronkenesse.

And there are bits of lively speech that may have given
Chaucer a hint for the incomparable dialogues between his
comic rogues, the Miller and the Reeve, or the Friar and
the Summoner, such as this, for instance, where in a narrative concerning the vicissitudes of Fortune after Crœsus
has recounted to his daughter a vainglorious dream, she
replies,

> *Beau-père . . .*
> *Cy a douloureuse nouvelle,*
> *Votre orgeuil ne vault une coque;*
> *Scachiez que Fortune vous mocque.*

Certainly Chaucer noticed this, for he borrowed the Crœsus
story, as well as one concerning Nero, for *The Monk's Tale.*
Guillaume de Lorris may have affected Chaucer in the
latter's early poetry more than Jean did, but Jean influenced
Chaucer all his life; in fact, one might say that in a way
Jean de Meung was Chaucer's favorite poet. He took *The
Physician's Tale* from him, and it apparently was from Jean
that he conceived the idea of translating Boethius' *De Consolatione Philosophiæ.*

Another French poet, Guillaume de Deguilleville, influenced Chaucer, to this extent, at least, that Chaucer
translated, very freely, a prayer contained in a long poem by
the Frenchman. It is called an *A. B. C.*, because the first
line of the first stanza begins with an *A,* and the first line
of the second stanza with a *B,* and so on. The poem is only
interesting to scholars. Chaucer was free from every touch,
or taint, if you prefer, of mysticism, he had no religious

[62]

fervor, he had no curiosity of soul that yearns for communion with reality behind appearance, no passion for things
of the spirit. At that time, although the medieval devotion
to the Virgin had died down, she was still the symbol of
the sweetest qualities of the Godhead, mercy, benignity,
tenderness, purity, still the fountain of spiritual hopes, and
in her double character of mother and maid appealed to what
was best in a man's heart. But even the Virgin seems scarce
to have touched Chaucer. The *Invocacio ad Mariam* in *The
Seconde Nonnes Tale* owes what dignity and nobleness it
has to its model, Saint Bernard's prayer in Dante, which is
the ripest fruit of religious poetry. Nor was this lack of
interest in mystical religion due to the times, though ra-
tionalism was coming in, for Chaucer's life falls between
Richard Rolle and Thomas à Kempis, two pillars of mysticism. Chaucer's mind was quite of another cast; and
because it was of an opposite cast, he was able to perceive
and to describe the Canterbury pilgrims. To the unscholarly
person the chief, perhaps the only, interest in this religious
poem—for such verses as

> Help and releeve, thou mighti debonayre,
> Have mercy on my perilous langour!
> Venquisshed me hath my cruel adversaire,

are out of tune with our taste—the only interest, I say, lies
in the versification, for that shows how much and to what
good purpose Chaucer had studied French poetry. Each
stanza contains eight lines, of three rhymes, a b a b b c b c,
and ten syllables in each line. His use of this difficult form
helps one to understand how diligently he worked at his
craft, and that his success was as much due to hard labor,
as to a nice ear.

CHAPTER VIII

POETRY, text-books tell us, is distinguished from prose by rhythm, by an arrangement of syllables that stirs our sympathies, our imagination, our memories, our longings, more readily and more intensely than an unrhythmical order can. The reason for this I do not know; I suppose it is due to our bodily structure, to the beat of our hearts, or because our nerves are sensitive to rhythmic stimuli. Poetry, true poetry, of course, has other qualities than rhythm to distinguish it from prose, but the rhythm, the arrangement of words, is what concerns us now. Samuel Taylor Coleridge says that poetry is the best words arranged in the best order. No doubt he would agree that what constitutes the best order will shift according to the subject-matter. To choose the right rhythm is the business of the poet. Poetry need not, of course, have rhyme; blank verse, *Samson Agonistes,* Collins' *Ode to Evening,* Tennyson's *Tears, idle tears,* and multitudinous verses more, show that; nor need it, provided it have other necessary qualities, have any regular recurrent rhythm. In the English Bible there are many passages, which one would class as poetry, because in addition to other necessary qualities, they have a rhythm, irregular and uncertain but still marked, for instance:

> Come unto me,
> All ye that labour
> And are heavy laden,
> And I will give you rest.

Take my yoke upon you,
And learn of me;
For I am meek and lowly in heart:
And ye shall find rest unto your souls.
For my yoke is easy,
And my burden light.

> St. Matt., XI: 28-30.

Or again,

Hearken to me,
Ye that follow after righteousness,
Ye that seek the Lord:
Look unto the rock whence ye are hewn,
And to the hole of the pit whence ye are digged.

* * * * *

Lift up your eyes to the heavens,
And look upon the earth beneath:
For the heavens shall vanish away like smoke,
And the earth shall wax old like a garment,
And they that dwell therein shall die in like manner:
But my salvation shall be for ever,
And my righteousness shall not be abolished.

> Isaiah, LI: 1,6.

This is the language of passion, and, as it rides aloft on its subject-matter, needs very little rhythm. At the other extremity of poetry, where there is no passion and but little sentiment, if any, there is need of great artifice, and you will find, as with Guillaume de Machaut, or in Charles d'Orléans, or generally in *vers de société,* a very meager amount of human interest and great intricacy and dexterity of rhythm. Between these two extremes, between passionate language that sustains itself, and artifice that makes a great virtue of dexterity, lie all the meters one finds in poetry:

[65]

blank verse, ballad meter, Spenserian stanza, the Petrarchian sonnet, meters adopted from the Greek and so on.

Chaucer, on the one hand, never touches passion as Shakespeare, Dante or Isaiah do, and, on the other hand, he never loosens his hold upon the realities of life so far as to lose himself in the virtuosity of artificial verse, as Guillaume de Machaut does. He usually walks in the mean between these two extremes; his highest achievement in pathos is in *Troilus and Criseyde* and his most conspicuous employment of artifical verse, let us say, is in *A Compleint to his Lady*. He has tried over a dozen meters, I believe, most of which he took from the French; among these he has employed stanzas of five, six, seven, eight, nine and ten lines, respectively. These various meters the serious student will study, and no doubt he will derive much pleasure from the art with which Chaucer, after he became proficient in craftsmanship, adapted his meter to his subject. But we—dilettanti and novices—need concern ourselves only with the verse in his most familiar measures, in the heroic couplet, the rhyme-royal, and the octosyllabic verse. The structure of the verse in these measures is the same, except that in the two former, both of which he contributed to English prosody, there are five beats, and in the last there are four.

Let us accept a suggestion that Coleridge makes. He says, "Let a few plain rules be given for sounding the final *e* of syllables, and for expressing the termination of such words as o-*ce-an* and na-*ti-on,* etc., as dis-syllables—or let the syllables to be sounded in such cases be marked by a competent metrist. This simple expedient would, with a few trifling exceptions—enable any reader to feel the perfect smoothness and harmony of Chaucer's verse." James Russell Lowell, also, has some good advice: "The best school for learning to understand Chaucer's elisions, compressions, slurrings-over and running-together of syllables is to listen

[66]

to the habitual speech of rustics with whom language is still plastic to meaning, and hurries or prolongs itself accordingly."

And then he advises readers to be guided by the ear, to impute to careless copyists the causes of our difficulties. Here he builds too much, perhaps, on the inaccuracy of scriveners like Adam, whom Chaucer berates so severely:

Adam scriveyn, if ever it thee bifalle
Boece or Troylus for to wryten newe,
Under thy long lokkes [of hair] thou most have the scalle,
But [unless] after my makyng thou wryte more trewe;
So ofte a-daye I mot [must] thy werk renewe,
It to correcte and eek to rubbe and scrape;
And al is thorugh thy negligence and rape [haste].

I imagine that Chaucer's handwriting may have presented difficulties, and, possibly, the curse of a scabby disease upon Adam's scalp for misinterpreting it, if seriously invoked, would have been harsh.

Let us look at Chaucer's practise in dealing with meter. It is very much like that of other poets. All poets have a common purpose of putting words in such sequence as to make the sounds affect us more forcibly, more vivaciously, more delicately, more emotionally, than prose. Take his heroic couplet. The normal verse has ten syllables with an accent on the second, fourth, sixth, eighth and tenth, *e. g.,*

Her lítel chíld lay wépyng ín hir árm.

But a long succession of such verses would be monotonous, so Chaucer asserts his right as an Englishman to be master of his own meter; his lines succeed one another like waves, hollow and crest, hollow and crest, but they are crossed and

[67]

varied by sundry irregularities. He endeavors to place his accented and his unaccented syllables in the order that best suits his narrative.

His most common variation from the normal ten-syllable verse is to put an unaccented syllable at the end of the verse, after the fifth beat, e. g.,

> Whan thát Aprílle wíth his shóures sóot*e* ;

or, within the verse he suppresses a final e, and sometimes another final vowel, before words beginning with a vowel, or in case of the *e,* before words beginning with an *h,* what scholars call, I believe, apocopation, e. g.,

> The dróght*e* of Márch hath pérced tó the roóte ;

or, he starts with an accented syllable, omitting the unaccented syllable that should have come before it, e. g.,

> "Móder," quód sh*e,* "and máyde bríght, Marý-e,"
>   *   *
> Twénty boókes, clád in blák or réed ;

or, he may shift or reverse the accent—nice meters curtsy to great poets—putting the crest of the wave where the hollow normally would be, e. g.,

> "Pées litel sóne, I wól do thée noon hárm" ;

or, he slurs an unimportant *e,*

> And óver his lítel eý-en shé it léyd-e.

You will find the same procedure in many poets.

Let us then merely note Chaucer's usage in these few particulars:

1. He sometimes omits the first syllable of his first foot and starts with the second, which carries an accent.
2. At the end of the line, there is often an extra syllable, usually an *e,* but sometimes *es, ed, en, et,* which is pronounced but not accented.
3. Sometimes there is an extra syllable before the cæsura.
4. An *e* at the end of a word, such as modern spelling no longer uses, is generally pronounced unless it comes before a vowel or an *h.*
5. An insignificant *e* in the verse is sometimes slurred over.

My advice is to keep the beat and slur ambiguous syllables, until you are sufficiently familiar with his verse to know when to pronounce and when to elide. What a novice should try to get is the hang of the verse, the lilt of the line.

Let me show you how the beat falls in a stanza, written in what they call rhyme royal—"surely it is a royalle kinde of verse,"—from *The Man of Law's Tale,* where the ill-fated Custance is put with her baby alone into a ship and cast adrift:

Hir lítel chíld lay wépyng ín hir árm,
And knélynge, pítouslý to hým she séyd-e,
"Pées, litel sóne, I wól do thée noon hárm."
With thát hir cóverchief óf [off] hir heéd she bréyd-e [took],
And óver his lítel eý-en [eyes] she it léyde,
And ín her árm she lúlleth ít ful fáste,
And ín-to hévene [hev'n'] hire eý-en úp she cáste.

Disciples of Epicurus, however, do not boggle over rules, they take verses as they would hurdles, in an easy even stride, and if one chances to kick a hurdle down, no matter. It is better to enjoy the thought, than to balk at a cæsura or a shift of accent. The point to remember is that the verse will scan if the reader will take the pains to note the value of each syllable; but for the novice, who seeks pleasure and lacks the ambition to become a Chaucerian scholar, it is best to take meter lightly, for, after all, the purpose of meter is to present the matter to the mind in the most effective way.

CHAPTER IX

THE BOOK OF THE DUCHESS

CHAUCER'S period of studious application to French poetry and French prosody was happily interrupted by political events. Had he continued to live quietly doing his duties in the royal household and spending his times of leisure upon his books, he might have become an eminent poet, he might have written *The Knight's Tale, Troilus and Criseyde,* and such, admirable in their way, but he would never have acquired his large knowledge of human nature, his brave tolerance of its failings, and his kindly sympathy with its sorrows, which enabled him to write one of the great books in the world's literature, *The Canterbury Tales.* His career is a contradiction of Goethe's saying,

> *Es bildet ein Talent sich in der Stille,*

for Chaucer's talent was fashioned not in quiet, but in the main stream of English military, diplomatic and business life.

The Peace of Brétigny had not proved a success. France had been horribly devastated before the Peace by English troops, and after the Peace by freebooters, and had found it impossible to pay the vast sums of money that she had promised; and, besides that, the operation of turning over to the English French towns, villages and castles, against the will of the inhabitants, proved a very difficult task. The English believed that the French were not dealing honestly; but in fact there was often real doubt as to what was in-

[71]

cluded in the cession. Mutual suspicion caused bad blood all along the border. But the pot boiled over in consequence of quite a different matter. The Prince of Wales had been acting for several years as viceroy of the Duchy of Aquitaine, when he was asked to intervene in the civil war between Don Pedro, the legitimate King of Castile, and his bastard brother, Enrique of Trastamare. The bastard, with the aid of French adventurers, had ousted Don Pedro. Various political considerations made English intervention desirable, so the Prince of Wales led an army through the Pass of Roncevaux into Castile, defeated the bastard in a smashing victory, set Don Pedro on his throne and went back to Aquitaine. It was now the month of August, 1367. But Don Pedro did not pay the money that he had promised for the Prince's intervention, and the Prince's mercenary army had to be paid, or it would pay itself. The Prince, his pockets very empty, was forced to levy a hearth tax upon his Gascon subjects, which at once provoked expostulation, refusal and rebellion. The Gascon lords complained to King Charles V, on the pretext that he was their suzerain lord. This happened in April, 1368, and the news must have reached England after a few w..ks, and rendered it apparent to King Edward that the Peace of Brétigny would soon become a dead letter, and that he must prepare for war.

One consequence arising from this general situation was that Chaucer was sent on some errand to France. What it was we can only guess. The record merely states that on July seventeenth he received a passport from Dover, and a grant of ten pounds for his expenses. When he came back, or perhaps before going, he was enrolled among the esquires of the King's household, probably because his former patron, Prince Lionel, had gone away. Evidently he was well thought of. Perhaps this favor was mainly due to his wife, but Chaucer's intelligence, his common sense and his ability to make friends commended him still more.

War, according to expectation, was soon renewed. Charles V had acted warily, but in January, 1369, he summoned the Prince of Wales to appear before the Chamber of Peers in Paris, and answer the complaints of the Gascon lords. According to the story, the Prince replied that he would come with sixty thousand men at his back. In May, King Charles *fit deffier Edouard le roi d'Angleterre,* and King Edward resumed the title of King of France, and hurried on preparations to send an army across the Channel. In July, John of Gaunt, with six hundred men-at-arms and fifteen hundred archers, together with Sir Walter Manny, the Earls of Warwick and Salisbury, and Sir Henry Percy, landed at Calais. Among those *equitantibus de guerra in partibus Francie* was, it seems, Geoffrey Chaucer. The Duke harried the countryside from Calais to Boulogne, and then, learning that a French army under Philippe le Hardi of Burgundy was approaching, stood on the defensive. The French, obedient to Du Guesclin's policy of avoiding a pitched battle, stayed in their camp, opposite the English, from August twenty-fifth to September twelfth, and then retreated. The English, finding themselves unopposed, marched along the coast ravaging as they went. Unable to take walled towns, they passed by Saint Omer, and Saint Pol, crossed the River Somme, near Abbeville, and proceeding parallel to the coast burned, pillaged and harried as far as Harfleur; there they turned round, and following another route in order to find fresh towns to rob and fresh fields to destroy, went back to Calais, and crossed over to England in November.

The bad news must have greeted them at Calais. Queen Philippa had died in August, and the Duchess of Lancaster had died on September twelfth. This was sad tidings to Chaucer, as well as to John of Gaunt. The Queen had been a kind friend to Philippa, and the Duchess had been a loving wife to the Duke. Through Blanche, John of Gaunt had inherited the Duchy of Lancaster and become the richest subject in England; they had had five children, of whom two died in infancy, and a third, Henry Bolingbroke, lived to be King Henry IV. The Duke had loved her. When, nearly thirty years afterward, he came to draw his will, he made provision to be buried beside her ashes, although he had been twice married since her death: *"En primes jeo devise m'alme a Dieu et a sa tres douce miere seinte Marie et a le joy du ciel, et mon corps a estre enselevez en l'esglise cathedrale de Seinte Poule de Londres, pres de l'autier principale de mesme l'eglise, juxte ma tres chere jadys compaigne Blanch illeoq's enterre."* Two priests were to chaunt continuously masses for her soul, and every year on the anniversary of her death, a solemn service was held in Saint Paul's at which the Duke attended, if he was in England, and if not, some officers of high rank took his place.

The Duke came back from Calais to desolation and widowerhood. Whether he commanded Chaucer to write an elegy upon the Duchess, as Professor Kittredge says, or whether Chaucer, feeling an emotional impulse to express his own sorrow as well, offered to write an elegy, I don't know, but in either case it is apparent that Chaucer already had a reputation as a poet, and that he was on friendly terms, almost intimate one might say, with the Duke. Possibly, if Froissart had been in England, he might have been asked, for his reputation as a poet was well established, and the Duke might have been as much pleased with a French poem as an English. Indeed, Chaucer, never having attempted an elegy before and puzzled as to how to begin, borrows his opening lines from Froissart's *Le Paradys d'Amour.* I will quote them to show you both how close and how free his translation is:

> I have gret wonder, be this lyght,
> How that I lyve, for day ne nyght
> I may nat slepe wel nygh noght;
> I have so many an ydel thoght,
> Purely for defaute of slep,
> That, by my trouthe, I take no kep
> Of nothing, how hyt cometh or gooth,
> Ne me nys nothyng leef nor looth.

> *Je sui de moi en grant merveille*
> *Comment je vifs, quant tant je veille,*
> *Et on ne porrait en veillant*
> *Trouver de moi plus travaillant;*
> *Car bien sacies que pour veiller*
> *Me viennent souvent travailler*
> *Pensees et melancolies——.*

This elegy, called *The Book of the Duchess,* is a fairly long poem, of 1,334 lines, six times as long as *Lycidas,* and four times as long as *Adonais.* A distinguished scholar with reference to it speaks of Chaucer's "exquisite and admirable art," but the unscholarly reader is rather impressed by the complicated artifice of approach before the poet reaches the purpose of the poem, praise of the Duchess. He begins by saying that he can not sleep. One does not expect lines like,

> O sleep, O gentle sleep,
> Nature's soft nurse! how have I frighted thee,
> That thou no more wilt weigh my eyelids down
> And steep my senses in forgetfulness?

[75]

But, on being warned of "exquisite and admirable art," one's expectations are high. The lines read:

> Defaute of slep and hevynesse
> Hath sleyn my spirit of quyknesse,
> That I have lost al lustyhede.

The commentators bid us compare this passage with some lines of Guillaume de Machaut:

> *Et pour ce que merencolie*
> *Esteint toute pensée lie,*
> *Et aussi que je bien vëoie*
> *Que mettre conseil n'i pooie——*

Then the poet, unable to sleep, takes up the book of Ovid's *Metamorphoses* and reads the story of Alcyone and Ceÿx, how Morpheus can make any one sleep, and how Alcyone learned in a dream that Ceÿx had been drowned and how both were turned into sea birds. Stirred by the knowledge that Morpheus has the power of giving sleep, the poet, following a passage by Machaut in the *Fonteinne Amoureuse,* in which the would-be sleeper promises to Morpheus a night-cap of peacock's feathers and a bed stuffed with gyrfalcons' plumage, Chaucer's sleepless poet promises to the God a feather-bed of pigeons' down, striped with gold and covered with fine black satin from across the sea. The poet's prayer is granted, he sleeps and dreams a dream. This is the connecting link between the story of Alcyone and Ceÿx and the elegy upon the Duchess. It seems to me rather artifice than art, the experiment of an apprentice. A dream was a convention of the strictest obligation. So the poet dreamt, and dreamt that he heard the noises of a hunt, of hounds and horn. Up he gets, mounts his horse and rides

[76]

after. The quarry escapes, and the master of the hunt sounds a blast of recall. And here is the most characteristic Chaucerian bit in the whole poem:

> A whelp, that fauned me as I stood,
> That hadde yfolowed, and koude [knew] no good.
> Hyt [it] com and crepte to me as lowe
> Ryght as hyt [it] hadde me yknowe,
> Helde down hys hed and joyned hys eres,
> And leyde al smothe doun hys heres [hairs].
> I wolde have kaught hyt, and anoon
> Hyt fledde, and was fro me goon.

This is a touch of the Chaucer that we know, the poet of *The Canterbury Tales,* who for the nonce frees himself from the medieval manner. The idea of the whelp came from Machaut, but Chaucer was not content to translate

> *Le petit chien*
> *Prist a glatir* [began to yelp],

he describes a real live puppy. The poet goes on his way, enters a wood, and comes upon a man in black, "a wonder wel-farynge knyght"—sitting under an oak, making sad rhymes,

> . . . a compleynte to hymselve,
> The moste pitee, the moste rowthe [piteous],
> That ever I herde . . .

This black knight is all woebegone,

> The blood was fled for pure drede
> Doun to hys herte, to make hym warm—

at which a commentator unwisely, for it is not fair to set Shakespeare's mastery side by side with Chaucer's prentice hand, recalls the line,

Why does the blood thus muster to my heart?

The poet persuades the black knight to speak of his lost lady. Here Chaucer incorporates bits of Machaut or of the *Roman de la Rose,* almost word for word. There was no more question of plagiary than there was of copyright. All poets culled where they chose; they cited the bees that go from flower to flower gathering honey. The concernancy lay in the success of the verse, or the idea appropriated; did it fit in among the poet's other verses, did it sweeten the melody, did it heighten the effect? The black knight, whom every reader would recognize as John of Gaunt, then tells how he fell in love with Blanche, how he composed lyrics in her honor, how she loved him and "took him in her governaunce," and how happy they were:

> "Therewyth she was alway so trewe,
> Our joye was ever ylyche [alike] newe;
> Our hertes wern so evene a payre,
> That never nas that oon contrayre
> To that other, for no woo.
> For sothe, ylyche they suffred thoo
> Oo blysse, and eke oo sorwe bothe;
> Ylyche they were bothe glad and wrothe;
> Al was us oon, withoute were [doubt].
> And thus we lyved ful many a yere
> So wel, I kan nat telle how."

Did this depict the Duke's real feelings? I can not tell. I believe that it did. All the court knew what the Duke's real feelings toward his wife were, and it would have been rash

[78]

to misrepresent them. But whether their happiness so depicted was true or not, it was singularly like the happiness
described by the lady in *Le Jugement dou Roy de Behaigne*

> *Ne riens desplaire*
> *Ne li peüst qui a moy deeist plaire.*
> *De nos deus cuers [cœurs] estoit si juste paire*
> *Qu'onques ne fu l'un à l'autre contraire;*
> *Einsois [unis] estoient*
> *Tuit d'un acort, une pensée avoient,*
> *De volonté, de désir se sambloient;*
> *Un bien, un mal, une joie sentoient*
> *Conjointement.*

It is prettily said, more so by the French poet, I think, but
artifice hovers over all the lines, and one sees how far away
artifice is from art at its highest, if one stops to read Homer's lines,

> οὐ μὲν γὰρ τοῦ γε κρεῖσσον καὶ ἄρειον,
> ἢ ὅθ' ὁμοφρονέοντε νοήμασιν οἶκον ἔχητον
> ἀνὴρ ἠδὲ γυνή,

For than this, I mean, there is nothing greater
Nor better, than when man and wife dwell together
Of one will in all their thoughts.

After this the end comes abruptly. The poet, asks the black
knight "where is she now?" and learns that she is dead.
"Be God, hyt ys routhe!" the poet cries, and, as if startled by
these words, the huntsmen begin to ride homeward to a
castle, from which a bell rang out and woke the poet, who
found himself lying in bed with Ovid in his hand.
There, you have a skeleton of the poem. My theory, in
this little book, is to lay Chaucer's poems, in the roughest

possible outline, before the unscholarly reader, and to say no more than what may be necessary for him to decide whether it is worth his while to read this one, or that, or all of them. Before advising him to read *The Book of the Duchess,* I should ask him first, "Have you read *Lycidas, Adonais, Thyrsis?*" If so, you will be disappointed; here is an elegy of a very different quality. But as a student of Chaucer, you will see what problems confronted him, and how he faced them. He had never written an elegy before, and he was unexpectedly called upon to commemorate the death of the first lady in the realm after the Princess of Wales. It would hardly do to make experiments, to give rein to his own opinion of what an elegy should be. The only safe and courteous course was to follow existing models, and adapt conventional ideas to the circumstances of the case, to consider what would be the most courtly fashion to express grief at this lady's death? Chaucer was essentially circumspect, he was not impetuous, hasty, not at all *primesautier* like his acquaintance Froissart; he was sensible, cautious and deliberate. He decided to take what he could from the poems he was familiar with, and to do more or less what a French poet would do for the occasion. He got his first clue from Froissart, sleeplessness. He followed this up with Ovid, this brings him to sleep, and to dream. The sleep, the dream, the landscape, the month of May, the *smale foules,* are what the Duke of Lancaster and all those of the royal household interested in letters would expect. The charming part is the description of the Duchess and the love between her and her husband; that, too, was a very delicate matter; the poet had to be personal enough to describe the Duchess so that every one would recognize her, and yet conventional enough not to overstep the bounds of delicacy and the observances due to her exalted rank.

The poem is interesting, then, to the general reader because he can discover, if he takes the trouble to look at the French poems referred to by the commentators, how Chaucer used his precedents, how he combined borrowed verses and imitated ideas with the matter of his own imagination; and also because this poem, more than any other, reveals what the relations were between Chaucer and the Duke, how intimate, how honorable for both.

CHAPTER X

ITALY

THE elegy seems to have given satisfaction to the Duke; and it is fair to suppose that the Duke's friendship was an important factor in Chaucer's rising fortunes. Chaucer's old friends at court, for I think one may call them so, Queen Philippa, Prince Lionel, the Countess of Ulster, the Duchess Blanche, were all dead, the King was in the hands of his mistress, Alice Perrers, and had it not been for the Duke's patronage, it is quite possible that Chaucer would have been forced to follow his family footsteps and seek his livelihood in the wine trade. But the Duke's patronage gave him the opportunity, and his own abilities took advantage of it.

I assume that the elegy gave the Duke satisfaction, for within six months Chaucer was sent abroad to Brussels in company with Sir Richard Stury on some diplomatic errand; his safe conduct was made out from June twentieth to Michaelmas. What this errand was, nobody knows. In the meantime the Duke of Lancaster had not abandoned himself to grief, but busied himself with collecting soldiers to go to the help of the Black Prince, who was sore pressed by the French all along the borders of Aquitaine. He sailed early in June, some weeks or more before Chaucer had left Dover. But the great career of the Black Prince had come to its end; illness forced him to go home, and his brother took his place as lord lieutenant. Six months later, John of Gaunt also resigned. Whether from a desire to forget his grief, or to gratify a naturally covetous spirit, he conceived a royal ambition. I have told how Don Pedro had been

[82]

reseated upon his throne by the Black Prince; but after the Prince had returned to Aquitaine, Du Guesclin went back with a troop of French mercenaries to aid Don Enrique. Don Pedro was defeated, captured and murdered, and Don Enrique became King. John of Gaunt thought that here lay his opportunity for a crown; he married Don Pedro's eldest daughter, Constance (September, 1371), and assumed the title of King of Castile, hoping to be able in course of time to make good his claim by the aid of an English army. He returned to England with his bride in November, and at once took an active part in English politics; a strong party at his back, he judged, would serve as a stepping-stone to the coveted throne. He found parliament eager to prosecute the war, and in June, 1372, his brother-in-law, the Earl of Pembroke, was dispatched with a fleet to La Rochelle.

Don Enrique, to protect himself from the English, had allied himself with the King of France, and on his part had promised to send the Castilian fleet in support of his ally. He was as good as his word. Spanish merchant ships, accustomed to sail from Cadiz, Seville and Coruña to the ports of the Low Countries, were readily convertible into men-of-war, and Spanish mariners were excellent seamen. This Castilian fleet encountered the English squadron under the Earl of Pembroke off La Rochelle, and won a complete victory; all the English vessels were sunk or captured (June, 1372). I am now coming to what I conceive the connection to be between these political events and Chaucer's journey to Italy, which in its broadening and deepening experience, has been compared to Goethe's *Italienische Reise*.

The situation of England at sea was serious. The French and Castilian fleets united could control the Channel, and interfere seriously not only with the Flemish trade but also with sending troops and munitions to the English army in

France. To meet this danger, King Edward, together with other projects, endeavored to tighten his friendly relations with Genoa. At that time, Genoa was an important sea power; she had scores of mercantile establishments in ports all along the shores of the Mediterranean, in Greece, in Syria, on the African coast, and in the Black Sea, and her galleys sailed out into the Atlantic to trade with Flanders and England. And it had been her habit to furnish mercenary crossbowmen for service by land or sea. She could be very useful to England. Unfortunately, not very long before this, it had happened that a Genoese ship sailing up the Channel had been robbed by English sailors, piratical fellows from Devon and Cornwall. You remember the Shipman among the Canterbury pilgrims,

Of nyce conscience took he no keep.

And the Doge of Genoa, Domenico de Campofregoso, in this very year, 1372, had sent his envoy, Marco Gentile, to obtain restitution of the booty taken. The English government, prudently, with an eye to the general political situation, acknowledged the fault and paid two thousand silver marks. Then, in order to confirm and extend friendly relations, King Edward's government appointed commissioners to agree with the Genoese government upon an English port where the Genoese merchants should establish themselves. As this embassy was fraught with such consequence to Chaucer's political career, I will quote the document of appointment at length:

"The King, to all and each, to whose notice these presents come, greeting,

"Please take notice that we, having complete confidence in the fidelity, circumspection and prudence of our beloved and trusty James de Provan, John de Mari, a citizen of Genoa, and Geoffrey Chaucer, our esquire, do hereby appoint and constitute the aforesaid, James, John and Geoffrey, or two of them, of whom we wish John to be one, our special envoys and representatives, giving and granting to them by these presents full authority and particular mandate, to treat for us and in our name with his Excellency, Domenico de Campofregoso, Doge of Genoa, and his council, as well as with the citizens, the honorable men and the corporation of the City of Genoa, upon the following matters, towit: that these citizens, honorable men, and merchants of Genoa may have a suitable and satisfactory place to themselves in some town or port on the coast in our realm of England, for the accommodation of carracks and other vessels from the city aforesaid, and of the wares and merchandise belonging to those citizens,

"And also as to a grant of franchises, liberties, immunities and privileges to those citizens and merchants in such place aforesaid, when they shall come for the sake of trading or to sojourn a while, according as these matters shall be agreed upon with the said Doge and his Council, the citizens, merchants and corporation aforesaid,

"And definitely and clearly to certify this same.

"In testimony whereof etc.

"Given at Westminister, the 12th day of November, in the 33rd year of Our reign in France and the 46th of Our reign in England."

John de Mari was a citizen of Genoa, and presumably was appointed on the commission on that account, as an act of graciousness or policy. But as to James de Provan, it is a little strange to find that ten days later, he was appointed to quite a different office by the King. On November twenty-second, official notice was given to all the royal admirals,

[85]

captains and officers, that the King had appointed his Eminence Peter de Campofregoso, brother to the Doge, admiral of the fleet of galleys that was to come from Genoa to aid the English, and that he had conferred upon the said Peter full power to appoint James de Provan [Pronan], knight, as his lieutenant or vice-admiral of the fleet aforesaid and that Peter was to appoint James to that position. The next day, presumably in order to place Provan's authority beyond cavil, the King appointed him lieutenant and vice-admiral to Peter de Campofregoso in the fleet aforesaid.

The naval agreement that obtained the help of a Genoese fleet was subsequently supplemented by a military agreement with two Genoese gentlemen adventurers, freebooting captains, I suppose, who were to provide fifty crossbowmen and fifty seamen and two officers besides themselves, for a year. These documents show that the English government was making a sort of tripartite treaty with Genoa, naval, military, and mercantile; and it would seem as if Chaucer, after James de Provan had been taken from the commission, was under a good deal of responsibility. He was sent with one Genoese citizen to Genoa to draft the terms of an important mercantile treaty; and one conjectures that through Italian friends in London he already may have acquired some knowledge of the Italian language.

However that may be, the appointment was highly honorable, and it is hard to believe that Chaucer was not indebted to the Duke of Lancaster for it. The King paid little heed to directing policy, the Black Prince was ill, Lionel was dead, Prince Edmund was an indolent person, and Thomas of Woodstock (subsequently Duke of Gloucester), very much younger, so it seems as if such appointments would lie in the Duke's hands. The Duke had known Chaucer for nearly fifteen years, and probably familiarly; their sons, Harry Bolingbroke and young Thomas Chaucer, seem to have been

[86]

about of an age; and Philippa had been in attendance, not only on the Duke's mother, but on his wife. Quite apart from Chaucer's practical abilities, and his presumable knowledge of Italian, there seem to be motives enough to explain why the Duke should pick him for the embassy, and I think that it will not be scandalous, too scandalous, to mention another probable factor in the Duke of Lancaster's patronage of Chaucer. The Duke's second marriage was for ambition, not for love, and it is to be feared that he sadly neglected the forlorn little Spanish lady, who, truth to tell, was illegitimate, in favor of Philippa's sister, Katharine Swynford, who was but twenty-two years old and according to repute, very pretty, and acting as governess to his two daughters. Sir Hugh Swynford, her husband, was at this time away in Aquitaine, and perhaps already killed. The Duke's admiration rapidly ripened into a stronger feeling. Remember that the respectable days of Queen Philippa were over and gone, and that Alice Perrers, of whom the chroniclers speak harshly, was lording it in the royal court with a shameless hand. The Duke's accounts tell the story. On May 1, 1372, he gave ten pounds to the lady; on May fifteenth, an annuity of fifty marks (a mark was worth about two-thirds of a pound, that is, perhaps a hundred dollars in our currency) in exchange for a former annuity of twenty marks; on June twentieth, a grant to her of the wardship of the lands of her late husband; in August, to her sister, Philippa Chaucer, a pension of ten pounds, in reward, or so expressed to be, of her services to the Duchess Constance, and much more. That the Duke's attachment was no passing fancy, but a deep and constant affection, is shown by the fact that, after a liaison of twenty-odd years, when she was forty-five years old, and he a widower for the second time, he married her, and thereby he and Chaucer became brothers-in-law. But however much the Duke liked Chaucer, however much

[87]

he may have loved Mrs. Chaucer's sister, Chaucer would never have received the missions conferred upon him had he not been a capable man of affairs.

Chaucer left London December 1, 1372, and presumably in the company of his fellow commissioner, John de Mari. All that the records show of this memorable journey is that he went to Genoa and to Florence, and did not return until May 23, 1373, and that he received one hundred and thirty-eight marks for his expenses, a sum reckoned at thirteen thousand dollars of modern money. The rest we can only infer, as an archeologist deduces a whole edifice from some scattered stones. He probably went on to Florence, after having transacted his business in Genoa, in order to borrow money for the King from Florentine bankers, a task that shows how great confidence was placed in his diplomatic skill, for every business man in Florence must have known that King Edward had ruined the great banking houses of the Peruzzi and of the Bardi by not repaying the immense loans they had made to him. But whether Chaucer placed a loan or not, what agreement he came to with the Doge of Genoa, what quarters for habitation, what wharves and docks, what franchises and immunities may have been conceded to Genoese merchants and seamen, is of little interest now; the importance of King Edward's embassy lies in Chaucer's acquaintance with Italy, in the spiritual and intellectual effect that Italy produced upon him. I do not think that Chaucer is comparable to Goethe, either as a man or as a poet, but one need not go to Goethe to measure the influence of Italy upon a spirit, foreign born and foreign bred. Even the common man of little soul knows well how his first visit to Italy touched his heart and lifted it high, when he first listened to the waters of the Mediterranean lap the Lavinian shore, and beheld old towers reflected in the waves' intenser day, when he first smelt the odor of orange blos-

[88]

soms and saw the golden fruit, while the green-gray olive leaves turned their silvery backs in the breeze, and black-eyed Tuscan girls wished him *"Buon giorno,"*—how Italy disclosed to him a beauty, a grace, a charm, not merely of sky, of sea, of purple Apennines, not merely of nature in melodramatic splendor or in childlike loveliness, but rather of that intellectual beauty, of that spiritual radiance which Shelley apostrophizes:

> Thy light alone—like mist o'er mountains driven,
>   Or music by the night wind sent,
> Thro' strings of some still instrument,
>   Or moonlight on a mountain stream,
> Gives grace and truth to life's unquiet dream.

Every newcomer to Italy is the thrall, not only of nature, but of the noble imagination that expressed itself in architecture, painting and sculpture. Chaucer, more sensitive than common men, must have felt all this more deeply, more delicately, than they. He found a civilization much riper than that he had known in the north. When he traveled from Genoa to Florence, he must have gone through Pisa and seen the Cathedral, that on summer days seems to be built of sunlight, the Baptistry, the leaning Tower, the Campo Santo with its dread frescos of the Triumph of Death, and the glittering Arno as it wound through the palaced streets. Perhaps he rode through Pistoia and Prato. At Florence he saw the Palazzo Vecchio, the Baptistry, the Bargello, the Duomo partly up, the Campanile gloriously simple in its many-colored marbles, line sweetly married to color, Santa Croce, Santa Maria Novella, the Guelf Towers, the dreaming river,—lovely when the full orbed moon hung over Fiesole, and lovelier still under the purple tints of evening,—the Ponte Vecchio, the Ponte Rubaconte, the frescos of Giotto and Orcagna; these sights must have whetted his curiosity to learn, if he had not known before, what literature accompanied such great achievements. And so he proceeded to make the acquaintance of Italian literature. The critics, however, say that the effect of Italy did not come to full ripeness in his poetry, until after a second journey in 1378.

CHAPTER XI

DANTE

CHAUCER was a scholar, a poet, a man of letters, and in those Tuscan evenings, after he had discussed business with the bankers, he must have asked, or his hosts have thrust upon him, much about Dante. The bones of the great poet had lain at Ravenna for fifty years, but his fame had been steadily growing, and Florence was proud of her greatest son. Chaucer had read some Latin classics, but in the *Divine Comedy* he read poetry such as he had never read before. Never, from the golden days of Hellas had Dante at his best been equaled, nor has he since, except by Shakespeare. Nor is Shakespeare ever as fierce as Dante, nor in his tenderness does he exceed Dante's tenderness. Here was allegory very different from that with which Chaucer was familiar in Guillaume de Lorris, or Machaut, or Deschamps, or Froissart. But Chaucer's genius was so different from Dante's genius that I find it hard to believe that he cared greatly for the *Divine Comedy*. That poem, in its essence, is a passionate lyrical utterance of the poet's deepest convictions concerning God and right and wrong. Chaucer, to my thinking, never had any strong emotional feeling about God, or about right and wrong; his deepest sympathies were with the sorrows of life and with its comedy. I take it that what he valued most in Dante is his power of presenting a fact, all raw and red, or all soft and beautiful, as God had made it, and next, the dramatic episodes of Francesca da Rimini, of Ugolino, of Ulysses, and so on. Indeed, Chaucer recognized so completely how alien Dante's

qualities were to his own that he never attempts to do anything in a Dantesque way. When commentators, as they
sometimes do, speak without due qualifications of Dante's
influence upon Chaucer, they puzzle and mislead their
readers. Dante stands on the farther side of the great ridge
that separates the medieval from the modern world, and
Chaucer stands on this. Dante's passion for establishing
God's kingdom on earth, in one spiritual and secular union,
and his emotional conviction that God's will is embodied in
human ethics, found but scant response in Chaucer; and
Dante would have been angry with Chaucer's indifference
to God's righteousness, with his insular nationalism, his
content to have Christendom broken into fragments, and
he would have scorned Chaucer's delight in the humor and
jocosity of the *comédie humaine*. Perhaps as good an illustration as any of the spiritual difference between the two is
that Chaucer takes the very words that Dante puts into Saint
Bernard's mouth when he prays to the Virgin Mary—holy
words, according to every possible standard of holiness—
and gives them to Troilus for his thanksgiving to Venus,
when she brings him to bed with Criseyde:

Benigne Love, thow holy bond of thynges,
Whoso wol grace, and list the nought [not] honouren,
Lo, his desir wol fle withouten wynges.

Chaucer did appreciate the music of Dante's Italian syllables,
and the nearest he comes to an attempt to imitate Dante is
in his efforts to give to his own verses as much of that
cello-like melody as English words would allow.

However, the commentators have spoken so frequently of
Dante in relation to certain poems of Chaucer's that we had
better see what they mean. Let us take *The House of Fame*,
written some time after this Italian journey, for Professor

[92]

French says, "No poem of Chaucer's shows more striking evidence of the influence of the *Divine Comedy* than *The Hous of Fame*," and Professor Robinson, ". . . he makes so much use of Dante that the poem has been regarded—unjustifiably, to be sure—as an imitation of the *Divine Comedy*," and, to go much farther back, Chaucer's disciple, Lydgate, uses the expression "Dante in English" which later scholars applied, whether rightly or wrongly, to *The House of Fame*.

As I think it a great error to praise a poet for qualities that he has not got, for achievements to which he does not aspire, I shall ask the reader to run through this poem, more especially as professional critics praise it highly. It opens with a discussion of the nature of dreams, which is followed by an invocation to the God of Sleep, praying that he will speed the poet to tell his dream aright, and calling down maledictions on the head of any one that may dislike the way he tells it:

> . . . whoso, thorgh presumpcion,
> Or hate, or skorn, or thorgh envye,
> Dispit, or jape [jest], or vilanye [bad manners],
> Mysdeme [despise] hyt, pray I Jesus God
> That (dreme he barefot, dreme he shod),
> That every harm that any man
> Hath had, syth the world began,
> Befalle hym thereof, or [before] he sterve [die] . . .

The poet then proceeds to tell his dream. He found himself within the temple of Venus, and on the walls the story of the Æneid depicted, and written on a table of brass, these words:

> "I wol now singen, yif I kan,
> The armes, and also the man
> That first cam, thurgh his destinee,

Fugityf of Troy contree,
In Itayle, with ful moche pyne
Unto the strondes of Lavyne."

I do not find in this translation of the opening lines of the
Æneid any appreciation of the grand manner of Virgil's
verse, and I should infer a similar lack of appreciation in
Chaucer of Dante's spiritual intensity, of Dante's violent
attempt to take heaven by force, if *The House of Fame* were
in any respect an imitation of Dante; it is not, it is an
ironical, satirical and humorous poem.

After looking at the pictures of Æneas, the poet goes
out of the temple into a field; an eagle swoops down and,
catching him fast, soars up again, and frightens him so badly
that the eagle thought him asleep:

. . . "Awak," to me he seyde,
Ryght in the same vois and stevene [sound]
That useth oon [one] I koude nevene [name];
And with that vois, soth for to seyn,
My mynde cam to me ageyn,
For hyt [it] was goodly [kindly] seyd to me,
So nas [was] hyt never wont to be.

This impolite and dull joke about his wife has punished
Chaucer by giving rise to the hypothesis that he and she
were not happy together. Mr. Masefield, taking these verses
in connection with a number of other satirical passages concerning wives and women in general, believes the hypothesis;
but most commentators find no more than a little commonplace medieval vulgarity here. The excuse is that the whole
tone of the poem is jocose. The eagle then talks, introducing a vast amount of medieval erudition; this talk, according
to Saintsbury, is as humorous as *The Canterbury Tales,* and,

[94]

according to Professor Kittredge, "intensely amusing." The eagle carries the poet up to the House of Fame. The poet then comes into the presence of Fame, herself, and witnesses the nonsensical way in which she distributes or withholds fame, quite regardless whether the swarming crowds that come before her want it or not, or what kind they want, good or bad. From here the poet goes to another house, the House of Rumor, sixty miles long, made of wicker work, that is whirling round and round with immense rapidity, while in and out rush a tumultuous multitude of tidings, true and false, of wars, of peace, of marriages, of repose, of labor, of travels, of love, hate, concord, strife, health, sickness and so forth. The house, too, is full of shipmen, pilgrims, pardoners, couriers, messengers, all with pouches full of lies and such like. And while the poet is going about to learn what he can, and begins to question a stranger, the story ends abruptly leaving scholars to guess of what and how much it is truncated.

I must admit that I find the poem extremely tedious, but Professor Kittredge says, "The poem is a humorous study of mankind from the point of view of a ruling passion. In substance it is a kind of epitome of the author's knowledge and culture in science and art and philosophy, in French and Italian and Latin. It is composed in small and great with astonishing virtuosity. It is full of spirit and originality, and instinct throughout with conscious power—a poem not only of sufficient merit in itself to approach the rank of a masterpiece, but also in the highest degree remarkable for what it indicates."

Professor Lowes is still more enthusiastic about the poem even than Kittredge or Saintsbury. Let me quote from his delightful lectures: "Book II is a racy and vivid masterpiece, sparkling with humour and wit. . . . [from the swoop of the eagle] to the end, without a tedious moment, the poem runs its swift and brilliant way. . . . Even Chaucer himself never surpassed the grasp of the potentialities of a situation, or the swiftness and lightness of touch which he displayed in that incomparable yarn. I am giving loose rein to superlatives I know, but the thing in its kind *is* superlative."

Is not this enthusiasm charming? Am I not right to say that there is a touch of Romeo in every true scholar? How he gallops "giving loose rein," like a *troubadour brûlant d'amour!* Great learning has given him the philosopher's stone, by whose virtue he transmutes medieval fancy and outmoded allegory into wit, humor and superlativity. But I warn you, Gentle Readers, before you shall have such a philosopher's stone, you must read twenty-two thousand lines of the *Roman de la Rose,* eighty thousand lines of Guillaume de Machaut, I don't know how many books of Froissart and Deschamps, volume upon volume of Benoît de Sainte-Maure and Guido delle Colonne, *Les romans de Thèbes, d'Eneas, de Jules Cesar,* most other medieval literature and all classical literature, and having done that, if you are very intelligent and gifted with rare enthusiasm and with faith, you will discover those superlative qualities in *The House of Fame* that Professor Lowes speaks of.

There are of course in *The House of Fame* many ideas such as an eagle carrying the poet up, and phrases, similes, words that Chaucer has read in Dante and uses when occasion serves. Scholars hunt these up; that is their business and their pleasure. But I shall pass these "borrowings" by, and proceed to other poems, which are cited as showing Dante's influence, and speak of one of two long passages which are indeed taken or imitated from Dante. The first shall be the prayer to the Virgin in the *Prologue to the Second Nun's Tale,* which is in part a translation of Saint

[96]

Bernard's prayer to her at the close of the *Paradiso*. I have already alluded to it.

> Thow Mayde and Mooder, doghter of thy Sone,
> *Thow welle of mercy, synful soules cure,
> *In whom that God for bountee chees to wone [dwell],
> Thow humble, and heigh over every creature,
> Thou nobledest so ferforth oure nature,
> That no desdeyn the Makere hadde of kynde [human nature]
> His Sone in blood and flessh to clothe and wynde [wrap.]

> *Vergine madre, figlia del tuo Figlio,*
> *Umile ed alta più che creatura,*
> **Termine fisso d'eterno consiglio,*
> *Tu sei colei che l'umana natura*
> *Nobilitasti sì, che il suo Fattore*
> *Non disdegnò di farsi sua fattura.*

I have put asterisks before the two lines of Chaucer not translated from Dante, and before the line of Dante not translated by Chaucer, thus leaving five lines translating five lines. In the two versions I see little equality. The *Tu sei colei*—"Thou art she that rendered human nature so noble that its Creator did not disdain to make *himself* his creature"—of the Italian, seems to my ear more melodious than the English words, and to my mind more simple, direct and majestic in its mystical theology. I continue:

> Withinne the cloistre blisful of thye sydis
> Took mannes shap the eterneel love and pees,
> That of the tryne compas lord and gyde is,
> Whom erthe and see and heven, out of relees,
> Ay heryen [praise]; and thou, Virgine wemmelees,
> Baar of thy body—and dweltest mayden pure—
> The Creatour of every creature.

[97]

Nel ventre tuo si raccese l'amore,
Per lo cui caldo nell' eterna pace
Così è germinato questo fiore.
Qui sei a noi meridiana face
Di caritate, e giuso intra i mortali
Sei di speranza fontana vivace.

Here, you see, Chaucer's first two lines only are a translation and, his matter being unsuited to Dante's context, not a very close translation.

I quote still a third stanza, for I reiterate that the pleasure we derive from a poet is closely allied to a just appreciation of his qualities, and we do him harm rather than advantage if we assign him to that circle in the heaven of poetry to which he does not belong. Dante is the great Christian religious poet, religious in his profound conception that spiritual life depends on a consciousness of God, and no poet is to be compared to him; whereas Chaucer is a poet of this beautiful earth and of the human comedy. The difference between them will appear, I think, to those who know Italian.

Assembled is in thee magnificence
With mercy, goodnesse, and with swich pitee
That thou, that art the sonne of excellence,
Nat oonly helpest hem [them] that preyen thee,
But often tyme, of thy benygnytee,
Ful frely, er that men thyn help biseche,
Thou goost biforn, and art hir [their] lyves leche.

La tua benignità non pur soccorre
A chi dimanda, ma molte fiate
Liberamente al domandar precorre.
In te misericordia, in te pietate,
In te magnificenza, in te s'aduna
Quantunque in creatura è di bontate.

[98]

Here Chaucer's first three lines translate Dante's last three, and his last four, Dante's first three. Mr. John Livingston Lowes has pointed out that Chaucer took some lines from a Latin poem, *Anticlaudianus,* by Alain de Lille. Such search into sources I leave to scholars, the point I wish to make is that the very combination of Dante and Alain de Lille, of Dante and Machaut, proves that Chaucer had no appreciation of the fact that every verse of Dante is bathed in the awful radiance of God's presence, and that it is impossible to take verses here and there from Dante to put in a comic poem, without the loss of their essential significance. Dan Chaucer found this glorious, murky, joyful, dolorous, workaday world good enough for him, and had little or no interest in that spiritual world in which Dante was passionately absorbed.

There is one other passage that I should refer to. In *The Monk's Tale,* Chaucer tells sad stories of famous men maltreated by Fortune, and among others that of "Erl Hugelyn of Pyze," none other than Dante's Ugolino, who together with his children was starved to death in a tower by Archbishop Ruggieri. Chaucer tells the tale in seven stanzas. Each stanza contains eight lines of ten syllables with five beats, rhyming a b a b b c b c, and it may be, perhaps owing to the comparative scarcity of English rhymes, that this metrical form is hampered by the four b rhymes, and is, of its nature, less effective for the expression of horror than the Italian *terza rima,* which is able to draw upon a prodigal supply of rhyming syllables. It seems to me also that such phrases as

Io non piangeva: si dentro impietrai
(I did not weep, so turned I to stone within),

and the question asked by the starving boy,

> *Padre mio, che non m'aiuti,*
> (My father, why do you not help me?)

have no equivalent in Chaucer's English; moreover, Dante has no such feeble lines as Earl Hugolin's

> Allas! Fortune! and weylaway!
> Thy false wheel my wo al may I wyte [blame].

Mr. Theodore Spencer says, "There is nothing of Dante's terrible concision and intensity which makes so indelible impression on the mind." And, that the passage "does not represent Chaucer at his best."

My excuse for dwelling upon the unlikeness of the two poets is that the casual reader hearing scholars talk of the *influence* of Dante upon Chaucer, may think the word refers to qualities of importance and not to the mere borrowing of an idea, an episode or a few phrases. Dante is very Italian and supreme in his way, and Chaucer is very English and very great in his way; but the two ways are quite different. And, after all, what other poet is there that has ever said words like these at the end of Saint Bernard's Prayer, of which we have been speaking,

> *Vedi Beatrice con quanti Beati*
> *Per li miei preghi ti chiudon le mani?*

CHAPTER XII

PETRARCH

I MAKE no doubt that Chaucer enjoyed his stay in Florence, even his talks with the wary bankers, that he loved to saunter through the city, look up at Giotto's tower that swayed, or seemed to sway, like a timid lily when the clouds wandered swiftly above it, or to consider the change that was coming over painting, as he compared his memories of pictured walls in English churches with the work of Gaddo Gaddi, Giotto and Orcagna. But though he took delight, as his poems show, in painted images, his central interest lay in letters, in scholarship and poetry, and certainly he must have heard great talk of Florence's most distinguished living son, Francesco Petrarca.

It is so pleasant to suppose that Chaucer met the other famous poets living in his time, that, as I have done in the case of Guillaume de Machaut, biographers used to say that the two poets, Chaucer and Petrarch, actually did meet, and James Russell Lowell refused to give up the belief. The only basis for the hypothesis, apart from romantic desire, lies in the statement by the Clerk at Oxenford in *The Canterbury Tales,* when it came his turn to tell a story to his fellow pilgrims,

> I wol yow telle a tale which that I
> Lerned at Padowe [Padua] of a worthy clerk, . . .
>   Frraunceys Petrak, the lauriat poete
> . . . whos rethorike sweete
> Enlumyned al Ytaille of poetrie.

This avowal, put into the mouth of one of his characters, gives but slim support to the theory; but romantic scholars, such as James Russell Lowell, argued that it was impossible to suppose that Chaucer, with all his interest in Italian poetry, had not ridden from Florence to Padua where Petrarch was residing at the time. And there is something in the argument. Petrarch was the most distinguished man in Europe. The Black Prince was renowned among soldiers, freebooters, armorers, and in general among young gentlemen devoted to matters military, but Petrarch was honored wherever letters were known, both as a scholar and a poet. In his charming and radiant youth he had written sonnets that fly in the air like winged things, and had received the laurel crown on the Capitol in Rome, almost at the time that Chaucer was born, and since then he had become the foremost humanist in Italy; the Pope had asked him to be a papal secretary, the King of France had invited him to Paris, the Emperor had bidden him to Prague, King Robert of Naples had entertained him, the Visconti were eager to have him in Milan, the Correggi in Parma, the Carraresi in Padua, Florence had offered him a chair in her university, Venice had given him a house. He was a very great personage, and Chaucer must have wanted to see him. His home at that time was at the mountain village of Arquà, near Padua, where he lived in a little house that he had built, surrounded by vines and olive trees, and in it he kept four or five scriveners at work, copying Latin manuscripts, several servants to minister to his growing infirmities, for he was sixty years old, and horses to drive him and his companion, an aged priest, to Padua, where as one of the canons he had Sunday duties to perform. It happened, however, that during the year before this war had broken out between the Tyrant of Padua and the Venetian Republic, and, apparently just before Chaucer left England, Petrarch had sought safety within the walls of Padua. If there had been a meeting between the two poets, it must have been of Chaucer's seeking. The passes over the Apennines were all guarded, even letters were intercepted, and it would have been difficult and dangerous for Chaucer to try to reach Padua, even if he had deemed it compatible with his duties as English envoy to the Doge of Genoa and to Florentine bankers.

A meeting between the two lies beyond the reach of even the most audacious guess. But to give you an idea of the social atmosphere, which Chaucer recognized at once as far more civilized than that to which he had been used, I will quote from a letter of Petrarch's to Boccaccio written this very year that Chaucer was in Italy. It was not only Italian literature that lifted Chaucer from what scholars call his French period to his Italian period, it was the whole union of nature and art, and of men interested in the humanities, in the problems of art, men of mercantile consequence talking, gesticulating, disputing, over rhyme and meter, over harmony and contrast, tradition and novelty, whereas at Westminster he had listened to Sir James Audeley and Sir Walter Manny argue over the relative merits of archers and men-at-arms, or how far steel plates might advantageously be added to chain armor.

In this letter, Petrarch tells how he had come upon a copy of the *Decameron,* and of the very tale which Chaucer put into verse for the Clerk of Oxenford to tell:

"June 4, 1373

"(Dear Giovanni)

"There has come into my hands, but how or from whom I don't know, a book in our mother tongue that you wrote, as I think, in your young years. I should be telling a lie if I were to say that I had read it. The size of the book, and

[103]

seeing it written in prose for popular reading, were my reasons for not abandoning more serious occupations, and taking up some of the very little time that is left to me. Besides I am distressed and worried by this war, that, as you know, is raging round us. For that reason, though I have nothing to do with it, I can not sit quiet in the midst of all this political topsyturviness. So, do you know what I did? I ran my eye over the book rapidly, stopping here and there like a hurried traveler who looks about him as he walks. Running through it in this fashion, I liked it very much. And if at times I was offended by something too free, too immodest, I thought of the excuses that could be made, the age you were when you wrote, the language, the style, the lightness of the subject, and above all the sort of readers for whom it is written. It is very pertinent to know for whom a book is written, for a difference in the culture of one's readers justifies a difference in style. Among many jocose, flippant tales, I came upon some that were serious and moral. However, I can not give you my precise opinion because I did not read very attentively. But, as usually happens when one makes a hasty examination, I paused most at the beginning and at the end of the book. I read the description of that horrible plague, that filled this age with unprecedented pain and misery, and I thought the skill with which you tell about that catastrophe to our country very remarkable. Then, at the end of the book, I read the last of your stories that seemed to me very different from the others, and I liked and enjoyed it so much, that even in the midst of the thousand and one cares which make me almost forget myself, I wanted to learn it by heart and I often said it over to myself with great pleasure, and I proposed to recite it to my friends the first time that it should be relevant to our conversation. A little while afterward I did just that, and I noticed that they all enjoyed it; so it occurred to me it would be nice to translate the tale for those who did not understand Italian. One day, therefore, while my mind was hovering over a thousand thoughts of this and that, I drove them all disdainfully away, snatched up a pen, and began to retell the very story you told, and I felt no doubt but that you would be pleased to have me translate your things, for I certainly would not do so for those of any other man whatever. I did this for my love of you, and for the beauty of your story, and in doing it, I followed Horace's precept, not to be too exact as it is impossible to translate word for word. The story is yours, the words are mine." And Petrarch copies out the whole story of Patient Grissel.

It seems that, after this letter was written, as Petrarch had made erasures and corrections in it, it was given to a friend to copy, and that, before it was dispatched, a letter came from Boccaccio telling Petrarch with a great deal of flattery to be careful of his health, and added that as for himself, his financial affairs were not brilliant. Petrarch, now at Padua, at once wrote an answer. He bade Boccaccio remember that all things come from God, and that, if in the gifts of fortune Boccaccio was poor, he had been enriched by most brilliant talents; and asked him with what man in the wide world he would exchange his lot. Then, continuing, he said: "Now I will address myself to that part of your letter that concerns me. I have told you the same thing so often that it irks me to repeat it. My circumstances are prosperous and happy, yours are meager. Assume this latter for a fact; but as to me, make a little change. In place of *prosperous* write *fair,* in place of *happy* write *not painful,* and you will be nearer the truth. But however that may be, remember what I have told you so often that I don't like to say it again. If I had but one loaf of bread, I should rejoice to share it with you. One loaf was enough for those famous hermits, Paul and Anthony, why should it not be enough for us? To be sure we are not worthy of heavenly bread; but bread, flavored by mutual affection will be sent to us by the same God, though perhaps not in a raven's beak. So, too, if I had but one pallet bed in my chamber, it would be big enough to invite us both to pleasant slumbers, and faithful refreshment from the day's cares. But I can tell you that we shall have more than one loaf, more than one bed; we shall lack nothing, if we are able to keep our souls calm and equable. And now I will speak of that passage in your letters which puzzles me. You say you suffer greatly for all that I am suffering. I am not surprised at that, because if one of us is ill, the other can not be well."

I need not quote more. Petrarch is a little pedantic, but in other respects the letters might have been written to-day. But there is no reference to an enthusiastic young Englishman, who had come from that foggy island on business but was more interested in poetry, none to England or any English mission. There are various other letters of Petrarch's that appear to have been written during his stay at Padua (November, 1372-October, 1373), one to Benvenuto da Imola in praise of poetry, a second to Giovanni of Ravenna, blaming him for his wandering ways, a third to Gaspar of Verona, telling him how he had been forced to leave Arquà, and go to Padua, a fourth to his brother, Gerardo, who had long been a Carthusian monk, a fifth to Lombardo da Serico, which dilates on the vices of city life and asserts that it is a great mistake to have a wife and children, a sixth to Francesco, a famous Siennese physician. But there is never a word of reference to Chaucer or to England. From the evidence then, the only reasonable inference is that the two poets never met.

Nevertheless Chaucer is indebted to Petrarch for *The*

Clerk's Tale about patient Grisilde, and in *Troilus and Criseyde* he has translated one of the sonnets as follows:

"If no love is, O God, what fele I so?
And if love is, what thing and which is he?
If love be good, from whennes cometh my woo?
If it be wikke [wicked], a wonder thynketh me,
When every torment and adversite
That cometh of hym, may to me savory thinke,
For ay thurst I, the more that ich it drynke.

"And if that at myn owen lust I brenne,
Fro whennes cometh my waillynge and my pleynte?
If harm agree me, wherto pleyne I thenne?
I noot [know not], ne whi unwery that I feynte.
O quike deth, O swete harm so queynte,
How may of the in me swich quantite,
But if that I consente that it be?

"And if that I consente, I wrongfully
Compleyne, iwis. Thus possed to and fro,
Al stereless withinne a boot am I
Amydde the see, bitwixen wyndes two,
That in contrarie stonden evere mo.
Allas! what is this wondre maladie?
For hete of cold, for cold of hete, I dye."

As this sonnet is numbered eighty-eight in the canon of Petrarch's lyrics, it is probable that Chaucer read and studied others. But the fact that he takes the tale of Patient Grissel from Petrarch instead of from Boccaccio, and that he cites Petrarch instead of Boccaccio as his authority for the episode about Zenobia in *The Monk's Tale,* shows that he had no very accurate information concerning Petrarch's works or Boccaccio's.

What Chaucer learned from Dante and Petrarch was reverence for art, for mastery of language, and a determination to labor on the use of words until he should be able to command them to do, not what Dante did, or Petrarch did, but what was suitable for his own needs.

CHAPTER XIII

BOCCACCIO

THE third of the three illustrious poets who raised the Tuscan dialect to be the language of Italy, and gave to Europe a literature that had no parallel since the days of Virgil and Cicero, is more closely connected with Chaucer's work than are Dante and Petrarch, more closely than anybody, even Jean de Meung. Dante was medieval, Petrarch, slightly ashamed of his sonnets and *canzoni* because they had been written in Italian, had thereafter confined himself to Latin, the language of the literate; both were really alien to Chaucer. But Boccaccio in his disposition and temperament, in his life and in his books bears strong resemblances to the English poet. Like Chaucer, Boccaccio belonged to the mercantile class, like Chaucer he had passed his adolescence and early manhood in attendance upon a royal court, and his stay in Naples in fashionable society had separated him from the bourgeoisie of Florence; somewhat as living among the French-speaking nobility had separated Chaucer from the bourgeois society of London. Boccaccio, also, had a public career. Before 1350 he had been sent as ambassador into the Romagna, *olim ambaxiator transmissus ad partes Romandiolae,* and again to Ravenna, when he carried ten golden florins from the Signory of Florence to Dante's daughter. He had gone on an embassy to the Court of the Tyrol, and to Pope Urban VI at Avignon. Chaucer, in his youth had been a servant to romantic ideas, and complains of eight years of unrequited love, and Boccaccio, in what I believe to be an equally imaginative mood, makes Fiammetta a heroine whom he aspires to rank with Beatrice and Laura. Chaucer's allusions to his wife have, as I said, persuaded people that he did not care for her, and Boccaccio never once mentions the mother of his five children. Both enjoyed the medieval banter about women and about friars. Both valued the virtues of wine; Chaucer being acquainted with Malvesye from Cyprus, Vernage, an Italian wine, the white and red wines of Bordeaux, the potent white Spanish wine from Lepe; and Boccaccio with those of Naples and Tuscany. Both were "good felawes," both were men of the world, both looked on life with a tolerant and tender approbation, and both united a taste for the elegance and delicacy of the old courtly romantic school with a taste for rollicking stories, that made raffish university students shout for joy, but called forth deprecation from the fastidious Petrarch. Both were true poets, and, though we English-speakers scoff at the idea of any parity between them, I dare say that Italians, such is the power of national bias, have the temerity to assert it.

When Chaucer was at Florence, Boccaccio was one of her foremost citizens, and Chaucer became familiar with Boccaccio's poems, and perhaps some of his prose. When he got back to England, he took Boccaccio's poem *Filostrato* which concerns the love of Troilus and Cressida, his constancy and her faithlessness, and out of it, following, translating, embroidering, cutting, condensing somewhat and expanding greatly, made his own beautiful poem of *Troilus and Criseyde*. He also took Boccaccio's poem *Il Teseide,* which relates how two Theban knights, Palamon and Arcite, fall in love with Emily, sister-in-law to the great Theseus, Duke of Athens, and condensing very greatly, also translating and imitating, made *The Knight's Tale*. These two poems of Chaucer's are, to my thinking, his most sympathetic, most melodious and most poetical. Besides these,

Chaucer took episodes from Boccaccio's Latin works, *De Casibus Virorum* and *De Claris Mulieribus,* for use in *The Monk's Tale* and also he borrowed something from Boccaccio's *De Genealogia Deorum,* for one of his heroines in *The Legend of Good Women,* and now and again in sundry of *The Canterbury Tales* there are episodes similar to episodes in the stories in the *Decameron,* but the commentators say that Chaucer never saw the *Decameron.*

It seems strange that not only the commentators but even the earlier and more sentimental biographers, who strove so hard to bring about a meeting between Chaucer and Petrarch, although Petrarch had left his native Arezzo as a baby, and had scarce ever been back in Tuscany except to pay Boccaccio a visit (in the latter's house across the Ponte Vecchio in *Oltrarno*), have not even ventured to guess that Chaucer and Boccaccio met, despite the facts that Boccaccio lived in or about Florence, except when off on a visit, and that Chaucer's debt to Boccaccio was twenty times what he owed Petrarch. This seems to be because Chaucer borrows nothing from the *Decameron,* ascribes the story of Patient Grissel to Petrarch and never mentions Boccaccio's name, and because they assume that, since Petrarch had not read the *Decameron* for twenty-five years after it had been written, few other people had done so, and Chaucer certainly not. This last reason carries no weight. After Laura's death in the plague of 1348,

Oimè il bel viso, oimè il soave sguardo!—

Petrarch dedicated himself, except for interruptions due to political tasks thrust upon him, to classical scholarship, and wholly forsook Italian for Latin, and all light and frivolous matters for serious pursuits; and it was most natural that, being so minded and far away from Florence, he had not

[111]

read the book. It is indeed odd that, if Chaucer had made Boccaccio's acquaintance, he does not mention his name, but it is not so odd as that, having appropriated to himself so much of *Il Filostrato* and the *Teseide,* he does not mention their author's name. But the visit to Italy affected him deeply, and he does not mention having been there. It was not the fourteenth-century custom.

Boccaccio's birthplace was Certaldo, a town about twenty miles from Florence, and that was his home. He had never been married, one at least of his children had died, no one knows what became of the others, he was now sixty years old, nearly destitute and suffering from various infirmities. It seems certain that he was in Certaldo during the time of Chaucer's visit to Florence; nevertheless, one must remember that, however much Chaucer may have wished to see Boccaccio, there was little or no reason why Boccaccio, old, weary and infirm, worried about the health of his dear friend Petrarch, should have gone even from Certaldo to Florence to see Chaucer. Possibly Chaucer did try to meet Boccaccio, and possibly the latter, in his poverty and weariness, meanly lodged in Certaldo, may have evaded the importunate young Englishman, and Chaucer felt himself snubbed and therefore never mentioned Boccaccio's name. Howbeit, considering what immense consequence this Italian journey was to Chaucer's intellectual and poetic development and that the record gives nothing but the dates of Chaucer's leaving England and of his return, together with a note of the moneys paid him for his expenses, guesses are more excusable than under other circumstances.

One at least may say that he met Boccaccio spiritually and became intimate with his imagination, his art, and his poetic numbers. And, since I, humbly following Dryden's lead, have likened Boccaccio in disposition and talents to Chaucer, and wish to show how charming and tender that disposition, common to the two men, displays itself in Boccaccio, there being no such convenient evidence in Chaucer's case, I will quote a letter from him to Petrarch.

"Florence, June 30 [1368]

"My illustrious Master,

"On March twenty-fourth I started from Certaldo for Venice, where you then were, in order to see you. But while I was in Florence, it rained steadily, and my friends urged me not to go, and alarming stories told by many travelers who had come back from Bologna made me delay so long, that to my own very great disappointment, you were called back to Padua. When I heard this, I was grieved indeed, and almost gave up going, and I had the best possible reason for not going. For although I wanted to see many things in Venice, these other motives would never have caused me to set out. However, in order not to disappoint the wishes of some friends, who had entrusted me with various troublesome matters, and because I had a great desire to see those two persons, whom you love so dearly, and for excellent cause, I mean Tullia and Francesco [Petrarch's daughter and her husband], whom I had never seen (though I think I have met all the others who are dearest to you), as soon as the weather became better, I went ahead with my journey, and with much weariness reached Venice. I think Francesco will have told you, how to my great delight I met him unexpectedly. After our hearty salutations and greetings, and I had learned that you were safe and sound and other good news concerning you, I paused to consider Francesco's great tall person, his placid face, his unembarrassed talk, his pleasant manners, and I was amazed and delighted to be acquainted with him. The moment I saw him, I approved your choice. But what have you ever done that I would not approve? However, I left him for the time being, as

[113]

I had things to do, and at daybreak I embarked in my little boat, and got out as soon as I reached land, and, as if I had sent word of my coming, all of a sudden a number of our Florentine citizens came around me. Every one of them begged me, as long as you were away, to lodge with him. I was bewildered, but I declined all their invitations, even that of our friend Donato, and went off with Francesco Allegri, for we had traveled together from Florence to Venice, and he had been particularly attentive to me, and I did not wish to repay his kind solicitude with a rebuff.

"I tell this at great length, so that you shall excuse me for not accepting that most generous proposition that you made in your letter. For, even if none of our friends had been there to take me in, I should have gone to an inn rather than lodge at Tullia's house, while her husband was away. Because, although you know the integrity of my feelings both in this case and many another toward you and yours, not everybody else knows it, and although, quite apart from my sense of honor, my white hairs, my advanced years and my body debilitated by too much fat, I thought it best to stay away so that the suspiciousness of people, always inclined to the worst interpretations, could not spy even the trace of a footprint where none had been made. You know very well that in such matters a false report prevails over the truth.

"After I had rested for a time, I went to pay my respects to Tullia. And, exactly as if it had been you yourself coming back, no sooner had she learned of my arrival, than she came out to meet me with the greatest cordiality, and the moment she saw me, a charming little flush came to her cheeks, she dropped her eyes, and then ran to throw her arms around me, with most modest filial affection and greetings. Good lord! I knew at once who had given the suggestion, and recognized your trusty kindness, and I rejoiced to be your friend. We said the usual things to each other, and then we sat in the little garden, together with several friends. Here we had a long friendly talk, and she offered me the freedom of the house, your books and all your belongings, maintaining always her lady-like dignity. While we were talking, your granddaughter Eletta came in, with a more demure carriage than belonged to her years, and before I knew who she was, looked at me with a smile. I picked her up in my arms, more than glad, greedily, and at first sight I imagined that she was the little girl that I lost. What shall I say? If you don't believe me, ask Doctor Guglielmo of Ravenna, and our dear Donato, who were there. I tell you that the little girl who was my Eletta had the same look as your Eletta, the same smile, the same lightsome eyes, the same movements, the same way of walking, the same carriage, although my child was a little bigger, as she was older, almost five and a half the last time I saw her. And if they had spoken the same dialect they would have said the very same words, in the very same childish way. Why do I write all this? I saw no difference between them, except that your grandchild is blonde, and my little girl had chestnut hair. Dear me! How often, as I held her in my arms and enjoyed her prattle, the memory of my lost baby brought tears to my eyes, but they passed off in sighs without any one noticing them. But you can understand how I cried over your Eletta, as if I were sad.

"If I were to tell you all I could about Francesco, my pen would not hold out. It would take long to narrate how eagerly and zealously he took pains to express all his kind feelings toward me, and how he continually came to see me, after he perceived that on no account I would become his guest, and how many invitations he honored me with, and how graciously. Let these few words suffice. Besides all this, as perhaps you don't know, when I was about to leave Venice, it was late in the evening, he took me aside in a room to ourselves, for he knew that I am poor, he held my little arm tight in his gigantic fist, and stammering out his words, forced me, in spite of myself and my blushes to accept a generous sum of money, and then, as if he were escaping, said good-by, went off and left me, to rail at myself and what I had submitted to. May God grant that I shall be able to repay him. . . .

"A few days after I got home, your letter written at Pavia in May reached me, forwarded by our friend Donato. I was overjoyed to receive it, and read it before anything else. I am most grateful for the place I occupy in your thoughts and in your letters, for I am sure that for this at any rate my name will be held in honor for many centuries. Intelligent men will comprehend that you would not have written so often and at such length to a man of little account, especially because your letters are so full of meat and in your graceful style. And it is near a year since, remarking how many letters I had had from you, I undertook to make a volume of them, putting them in the order that they were written, but I was obliged to stop for some never arrived, such as that beginning 'You have bestowed a gift on me,' and that which you wrote about Dante, and others perhaps; and lately I never got that which you say you wrote against astrologers, or that with the praises of your young protégé, or that in which you speak of your age, all which I want very much to add to the others so that, if I can't have all the collection of your letters, those at least may not be missing. I beg you, therefore, by your dear head that I venerate so, that you will have one of your secretaries copy those letters that I have named, and will send them to me, so that I may complete the unfinished volume. I have written enough, or rather too much. Please remember me to Francesco. Good-by, Best of men."

Is it not a pity that Chaucer and Boccaccio did not meet? They would have been such good friends.

CHAPTER XIV

THE CUSTOM-HOUSE

IN CHAUCER'S first period, as I have said, he was indebted to Guillaume de Lorris, Froissart, Deschamps and Guillaume de Machaut for the traditional matter of sentimental feelings among high-bred damsels and squires, and for a delicate, refined art of meter; in his second period, to Boccaccio, Petrarch and Dante, for material of various sorts and for a deeper understanding of the emotional values of rhythm and rhyme. This in the main, in addition to his careful study of some Latin authors, especially Ovid and Boethius, constituted his literary education. But Chaucer's real education, that which enabled him to write the *Prologue* and the junctional passages in *The Canterbury Tales* was acquired in the theater of workaday life.

The French poets taught him the art to write such sweet verses as these, where Ceÿx's ghost bids Alcyone good-bye:

"And farewel, swete, my worldes blysse!
I praye God youre sorwe [sorrow] lysse [lessen].
To lytel while our blysse lasteth!"
    With that hir eyen up she casteth
And saw noght. "Allas!" quod she for sorwe,
And deyede within the thridde morwe [morning].

And after Chaucer had digested all that the French poets taught him, and had studied the grander art of the Italians,

he could write such a stanza as this, where Criseyde yields
to Troilus's love:

And as the newe abaysed nyghtyngale,
That stynteth first whan she bygynneth to synge,
Whan that she hereth any herde [shepherd] tale,
Or in the hegges any wyght stirynge [stirring],
And after siker [securely] doth hire voys out rynge,
Right so Criseyde, whan hire drede [fear] stente [stopped],
Opned hire herte, and tolde hym hire entente.

But education is more than reading poetry; there must be
study of the businesses of life, of getting and spending, of
bargaining, of superintending, inspecting, measuring and
weighing, of obedience to superiors, of commands to in-
feriors, of calculation and foresight, and in so doing of an
intimate acquaintance with men and women of every rank
and station, with Tom, Dick and Harry, with lord and lady,
with farmers, plowmen, hedgers and landlords, with rogues
and honest men; Chaucer had need of this thorough education in the great university where men strive for their daily
bread, before he could write such a passage as this in *The
Nonnes Preestes Tale,* where there is a hue and cry after
the fox that is carrying off the widow's chauntecleer while
the hens cluck and groan:

This sely [poor] wydwe and eek hir doghtres two
Herden thise hennes crie and maken wo,
And out at dores stirten they anon,
And syen [see] the fox toward the grove gon [go],
And bar upon his bak the cok away,
And cryden, "Out! harrow! and weylaway!
Ha! ha! the fox!" and after hym they ran,
And eek with staves many another man.
Ran Colle oure dogge, and Talbot, and Gerland,
And Malkyn, with a dystaf in hir hand;

Ran cow and calf, and eek the verray hogges,
So fered [feared] for the berkyng of the dogges
And shoutyng of the men and wommen eeke,
They ronne so hem [dative] thoughte hir [their] herte breeke.
They yolleden as feendes doon in helle;
The dokes [ducks] cryden as [as if] men wolde hem quelle
      [kill];
The gees for feere flowen over the trees;
Out of the hyve cam the swarm of bees.

This passage shows the accuracy of a Van Eyck and the pictorial power of old Pieter Breughel, it proves that the poet had had the liberal education to which I have referred. No mere knowledge of cottages, crofts and granges, of husbandry, of chicken houses, could have sufficed for a passage of this character; such a poet must have had a wide observation of human life, from castle to cottage, from counting house to farm. It is only wide experience that can blend sympathy and irony, as Chaucer does. And fortunately the records show, meagerly enough, of what this liberal education of Chaucer's consisted.

At every stage in Chaucer's career, unless possibly it be at the end, his good luck shines bright. I remarked upon this in Chapter IV, and enumerated bits of fortune, and now I will mention others. *First,* his marriage, for though Mr. Masefield, in one of his less poetic moods, says, "We gather from the poems that Chaucer's own marriage was one of the utmost and liveliest unfortunate horror," and asks, "Can it be possible that the Wife of Bath is a portrait of Mrs. Chaucer?" Married scholars hold that he is quite wrong, and it is apparent, or highly likely, that Chaucer owed his promotion at court in great part to the Queen's partiality for his wife, and after that, as I believe, to the favor which her sister found in the Duke of Lancaster's eyes. *Second,*

[119]

in his mission to Italy; and *Third*, by being taken from the King's household and thrust into business. On June 8, 1374, he was appointed comptroller of the customs on wools in the Port of London. This appointment is so important in its effect upon Chaucer's political career, in that it took him from a life in which literary interests were predominant and plunged him into the active world, of what we conventionally call real life, where men wrestle with economic forces, that I will quote the document of appointment almost in full:

"Rex, omnibus ad quos etc. salutem: Sciatis quod concessimus dilecto nobis Galfrido Chaucer officium contrarolatoris custume et subsidii lanarum, coriorum, et pellium lanutarum, in Portu Londonie. . . . Ita quod idem Galfridus rotulos suos, dictum officium tangentes, manu sua propria scribat, et continue moretur ibidem, et omnia que ad officium illud pertinent in propria persona sua, et non per substitutum faciat et exequatur, etc."

Which in English is:

"The King to all whom it may concern greeting: Know ye that we have granted to our beloved Geoffrey Chaucer the office of Comptroller of the customs and subsidies on wool, hides, and wool-fells, in the Port of London. With the proviso that the said Geoffrey shall write out the accounts touching the said office with his own hand, and that he shall always stay there and do and perform all things that pertain to that office in his own person and not by a substitute, etc."

It seems that the requirements to write his reports with his own hand and to attend in person to his official business, was a regular clause in such appointments to public office, and perhaps, if human nature in the fourteenth century was similar to what it is to-day, not always strictly observed. This appointment necessitated a removal from whatever quarters he and his wife occupied while he was attached to the King's household into the city, and the records show that in anticipation of this office he had been given gratis by the City of London a lease for life of the dwelling over Aldgate. Again—for I think that the custom-house was more important to Chaucer of *The Canterbury Tales* even than Italy—I quote the terms of the lease:

"To all persons to whom this present indenture shall come, Adam de Bury, Mayor, the Aldermen and the Commonalty of the City of London, greeting: Know ye that we, of unanimous will and consent, have granted and released by these presents to Geoffrey Chaucer the whole of the dwelling-house above the Gate of Aldgate, with the rooms above, and the cellar beneath, the said gate, on the south side of said gate, and the appurtenances thereto, to have and to hold the whole house aforesaid with the rooms and cellar, unto the said Geoffrey Chaucer, for the whole of his, the said Geoffrey's life. And the said Geoffrey shall maintain and repair the whole house aforesaid etc. etc. "This 10th day of May, in the 48th year of the reign of King Edward, after the Conquest the Third (1374)."

This dwelling was part of the superstructure over Aldgate, which guarded the road leading out of the city to the east, and was protected by a double gate and a double portcullis. There was probably a storeroom in the pier on one side of the gate and a kitchen on the other, and bedrooms above, which were reached by circular stairways of stone. One of the up-stairs rooms must have been his library, with his sixty books on the shelves, and in it he must have sat up late at night reading his Latin, French and Italian authors. He describes his habit of life in *The House of Fame:*

> . . . when thy labour doon al ys,
> And hast mad alle thy rekenynges,
> In stede of reste and newe thynges,
> Thou goost hom to thy hous anoon;
> And, also domb as any stoon,
> Thou sittest at another book
> Tyl fully daswed [dazed] ys thy look,
> And lyvest thus as an heremyte . . .

Here, too, he probably wrote *Troilus and Criseyde* and *The Knight's Tale;* indeed he implies as much,

> . . . thou wolt make
> A-nyght ful ofte thyn hed to ake,
> In thy studye, so thou writest,
> And ever mo of love enditest.

Aldgate had been sometimes used, like other gates, as a prison, but it was stipulated in the lease that it should not be so used during Chaucer's tenancy. Aldgate was famous in history, for in the year 1215, the Barons of England, fresh from wresting Magna Charta from King John, which was enriched with the clause that "the city of London shall have all its old liberties and free customs both on land and on water," rode through it into London, and having made themselves safe by taking security from the citizens, proceeded to the Jew quarters, broke open the Jews' houses, filled their purses from Jewish coffers and then repaired the walls and gates of the city with stones quarried from the ruins they had made. But quite apart from any satisfaction in historic interest, the dwelling was convenient for Chaucer, it was a quarter of a mile from the Tower, and less than half a mile to his place of business.

The custom-house at that time was but a makeshift, some building or part of a building, hired for three pounds a year. I do not know where it was, but likely enough near the spot where a few years later the government hired better quarters on the quay called Wool-wharf in the Tower ward, between the quay of Paul Salesbury on the east and a lane called Watergate on the west. In the latter house, as I understand it, the bales of wool were examined and weighed on the ground floor, with a counting-room above, and over that chambers for the staff. The earlier quarters were simpler.

The walk from his house to his office and back took him through crowded parts of the city, where he met men of all sorts of occupation of far wider range than he had been used to in Westminster, and not Londoners only but merchants, chapmen, hucksters from out-of-town, bailiffs, reeves, manciples, on their masters' business, franklins, friars, clerks and so forth. The author of *Canterbury Tales* had a quick observant eye, and what he saw he noted in his tablets, at least in the tablets of a retentive memory. Of this there is one scrap of a record. While on the campaign in which he had been taken prisoner, he had been familiar with the heraldic design on the escutcheon of Sir Richard Lescrope, *"dazure oue (avec) une bende d'or"*; and one day, while walking through Friday Street in London, he noticed that an inn had put out a new sign bearing that heraldic device. He stopped to inquire how it happened that the Lescrope arms were on this sign, and he was told that they were not Lescrope but Grosvenor arms. And doubtless he noticed all the houses and people with the same quick perception. In *The House of Fame* he describes a crowd discussing a rumor:

> And every wight that I saugh there
> Rouned [whispered] everych in others ere
> A newe tydynge prively,
> Or elles tolde al openly
> Ryght thus, and seyde: "Nost not thou
> That ys betyd, lo, late or now?"
> "No," quod he, "telle me what."
> And than he tolde hym this and that,
> And swor thereto that hit was soth [true]—
> "Thus hath he sayd," and "Thus he doth,"
> "Thus shal hit be," "Thus herde y seye [say],"
> "That shal be founde," "That dar I leye [wager]"—

Probably he overheard just such talk among the folk along the wharf outside his office.

While at his task Chaucer must have been kept very busy. Great quantities of English wool were exported to Flanders, where the weavers of Ghent, Bruges, Ypres and Arras wove it into cloth. It was a very profitable business. No other country raised enough wool for export, except Spain, and Spanish wool was of poor quality, and as wool was virtually one of the necessities that people of the continent must have, England was able to add her export tax to the price of the wool, and—great object of ambition to all chancellors of the exchequer and secretaries of the treasury—oblige the foreigner to pay it. The industry was almost as profitable to the government as to the merchants, and the customs officers must have been kept busy. The export duty was so high that it paid in great measure for the cost of the war.

Chaucer's position as comptroller seems to imply that he acted as a check upon the collectors of customs, who were his superiors in office, and it certainly brought him into relation with the great export merchants. The collectors were appointed from the most eminent men in the city; for instance, in 1374, Nicholas de Brembre, who afterward became Lord Mayor, in 1375, Brembre again and William de Walworth, who also became mayor, and a little later John Philipot, he too, mayor. These three men belong to English history: you may read their lives in the National Biography. A comptroller of the customs in London, even if supported by princely influence, must have been selected on account of his business abilities.

CHAPTER XV

THE GOOD PARLIAMENT

POETS are not usually supposed to be good men of business, but it would be a fair inference from the finish, the precision, the careful craftsmanship, of Chaucer's poetry—Lowell says that he never has an imperfect line—that he would carry these same qualities into the execution of any duties assigned to him. But there is no need of going to those premises for any such inference; Chaucer's public employments are evidence enough that what he had already done he had done well. And, making assurance doubly sure, it is on record that after seven years' service he received a special reward of ten marks (one thousand dollars) for diligence in the execution of his office.

It is necessary, I think, to lay stress upon Chaucer's practical abilities and his faithfulness, for it is hard to suppose that he was not largely indebted for his good fortunes to the Duke of Lancaster. In the year 1374, he received on April twenty-eighth, the feast of Saint George, the grant of a pitcher of wine, nominally from the King, to be delivered to him daily, a grant worth some twenty marks, on June eighth his appointment as comptroller of customs, and on June thirteenth, he and his wife received, as I have said, an annuity of ten pounds from the Duke. The grant of this annuity reads as follows:

"Johan, par la grace de dieu Roy de Castile faisons savoir que nous, de nostre grace especial et pur la bone et agreable service que nostre bien ame Geffray Chaucer nous ad fait,

et auxint pour la bon service que nostre bien ame Philippe,
sa femme, ad fait a nostre tres honoure dame et Mere, la
Royne (que dieu pardoigne) et a nostre tres-ame compaigne
la Royne, avons grante au dit Geffray, X livres, par an, a
terme de sa vie, apprendre annuelment le course de sa vie
durant, a nostre Manoir de la Sauvoye, prese Loundres, etc.
—leXIII jour de Juin, l'an XLVIII (of the King's reign)

(We, John by the grace of God King of Castile, make it
known, that of our especial grace and for the good and
satisfactory services that our well beloved Geoffrey Chaucer
has rendered to us, and also for the good services that our
well beloved Philippa, his wife, has rendered to our very
honored Lady and Mother, the Queen (on whom God have
mercy) and to our much loved companion the Queen, we
have granted to the said Geoffrey ten pounds a year for the
term of his life to be paid annually during the continuance
of his life, at our House of Savoy, near London, etc.
—this Thirteenth day of June, year XLVIII etc. [1374])

The consideration for this grant strikes even the casual
reader as a little peculiar, for the Queen Mother had been
dead for five years, and Mrs. Chaucer, residing at Aldgate,
could hardly have rendered much service to the poor little
Spanish lady, the Duke's wife, who resided at the Savoy
House, which lay out beyond the walls on the farther side
of London on the way to Westminster. These three gifts,
the wine, the comptrollership and the annuity were given
while the Duke was still away, but his partisans were in
power, for the old King was in his dotage and the Black
Prince lay very ill. The Duke came back in July and assumed control of the government, and a year was but little
more than gone, when Chaucer received still greater pecuniary favors. On November 8, 1375, he was made guardian

of a rich young Kentish gentleman, which office within two years brought him in one hundred and four pounds, equal to perhaps fifteen thousand dollars to-day and within six weeks thereafter on December twenty-eighth, he was made guardian of another young man under age, and besides these two favors, on July 12, 1376, he received the forfeit paid by a London merchant for cheating the revenue, to wit: £ 71-4-6, or let us say ten thousand dollars. One would have expected these pecuniary rewards to go to some henchman of the Duke, who had rendered, or was expected to render, the equivalent in political service. I do not believe that Chaucer rendered any such services to the Duke, but I can not put away the thought that Katharine Swynford's affection for her sister was instrumental in these matters. The wardships and the forfeit did not come out of the Duke's own pocket, but the annuity of ten pounds did, and I can not prevent myself, after reading the terms of the grant, from entertaining the suspicion that the Duke was rather put to it to give reasonable color to a gift made to please his mistress.

A further justification for supposing that the Duke of Lancaster was the efficient cause of these bounties to Chaucer, lies in the circumstance that many others of the Duke's friends profited at the public expense, so much so that there was great murmuring and indignation throughout the land. Mr. G. M. Trevelyan says that the Duke of Lancaster, supported by Mistress Perrers who dominated the doting old King, established "a system of official robbery, carried on for the benefit, not of a class or a party, but of a clique of his personal adherents. He was at the head of a small, but well-organized hierarchy of knaves, who made a science of extorting money from the public by a variety of ingenious methods." In this little clique were two eminent noblemen, Lord Latimer and Lord Neville, and a rich merchant of

London, Richard Lyons whom Trevelyan calls "the financier of the unscrupulous gang." It seems—to give as an instance of the advantages derived by these persons from possession of office—that Richard Lyons acted in this fashion. All exported wool according to law passed through Calais and was there taxed before it crossed the English frontier; but Lyons got permission from the Privy Council to carry his wool direct to other ports on the continent, and thereby not only avoided the tax but also got his goods more quickly to foreign markets. Mr. Trevelyan is very severe, "Besides these arch-thieves," he says, "there were sharks and dependents who received and bought concessions and privileges from the King's councillors and abused them to the full. One man was made Mayor of Calais, another Controller of the Customs at Yarmouth; both imitated those to whom they owed their nomination, by exacting illegal dues. A London merchant obtained through the agency of Richard Lyons a monopoly of the sale of wine in the capital, and, in the absence of all competition, raised the prices beyond the limit set by the regulations of the city. From top to bottom the system was all one structure, of which the Duke of Lancaster was the keystone. All depended on his supremacy at headquarters."

Nobody will suspect Chaucer of any dishonest conduct; the point I make is that when in April, 1376, the Good Parliament, as it is called from its high moral indignation, met and investigated this political ring, he must have suffered some disquiet in his mind lest he be thought to have acquired his office by political favor, and be dismissed or suffer some detriment in his reputation. But it is easy to exaggerate the influence of politics upon our lives; what is really of importance is that which goes on within one's house, and if one may judge from general impressions of serenity got from his poetry things went well in Chaucer's house.

The Good Parliament assembled in a mood of deep discontent. According to custom, if not to law, parliament should have been summoned every year, but none had been called for three years; expenses had been great; the Church had been extortionate; the peasants were disaffected; and a large majority of the members believed that military affairs had been badly mismanaged and that there had been great corruption in office. The Black Prince lay helpless on his bed, but his sympathies were all with the reformers. Supported by his immense prestige, the Commons acted with vigor. They refused supplies until their grievances should be redressed. They accused Richard Lyons of commercial and financial frauds, they charged Lord Latimer, Lord Neville, Sir Richard Stury, Adam de Bury, William Ellis and John Peachy, with many misdeeds, and laid various complaints against "a certain proud woman, called Alice Perrers, who by overmuch familiarity that she had with the King, was the cause of much mischief in the realm, persuading and dissuading in defence of matters" with which she had no business to meddle and "requesting things contrary to laws and honesty." Richard Lyons (according to report), "fearing for his skin," sent to the Prince of Wales a barrel labeled "sturgeons," which contained one thousand pounds; it was a singular mistake for a sagacious man to make. Lyons was committed to prison, Lord Latimer was deprived of his offices and his name stricken from the Privy Council, Lord Neville and Sir Richard were dismissed from about the King's person. Adam de Bury escaped to Flanders. Mistress Alice Perrers was also dismissed from about the King's person, under penalty of banishment, excommunication and confiscation of her property. There was a complete house-cleaning; and its effects came pretty near to Chaucer; Sir Richard Stury had been made prisoner on the campaign of 1359-1360 about the same time as he, and the two had been sent together on a diplomatic errand to Brussels in 1370. Adam de Bury, as Mayor of London, had granted him the lease of Aldgate, and as all the other delinquents were more or less closely connected with the Duke of Lancaster, they, too, must have been known to him.

But the eclipse of the Lancastrian party did not last long. The Black Prince died in July, and the Good Parliament, after having appointed a Council to govern the King and the Kingdom, separated; knights and burghers went home. The Duke of Lancaster returned promptly to power. The Good Parliament's Council was dissolved, Lord Latimer returned to court, Peter de la Mare, who had led the impeachment in the House of Commons, was thrown into prison; Mistress Alice Perrers returned to her royal lover; Sir Richard Stury came back. The Good Parliament was declared no parliament, all its acts were canceled, and the whole episode of reform was relegated to the chronicles of history.

CHAPTER XVI

FRANCE, AGAIN, AND ITALY

POLITICS, as I have said, returned to the *statu quo ante,* and the Duke of Lancaster, now the King's oldest living son, resumed the reins of government. He may have entertained long views of a policy that should ultimately set him on the throne of Castile, or he may have been guided by the present needs, but, whichever it was, it was obvious that peace with France was desirable. The cost of the war was enormous, and the English were losing. The people, to be sure, were for prosecuting the war, they felt that Aquitaine was a part of the realm, and that the subtle French, who could not stand up against them in a fair field, had falsely outwitted them. But in spite of an adverse public opinion the government made attempts at peace, and in the diplomatic proceedings to that end Chaucer was again employed. From this it is clear that the requirement directing the Comptroller of Customs to stay in his office, and act in person, was not of complete obligation. What this mission was is only to be guessed at; all we know is that at the end of 1376, Sir John Burley, then Captain of Calais and a brother to Sir James Burley, was sent abroad on the King's business, and Chaucer with him as his subordinate, and that the subordinate received exactly half as much salary as his chief.

A few weeks later, Sir Thomas Percy (who appears in *King Henry IV* as the Earl of Worcester), or possibly Sir Richard Stury as his substitute, was sent on a diplomatic errand to France, and Chaucer with him. They set forth on February 17, 1377, and went to Paris, Montreuil "and elsewhere," and did not get back till March twenty-fifth. Less than a month later, Chaucer went a third time, and remained in France from about May first to June twenty-sixth. It is reasonably certain that these embassies had to do with a proposed treaty of peace between the two countries, and as incidental thereto, with a marriage between young Prince Richard and the Princess Mary, daughter to King Charles V, a girl nine years old. Froissart says, "About Shrove-tide, a secret treaty was formed between the two kings for their ambassadors to meet at Montreuil-sur-mer; and the King of England sent to Calais Sir Guischard d'Angle, Sir Richard Stury, and Sir Geoffrey Chaucer. On the part of the French were the Lords de Coucy and de la Rivière, Sir Nicholas Brages (or Brake), and Nicholas Bracier (or le Mercier). For a long time they discussed the subject of the above marriage; and the French, as I was informed, made some offers, but the others demanded different terms, or refused treating. These lords returned, therefore, with their treaties to their sovereigns." Stow's account in his *Annales* (1590), is as follows: "About the same time the Earle of Salisbury and Sir Richard Anglisison [Sir Guischard d'Angle] and Poynton [? of Poitou], the Bishop of Saint Davids, the Bishop of Hereford, Geoffrey Chaucer (the famous poet of England), and others, were sent into France to treate a peace, or at least a truce for two yeere or more, but they could not obtaine any longer truce, than for one moneth, which they utterly refused, whereupon they stayed in France about these things, and some thinking they might safely have passed betwixt Calais and Dover, about fiftie taking shippe, were forthwith intercepted by the Galleys [i. e. French] and were all slain, two men and two women only excepted. The messengers returned into England, and brought nothing backe with them, but rumor and warre."

It is evident that nothing was accomplished. On his return Chaucer found the old King dead, and the boy Richard II king in his stead. For a time the Duke of Lancaster appears to have been occupied with his own matters, and Thomas of Woodstock, the youngest brother, controlled the affairs of the Kingdom. The change did not at first affect Chaucer. He was confirmed in his office as comptroller of customs and in his annuities, and continued to receive forty shillings a year to pay for his robes as the King's squire. And, once more, in the beginning of the year 1378, he was again in France, apparently on the same diplomatic errand, the negotiation of a treaty of peace and of a marriage between King Richard and a French Princess, but again nothing was accomplished, and the English government resolved to press the war. Thomas of Woodstock was always for war against France, whether it was that he wished to curry favor with the people, or that for some reason of his own he hated France, or merely desired to thwart his brother, John, whom he disliked.

European politics were almost as disturbed and complicated as they are now, and all countries were affected in some way by the war between France and England. Castile, we know, sided with France, and in consequence Portugal stood with the English. The Holy Roman Empire was compact of states too heterogeneous to act or to feel as a unit. The Emperor, Charles IV, was the last of the really medieval emperors; he had been crowned King of the Romans at Aachen, King of Burgundy at Arles, King of Lombardy at Milan, and Emperor in Rome. He was the son of the blind King of Bohemia who had lost his life at Crécy, and nephew by marriage to King Charles IV of France; he had married a sister of King Philip VI, successor to

Charles IV, and had spent seven years at the French court, and had fought at Crécy, so it might be supposed that his natural inclinations, if such exist in politics, would incline him to the French side, but he was now a very old man, and chiefly interested in the affairs of Bohemia. For the moment it seemed that English policy might disregard him. In Italy there was great diversity; England had secured Genoa's friendship, Venice was occupied with the East, and the Papacy, though it had but recently shifted its seat from Avignon back to Rome, was on the verge of the Great Schism, and no one could tell as yet what its attitude toward the conflict between England and France would be. But there remained the city of Milan, the richest city I presume in Europe; "the waveless plain of Lombardy" poured gold into the laps of the Visconti, and they spent it royally. Ten years before when Prince Lionel married Violante Visconti, the magnificence of the festivities was so splendid that, after two hundred years, old Stow, the annalist, records the story of it with astonishment: "At the comming of Leonell, such aboundance of treasure was in most bounteous manner spent, in making most sumptuous feasts, setting forth stately sightes, and honouring with rare gifts above two hundred Englishmen which accompanied his [Galeazzo Visconti's] son-in-law, as it seemed to surpasse the greatnesse of most wealthy Princes; for in the banquet whereat Francis Petrarch was present, amongst the chiefest guests, there were above thirtie courses of service at table, and betwixt every course, as many presents of wonderous price intermixed, all which John Galeasius [Gian Galeazzo], chiefe of the choice youth, bringing to the table did offer to Leonell. There were in one onely course seventy goodly horses, adorned with silke and silver furniture; and in the other silver vessels, falcons, hounds, armour for horses, costly coats of mayle, breastplates, glittering of massie steele, hel-

[135]

mets, and corselets decked with costly crestes, apparrell distinct with costly jewels, souldiors girdles, and lastly certain gemmes, by curious art set in gold, and of purple cloth of gold for mens apparrell in great abundance."

It was well worth while to secure the alliance of so rich a state, especially as it might be uncertain which way Bernabò, who on the death of his brother, Galeazzo II, had recently become sole Lord of Milan, would incline, whether to England or to France, for since Prince Lionel had died, perhaps of poison, perhaps of "untimely banquettings," Violanti's brother, Gian Galeazzo, "the chiefest among the choice youth of Milan," had married Isabella, sister to King Charles V. And, if Bernabò should wish, as it afterward turned out that he did, to renew the close relations between Milan and England by the marriage of one of his daughters to King Richard, it might be well to consider the plan, or at least to let him think that the English government was considering it. Such possibilities made it worth while to send envoys to Milan, and a further reason existed for doing so. There was an English adventurer of renown, a soldier of fortune, Sir John Hawkwood, who had made a great name for himself in the French wars and now was a power in Italy. He had collected a little army of soldiers (thrown out of employment by the truce, which John of Gaunt had made for two years or so in 1374) and organized it into an admirable fighting force, known as the White Company or sometimes the Holy Company. With these men at his back, Hawkwood had raided, robbed, burned, ravished, wherever resistance was least and booty best; and, after leaving a long wake of devastation in France, he had crossed the Alps and had been even more successful in Italy, hiring himself out to the highest bidder. At one time or another he served Pisa, the Pope, Milan, or Florence; you may see in the Duomo at Florence, on the wall there, a notable painting by Paolo Uccello of this terrible warrior, known to the Italians as Giovanni Acuto, seated on a horse, with a truncheon in his hand. A year before the English mission of which I am about to speak went to Milan, Hawkwood had married an illegitimate daughter of Bernabò Visconti, and was in the service of Milan. The English government may have hoped that a patriotic chord in the *condottiere's* breast might induce him to fight for England against France at a lower price than he would fight for France against England, or possibly it had some other favor to ask of him, for, as it happened a few years later, Sir John Hawkwood became English ambassador at the papal court.

At all events, whatever may have been the purpose of the English government, it sent Sir Edward de Berkeley to Italy to confer with these two redoubtable personages, and Chaucer with him. This is proof enough that Chaucer had fulfilled his former mission to Italy to the satisfaction of the government. The envoys left England on May 28, 1378. I presume that they crossed the Low Countries to Cologne, went up the Rhine by boat to Basle, and then crossed the Alps. No doubt Chaucer's knowledge of Italian, and the experience got on his earlier visit, proved useful to Sir Edward de Berkeley; as for Chaucer, himself, this second visit can hardly have been comparable to the first. Petrarch was dead, Boccaccio was dead, and no new poet had risen to take their place, and it hardly seems likely that he came upon any books that he did not know before, unless, possibly, Petrarch's translation of *Patient Grissel* or the *Cento Antiche Novelle*. Milan, itself, as a city was interesting; there was a castle, there was Sant'Ambrogio and Sant'Eustorgio, and the works of art within them, but what were they compared to the Palazzo Vecchio, the Baptistry, and Giotto's Campanile? Nevertheless, Chaucer did for Milan what he did not do for Florence or Genoa, he commemorated this visit by an episode in *The Monk's Tale:*

De Barnabo de Lumbardia

Off Melan grete Barnabo Viscounte,
God of delit, and scourge of Lumbardye,
Why sholde I nat thyn infortune acounte,
Sith in estaat thow cloumbe were so hye?
Thy brother sone, that was thy double allye,
For he thy nevew was, and sone-in-lawe,
Withinne his prisoun made thee to dye,—
But why, ne how, noot I that thou were slawe.

How Sir Edward executed his mission to Bernabò Visconti, I do not know, beyond this, that Richard II subsequently rejected the idea of marrying his daughter, even with a princely dowry. Nor do I know whether he had an interview with Hawkwood, but I presume that he did. About this time Hawkwood was leading the Milanese forces against the Scaligeri of Verona, and there would have been no great difficulty in visiting him at his headquarters. It was soon after this that he quarreled with Bernabò and took service with Florence. A few years later, as I said, he became English ambassador at the papal court. This is probably as near as we can get to an estimate of the success of the mission. The English envoys were back in England by September nineteenth.

CHAPTER XVII

WAT TYLER'S REBELLION

I HAVE quoted the joyous passage in *The Nonnes Preestes Tale,* which describes how Col Fox ran off with Chaunticleer and how the whole farm started in pursuit, the poor widow and her daughters, crying, "harrow! and weylaway!", the men with staves, Malkin with her distaff, cows, dogs, calf and pigs, and then the poet says:

> The gees for feere flowen over the trees;
> Out of the hyve cam the swarm of bees,
> So hydous was the noyse, a, *benedicitee!*
> Certes, he Jakke Straw and his meynee [followers]
> Ne made nevere shoutes half so shrille,
> Whan that they wolden any Flemyng kille,
> As thilke day was maad upon the fox.

This merry reference to perhaps the most horrible riot in London's history, sets in high relief one of the most delightful traits in Chaucer's character, the kindly, sweet, generous sympathy, the freedom from rancor and malice, that could remember the sufferings and the provocation of the rebels as well as the dire deeds they did, and liken their shouts to the noises of a barnyard chase. You might say that Chaucer had the fortitude necessary to bear the murder of Flemings; but the answer to that is that he also passes over the murder of Englishmen, and merely recalls, out of the tumultuous *res gestae,* what he can refer to with jesting irony. But picture to yourself Chaucer and his wife and their thirteen-year-old boy, and possibly a baby boy, in the upper story of Aldgate, when the angry, revengeful, swaggering mob, tramped through the gate, under his windows. Perhaps he went out into the streets, and saw sights that he never could forget, such as is recorded in these verses:

> Have ye nat seyn somtyme a pale face,
> Among a prees, of him that hath be lad [led]
> Toward his deeth, wheras hym gat no grace,
> And swich a colour in his face hath had,
> Men myghte knowe his face, that was bistad [troubled],
> Amonges alle the faces in that route?

These lines seem to record a lynching such as then took place, when the mob laid hold upon a man they disliked.

The revolt came about in this way. Ever since the Black Death there had been serious trouble between the landlord class and the proletariat. The dreadful mortality had depleted the ranks of labor so greatly that landowners could not get enough farm-hands; as a consequence there was competition for labor and wages went up. The landlords were outraged; they promptly made up their minds to resist any rise in wages, and their representatives in Parliament enacted the *Statute of Laborers,* which forbade employers to give, or laborers to receive, wages higher than those customary before the Black Death. For this the landlords had the excuse that their incomes had not gone up. But the attempt to run counter to the law of supply and demand failed. Wages, such as were paid before the Black Death, could not now support life, all prices had gone up, and when a landlord really needed labor he was obliged to pay enough to get it. But there was no end of contention. Villeins, who from time immemorial had been obliged to render certain services to the lord of the manor, chafed more than ever at the restrictions laid upon them; they wished to go into the market and demand as high wages for their services as the free laborers received. They grumbled over their feudal dues, and balked at paying the heriot (their best beast) when a tenant died, or the *merchet,* when the tenant married off his daughter, or at paying a farthing, when he sold a horse or a cow. In some manors the villeins ran away, in others they confederated and refused to perform their servile duties. Free laborers, who did not get the wages they asked, took French leave and went elsewhere; if they still could not get what they wanted, they became sturdy beggars, and sturdy beggars often turned into highwaymen and outlaws.

This state of things was bad, but worse happened. The war had been unsuccessful, according to common belief it had been mismanaged and the expenses were great. But the people, or at least the governing classes, were set on continuing the war, and more money was imperatively needed. In order to raise this money the Parliament of 1381 voted a poll tax, far heavier than before, of three groats, that is one shilling, on every lay person in the realm over fifteen years of age. The peasants protected themselves by making false returns. To judge by these returns the population of the country had fallen off twenty to fifty per cent. in four years. The government scented fraud and made inquiry; hardly a family but had rendered a false return. The government then sent commissioners to punish the wrong-doers and collect the tax. At this the discontent that lay smoldering burst into flame over half England; local leaders stood up on chairs and talked rebellion. But let me give you an incident, taken by Stow from the Chronicle of Saint Albans, to show the provocation. "One of the collectors of the groats, or polle money, coming to this house

[141]

of one John Tylar, in the towne of Dartford in Kent, demanded of the Tylar's wife [John was a tiler by trade as I
understand it] for her husband, her selfe, her servants and
for their daughter (a young mayden) every one of them
a grote, which the Tylar's wife denied not to pay, saving
for her daughter, who she said was but a child, not to be
counted a woman; quoth the collector, that will I soone wit
[know], and taking the mayden, turned her up—(in many
places they made the like triall) whereupon her mother cried
out, neighbors came running in: and her husband being at
worke in the same towne, tyling of an house, when hee
heard thereof, cought his lathing staffe in his hand, and
ranne reaking home, where reasoning with the collector,
who made him so bold, the collector answered him with
stout words, and strake at the Tylar, whereupon the Tylar
avoiding the blow, smote the collector with his lathing staffe,
that the braines flew out of his head, where-through great
noise arose in the streetes, and the poowre [poor] people
being glad, everyone prepared to support the said John
Tylar."

Incidents such as this roused the peasants to fury. But
the upper classes saw another aspect of the uprising, and
heard tell of massacres of gentlemen and burning of manor-
houses. One must suppose that Chaucer's sympathies would
naturally be with his class. Froissart expresses the upper-
class attitude. He says: "While these conferences [for
peace with France] were going forward, there happened in
England great commotions among the lower ranks of the
people, by which England was near ruined without resource.
Never was a country in such jeopardy as this was at that
period, and all through the *too great comfort of the commonalty*. Rebellion was stirred up, as it was formerly done
in France by the Jacques Bons-hommes, who did much evil,
and sore troubled the Kingdom of France. It is marvellous

from *what a trifle* this pestilence raged in England." But Froissart, in his chapters that give an account of the rebellion, does not seem to me unfair. I put two of his phrases in italics in order to show the atmosphere of opinion among the society in which Chaucer moved, and by doing so make clear the breadth of Chaucer's human sympathy. No other member of the upper classes, who had lived through the riots, would have likened the noises of the mob to a barnyard chase.

Chief among the agitators was a Kentish priest, John Ball. Froissart reports his preaching in these words: "My good friends, things cannot go on well in England, nor ever will until everything shall be in common; when there shall be neither vassal nor lord, and all distinctions levelled; when the lords shall be no more masters than ourselves. How ill they used us! And for what reason do they thus hold us in bondage? Are we not all descended from the same parents, Adam and Eve?

> When Adam dalf and Eve span,
> Who was then a gentleman?

And what can they show, or what reasons give, why they should be more the masters than ourselves? except, perhaps in making us labor and work, for them to spend. They are clothed in velvets and rich stuffs, ornamented with ermine and other furs, while we are forced to wear poor cloth. They have wines, spices, and fine bread, when we have only rye and the refuse of the straw; and, if we drink, it must be water. They have handsome seats and manors, when we must brave the wind and rain in our labours in the field; but it is from our labour they have wherewith to support their pomp. We are called slaves; and if we do not perform our service, we are beaten, and we have not any sov-

[143]

ereign to whom we can complain, or who wishes to hear us and do us justice. Let us go to our King, who is young, and remonstrate with him on our servitude, telling him we must have it otherwise, or that we shall find a remedy for it ourselves. If we wait on him in a body, all those who come under the appellation of slaves [villeins (?)], or are held in bondage, will follow us, in the hopes of being free. When the King shall see us, we shall obtain a favourable answer, or we must then seek ourselves to amend our condition."

He was listened to. A great multitude gathered together in bands and detachments, in various shires, and following John Ball's advice, marched toward London to see the King. The men from Kent were led by Wat Tyler, an old soldier of the French wars perhaps, and others by Jack Straw. They marched from Canterbury, and as their numbers increased and their confidence grew great "they beganne [I quote Stow] to shewe some such actes as they had considered in their mindes, and tooke in hand to behead all men of lawe, as well apprentices, as utter-barristers, and olde justices with all the jurers of the countrey, whom they might get into their hands, they spared none whom they thought to be learned especially if they found any to have pen and inke they pooled off his hood, and all with one voice of crying, 'Hale him out and cut off his head.' They also determined to burn all Court-rolles and old monuments that the memory of antiquities being taken away, their Lordes shoulde not be able to challenge any right on them, from that time forth."

On reaching Southwark the rioters broke open prisons, set the prisoners free, sacked the Archbishop's palace at Lambeth, burned the house of the Warden of the Marshalsea, and so forth. The propertied classes in London were in great alarm, especially as the royal uncles, the natural military leaders, were away, the Duke of Lancaster in Edinburgh, Thomas of Woodstock in the Welsh March, and Edmund of Cambridge had sailed for Portugal. The young King, together with his chief nobles including his Chancellor, Archbishop Sudbury, and his treasurer, Hales, the two best hated men in the Kingdom, for the rioters held them responsible for the poll tax, took to safety in the Tower. Mayor Walworth and the aldermen locked themselves in the Guildhall. There were, however, thousands of the poorer sort in the city who sympathized with the rebels, and some from among them let down the drawbridge to the Kentishmen, while others opened Aldgate to those from Essex. The mob, animated by hatred of the Duke of Lancaster, marched out to the Savoy, a palace to which "there was none in England to be compared in beauty and stateliness," broke their way in, hammered to bits plate and ornaments, smashed the furniture, flung the fragments out of the windows, tore up and rent carpets, hangings, and clothes, gutted every room, and then set the building on fire. They sacked the inns of Court where the hated lawyers were bred, they ravaged the Temple Church, they opened prisons, they burned various buildings, they murdered some eight score Flemings, and any other foreigners that they could lay hands on as well as some obnoxious Englishmen. Bands of marauders went about the streets, in the name of the "Commons," and stopped passers-by: "With whom hold ye?" If the poor fellow refused to say "With King Richard and the true Commons," they dragged him to a street corner, laid his neck on a block and chopped off his head. Chaucer's pleasant comparison of Jack Straw and his crew to the louts, dogs, cows, pigs, geese and bees, that pursued the culprit fox, sounds too buoyant and gay.

The King issued a proclamation bidding the rebels disperse, which they refused to do, and their leaders replied with counter propositions. Then there were pourparleys,

[145]

and it was finally agreed that the King should meet the rebels outside the walls at Smithfield, in an open square. Richard II was only fourteen but full of Plantagenet courage, a handsome, charming young man; and with a scanty band of attendants he rode out to keep the tryst. While he was gone, I will tell you what happened at the Tower, according to Stow, who follows earlier chroniclers: "The gates of the Tower being set open, a great multitude of them [the rebels] entred the same. There was the same time in the Tower six hundred warlike men furnished with armour and weapons, expert men in armes, and six hundred archers, all which did quaile in stomacke. For the basest of the rustickes, not many together, but every one by himselfe durst presume to enter the King's chamber, or his mother's with their weapons, to put in feare each of the men of warre, knights or other: many of them came into the King's privy chamber, and plaid the wantons, in sitting, lying and sporting them on the King's bed: and that more is, invited the King's mother to kisse with them, yet durst none of those menne of war [strange to be said] once withstand them: they came in and out like masters, that in times past were slaves of most vile condition. Whilst therefore these rusticks sought the Archbishop with terrible noise and fury running up and downe, at length finding one of his servants, they charge him to bring them where their master was, whom they named traytor, which servant daring doe none other, brought them to the Chappell—where the Archbishop was busie with his praiers, for not unknowing of their comming and purpose, hee hadde passed the last night in confessing of his sinnes, and in devout praiers— with that the tormentors entring cried, Where is the traitor: The Archbishop answered, behold, I am the Archbishop whom you seek, not a traitor. They therefore laid handes on him, and drew him out of the Chappell, they drew him

[146]

out of the Tower gates, to the Tower hill." There he be-
haved with dignity and Christian fortitude. "He died not
till being mangled with eight strockes in the necke, and in
the head, he fulfilled most worthy martyrdom." The mur-
derers fastened his head on a pole and set it up on London
Bridge. They also murdered Sir Robert Hales, the royal
treasurer, one John Legge, a sergeant at armes, also a Franciscan friar, the King's confessor, and a fourth. In the
city (as I have said) they beheaded more than eighty
Flemings and Englishmen, dragging them out of churches,
for no cause "but because it was a solemne pastime to
them."

Let us now proceed to Smithfield where the King and his
retinue were facing Wat Tyler and the rioters across the
square. I have disregarded a nice chronology. Stow says
that Wat Tyler played for time, because he proposed that
night to burn and sack the city of London. Very likely
Stow does him injustice; at all events Tyler boggled over
the terms sent to him by the King, and the King invited him
to come over and talk face to face. Stow then recounts
Tyler's first demand: "He would have a commission for
him and his to behead all lawyers, escheters, and other whatsoever that were learned in the law or communicated to the
law, by reason of their office, for hee hadde conceived in
his mind, that this being brought to passe, all things afterward should be ordered according to the fancy of the common people: and indeede it was sayde that with great pride
he had but the day before sayde, putting his hand to his
lips, that before 4 days came to an ende, all the lawes of
Englande shoulde proceede from his mouthe."

Tyler acceded, in boorish manner, to the King's message,
and rode across the square so near the King that his horse's
head touched the croup of Richard's horse. What happened
is told in different ways. Stow says this:

TYLER: Sir King, seest thou all yonder people?

THE KING: Yea truely, wherefore sayst thou so?

TYLER: Because they be all at my commandment, and have sworn to me faith and trueth, to doe all that I will have them.

THE KING: In good time, I will it be so.

TYLER: Believest thou, King, that these people, and as many moe as bee in London at my commandment, will departe from thee without thy letters?

THE KING: No, ye shall have them. They be ordeined for you and shall bee delivered to every each of them.

At this point Tyler became indignant because he saw Sir John Newton near him on horseback, carrying the King's sword, and said that it would be more suitable for Newton to be on foot in his presence. Sir John answered bruskly. Tyler called him traitor and drew his dagger. The knight said he lied, and drew his dagger. The King interfered and bade Sir John dismount, and give Tyler the dagger. Tyler demanded the sword also. The knight answered, "It is the King's sword, and thou art not worthy to have it; nor thou durst aske it of me, if here were no more but thou and I." "By my faith," cried Wat, "I shall never eate till I have thy head," and would have attacked Sir John. The King's retinue interposed, and Mayor Walworth said that Tyler ought to be arrested. The King bade him do so, and Walworth, in token of arrest, tapped him on the head. Tyler, furious, struck the Mayor with his dagger, but did not pierce the Mayor's corselet. Thereupon the Mayor drew his sword and struck Tyler on neck and head, and one of the King's esquires also smote him a deadly blow. Wat spurred his horse toward his comrades, but before fourscore feet fell off, dead. The rebels bent their bows. The young King rode his horse over to them and said: "What a work is this, my men, what meane you to doe, will you shoot at your King? I am your captain and leader, followe mee unto the fields, there to have whatsower you will require."

Meantime Walworth galloped back to the city, and there found that the conservative classes had rallied, and that Sir Robert Knolles with a thousand armed men was ready to ride out. The loyal forces surrounded the dismayed peasants, who straightway threw down their arms. The King knighted Mayor Walworth on the spot, although the Mayor protested that he was but a merchant and lived by his merchandise and was unworthy of such an honor. And then, at Walworth's request, the King also knighted Nicholas Brembre and John Philipot, and gave Walworth 100 pound land and to the others 40 pound land.

I need not continue. The upper classes reasserted their power, the rebellion was put down and the rebels were punished. "Jake Straw was hongyd and qwarterd." Richard, himself, after his astonishing escape rode to the Lady Princess, his mother, who was lodged in the Queen's Wardrobe near Barnard Castle where she had been for two days, sore abashed. When she saw him, she was greatly rejoiced and said, "Ah, fayre sonne, what great sorrow have I suffered for you this day." Richard answered, "Certainly, Madam, I know it well, but now rejoice and thank God, for I have this day recovered mine heritage and the realme of England which I had nearly lost."

One must remember that Chaucer's dwelling over Aldgate was not a quarter of a mile from the Tower, and that according to Froissart the rebels "did all they could to throw the town into such confusion that the lords and rich citizens might be murdered, and their houses pillaged and destroyed," and yet, throwing the cloak of a great charity over what might have happened to his wife, his son and himself, he compares the riot to a barnyard chase.

[149]

CHAPTER XVIII

WYCLIFFE

THERE was little enough recorded connection between Chaucer and Wat Tyler's rebellion, nothing beyond the reference in *The Nonnes Preestes Tale* and the occupancy of Aldgate, through which the rebels passed, but even that is more than the recorded connection between him and Wycliffe, and yet it is impossible that the moral disturbance caused by this precursor of Protestantism should not have affected the society in which Chaucer moved. We do know that the Princess of Wales and the Duke of Lancaster patronized Wycliffe, that Sir Richard Stury was a Lollard, or strongly suspected of Lollardry, and there must have many more among Chaucer's friends and acquaintances in the like case. And we know that Wycliffe was the most notable Englishman in this half-century, if notability is to be measured by social consequences, for his teachings reached thousands among succeeding generations, when Chaucer's poetry was read by not one in twenty out of each of those thousands, and when the Black Prince's renown was as remote in practical interest as the hatchments over his marble tomb in Canterbury Cathedral, and therefore every one who attempts to tell the story of Chaucer's life can not but refer, however briefly, to Wycliffe, and make some estimate of Chaucer's attitude toward Lollardry.

Chaucer, I have said, was not a religious man. He, perhaps, accepted Christianity as it was presented to him, attended mass, confessed some of his sins, walked in ecclesiastical processions, outwardly respected the bishops, admired

the good priests, despised rascally friars, and cordially disliked the whole system of papal taxation and of the Church's
intermeddling with politics. He probably felt on most ecclesiastical matters very much as all educated Londoners
did; they were all dissatisfied with the worldliness and corruption of the Church and wished for reform, some more,
some less; but Chaucer, not caring primarily for the soul
and enjoying intensely the human comedy, was probably
lukewarm about any drastic action. He certainly was not a
Wycliffite in any sectarian sense. So far as I remember, he
makes no reference to Wycliffe and but one to Wycliffe's
partisans, the Lollards. In *The Canterbury Tales,* Harry
Bailly, the Host of the Tabard, and master of ceremonies on
the pilgrimage, when he asks the Parson for a tale, begins:

"Sir Parisshe Prest," quod he, "for Goddes bones,
Telle us a tale,"

The Parson, displeased by this profanity, cries out "Benedicite!

What eyleth [aileth] the man, so synfully to swere?"

The Host, who was not a man to be readily snubbed, ex-
claims,

"O Jankin, be ye there?
I smelle a loller in the wynd."

And he shouts a warning to the company, "Now! goode
men, herkeneth [hearken ye to] me:

We schal han a predicacioun;
This Lollere heer wil prechen us somwhat."

[151]

The Shipman, who we have learned was "a good felawe"
and liked a "draughte of wyn," takes alarm, and bursts out
with

> "Nay, by my fader soule; that schal he nat!
> . . . heer schal he nat preche;
> He schal no gospel glosen here ne teche."

"We all believe in God," he explained, but the loller, he
feared, would sow tares in their good clean corn and make
trouble. These two men, Harry Bailly and the Shipman, in
their several ways, are typical Englishmen of the centuries
before Puritanism swept over the land: they respected religion, but wished it to keep its place in the pulpit and the
confessional, and not come out on week days to cast a
shadow over the gaieties of life. Chaucer, also being a typical Englishman, had some similar attitude toward religious
matters, and if he came into relations with the Wycliffites
at all, it was through his patron, the Duke of Lancaster.

Politics make strange bedfellows. When Lancaster came
back in 1374, after his great raid through France from
Calais to Bordeaux, he plunged into politics, and as the
King was too old and the Black Prince too ill, to take any
real part, he dominated the government. While, according
to Trevelyan's harsh judgment, he was building up a party
by lavish favors, he took advantage of the wide-spread discontent of the laity with what it regarded as the dispropor-
tionate riches of the clergy, and allied himself with this anti-
ecclesiastical faction; in this way the Duke found himself,
as it were, in comradeship with the saintly John Wycliffe,
and he made the most of it. Wycliffe was the most eminent
philosopher and scholar in England, he had been Master of
Balliol at Oxford, and enjoyed a reputation for learning,
that extended far beyond the university precincts. When
King Edward was engaged in his controversy with the

Papacy concerning the tribute promised by King John, Wycliffe upheld the national position. His argument, if I may call it so, is said to have been published in 1374. In April, 1374, the Duke, acting for the crown, presented him with the living of Lutterworth in Leicestershire; and that summer he was sent to Bruges, as one of the royal envoys, to discuss with papal commissioners sundry important matters in dispute between England and the Papacy. It was shortly after this that Chaucer was made comptroller of the customs in London. From this time Wycliffe's opposition to the existing ecclesiastical system became more and more outspoken; he contended that the Church had no concern with temporal matters, that priests should not possess (as I understand it) any worldly goods, but only have the usufruct and even that for no longer time than they should fulfil their duties in godliness and righteousness, and if they should fall away into sin or worldliness, the secular power had the right and the duty to take their temporal possessions away from them. This doctrine exactly suited the Duke of Lancaster, who was quite ready to lay hands upon the Church property.

The Church, of course, could not put up with these revolutionary doctrines. In February, 1377, shortly after the Lancastrian faction had triumphantly undone all that the Good Parliament had done, the Archbishop of Canterbury summoned Wycliffe to appear before the Bishop of London on the nineteenth of the month. Accordingly, in obedience to the summons, Wycliffe attended at the Lady Chapel of Saint Paul's Cathedral, but with him went the Duke of Lancaster, Lord Henry Percy, Hotspur's father, and a troop of retainers. The Bishop was a proud man and high words passed between him and the Duke. The dispute grew hot and the Duke threatened to drag the Bishop by the hair of his head. At this there was immense confusion, for the

[153]

citizens of London did not like the Duke, and rallied round their Bishop. And when news came that the Duke proposed in his packed Parliament to unseat the Lord Mayor and supplant him by an appointee of the crown, there was a riot, and in the confusion no attention was paid to Wycliffe. The city seethed that day, and on the next the mob marched out to the Savoy Palace. Stow says that the Duke and Sir Henry Percy were dining there, when a messenger rushed in to warn the Duke of his danger. The Duke leapt up from table, leaving his oysters, so hastily that he hurt both his legs against the table, and though the butler was just offering wine to wash down the oysters, he and Percy ran down to the river, jumped into a boat and never stopped rowing till they came to the Manor of Kennington, where the Princess of Wales and young Richard were living.

A year later (1378) Wycliffe was summoned before a council of prelates at Lambeth Palace, but this time the Princess of Wales, who was in accord with the Duke of Lancaster, sent a message forbidding the prelates to pass judgment upon him. It would have been more or less than human, if in return Wycliffe had not thought well of the Duke of Lancaster; and when that nobleman violated the sanctuary of Westminster, and was excommunicated by the Bishop of London, Wycliffe wrote a defense of the Duke's action. But from that time on the reformer grew more radical; he attacked the Papacy as a monarchy, he denounced sacerdotal power, and passing from institutions to theology, finally condemned the doctrine of transubstantiation. Heresy was a dangerous matter, and the Duke bade Wycliffe be silent; and, a year or two later, after Wat Tyler's terrifying uprising, when the conservatives suspected that seeds of rebellion lay in Wycliffe's teachings, the Duke sided with the propertied classes, and he and Wycliffe drifted apart. The alliance had been unnatural; Wycliffe was a spiritual reformer, John of Gaunt an ambitious politician.

Chaucer's mission to Paris with Sir Thomas Percy had taken him from England just two days before the convocation of bishops sat in Saint Paul's Cathedral to sit in judgment upon Wycliffe, so he was away when the mob set out for the Savoy Palace to wreak vengeance on the Duke. And I assume that he was not sorry to have missed the incident. And, when he was at home again, I take it that he stood aside from the whole controversy, busying himself with his duties at the custom-house during the day and with his reading at night. He probably looked on the reform movement with a mixture of sympathy and annoyance. However much he himself might belabor the rogues, who dressed themselves up in ecclesiastical garments—monks, friars, pardoners, summoners—he did not like the subversive and combative methods of this precursor of Martin Luther. Chaucer would have much preferred the intellectual, ironical and gentlemanlike behavior of such a man as Desiderius Erasmus.

CHAPTER XIX

The Parlement of Foules

WAT TYLER's rebellion was followed by such punishments as are usual for the victors in social strife to inflict upon the vanquished. The King, attended by five hundred spears and as many archers, proceeded from London to Canterbury, by the Pilgrims' Road; there was drowning, hanging, beheading and quartering, and so, John Stow says, "the countrey was in peace." The King, although somewhat set up by his success, continued obediently to follow the advice of his counselors, and the business of London again went on at its usual pace. Chaucer's friend, John Gower, a Kentish gentleman, whose estate was in the very thick of the rebellion, published a poem in Latin, *Vox Clamantis,* in which he gave expression to the fear and indignation caused to men of property by the rebellion. It begins with a vision and an allegory, in traditional fashion, and then passes on to a homily upon the vices of the age. Chaucer, more even-tempered or more magnanimous, turned his mind to a very different subject.

The reason that I have said so little of his poetry is that for the most part his poems are the autumnal fruit of his life, the riper harvest of experience and leisure. He may have written many poems in his younger days, but none have come down except the translation of the *Roman de la Rose, The Book of the Duchess* and *The House of Fame* to which I have referred, and a few short poems, complaints about one thing or another, and such. At about the time we have come to, when Chaucer was forty years old, he wrote

The Parlement of Foules, a poem concerning a wooing. It might be called an allegorical "The Wooing o't." The poem came about in this way, according to the usual interpretation, which I shall follow, although no one can be wholly blind to the strength of Haldeen Braddy's arguments opposing it.

After the failure of the negotiations for a French marriage, the royal uncles had been obliged to look elsewhere for a wife for young Richard. A princess from Hainaut would have been more popular in England, for the memory of good Queen Philippa was still fresh, but there were no marriageable princesses there; and, according to report, the Duke of Lancaster would have liked his daughter to be chosen, but the girl was the King's own cousin and that seemed too close a blood relation, and also there was a general feeling among the people that the King should by his marriage make an alliance advantageous to the country. So, some time before the rebellion, Sir Simon Burley, "a sage and valiant knight," who had been Richard's tutor and also a close friend to the Black Prince, and brother to Chaucer's friend, Sir John Burley, was selected to go to the Emperor and to propose terms of marriage between the King and the Emperor's daughter, Anne, a girl about the King's age or a few months older. Sir Simon left England with a great train and went to Brabant, where he was most hospitably received by the Duke and Duchess, the King's relations. They approved the match and gave Sir Simon letters to the Emperor; and the English embassy proceeded to Brussels, and then by way of Louvain to Cologne, and on from there to Prague.

The old Emperor, Charles IV, had died before the ambassador arrived and had been succeeded by his son, Wenceslaus, brother to the Princess Anne. Both brother and sister were agreeable to the proposal, but Bohemians were not very well acquainted with the remote island of Britain, and, unwilling

[157]

to marry their young Princess among an uncivilized people, sent an envoy to observe the state of England, and to make inquiries concerning the dowry and the marriage settlement. The envoy was much pleased with all he saw and heard, particularly with the pecuniary arrangements, and well he might, for according to report, King Richard, who had refused to think of the daughter of Bernabò Visconti, dowered though she was "with an inestimable sum of gold," gave the Emperor ten thousand pounds for his daughter as well as much else besides. The envoy liked Richard, himself— who had inherited his mother's beauty and in his youth was charming—also the uncles, John of Gaunt, and Edmund, Earl of Cambridge, and various lords of the English court, and went away promising to bring the marriage to a conclusion. He was as good as his word, everything was happily settled; and the Princess, attended by a goodly number of knights and damsels, took her way to England. They stopped at Brussels with Richard's relations, the Duke and Duchess. There they heard that Norman ships were cruising between Calais and Holland and they were afraid to embark, especially since rumor said that the ships were lying in wait for them, as the King of France was very ill pleased with the proposed marriage. They sent word to the French that it was not honorable to carry off a lady even in war; to which the French retorted that the Black Prince had set a precedent in carrying off the Duchess of Bourbon. Finally, however, the Duke of Brabant persuaded the French to grant passports to the Bohemian party, and the Norman ships were remanded to port. Thus reassured, the Princess proceeded by way of Ghent and Bruges to Gravelines and Calais, and then as soon as the winds were favorable embarked for Dover. She rested there two days, and then went to Canterbury, where Thomas of Woodstock, Earl of Buckingham, received her with befitting ceremony. In

London the little Princess of sixteen was welcomed by the whole city. The young couple were married in Westminster Abbey by the Archbishop of Canterbury, and the wedding was celebrated by great feastings, jousts and merrymaking. The King and Queen then went to Windsor, where they kept an open and noble house, and Froissart says that they were very happy together.

The commentators, as I have said, usually assume that Chaucer had this wooing in mind when he wrote *The Parlement of Foules,* and it may be that some confirmation of the theory is to be found in his appointment in the spring of that year, 1382, as comptroller of the petty customs in the Port of London, with permission to act by deputy. Such an office added to his other office must have been in the nature of a sinecure, and might well be, I should suppose, an acknowledgment of the King's satisfaction with the compliment. But we had better look at the poem and see whether or no it will justify the theory.

The introduction is, to me, a little enigmatical, and a very devious way of coming to the wooing. The first verse, which admirably translates the maxim of Hippocrates,

The lyf so short, the craft so long to lerne,

leads the poet to say that he often reads in books about Love's miracles and cruel anger, then he speaks of reading old books, and especially a book by Macrobius that contained Cicero's *The Dream of Scipio,* how the elder Africanus comes to his illustrious grandson and tells him that after this life there is a heaven where good men go, and the wicked, too, after their sins have been expiated and forgiven. But while reading, the light became too feeble for him to continue. So he went to bed and to sleep, and dreamt that old Africanus came to him and said that, as he saw

how well the poet had read Macrobius' book, he would reward him. At this time the poet prays Venus to help him
put his dream properly into rhyme. Then he tells the story.
Africanus led him to a double gate, with this inscription over
one-half, that I have quoted on the title page, at a suggestion contained in James Russell Lowell's essay,

> "Thorgh me men gon into that blysful place
> Of hertes hele [health] and dedly woundes cure,"

and this over the other half,

> "Thorgh me men gon . . .
> Unto the mortal strokes of the spere [sphere]
> Of which Disdayn and Daunger is the gyde . . ."

The poet is frightened and does not know whether to enter
the gate or not, but Africanus (with a touch of Chaucerian
irony) tells him that the inscriptions are only meant for
lovers, and not for such as he, who have lost all taste of
love, and takes him by the hand and pulls him in. Here
he sees,

> . . . treës clad with leves that ay shal laste,
> Ech in his kynde, of colour fresh and greene
> As emeraude, . . .

> The byldere ok, and ek the hardy asshe;
> The piler elm, the cofre unto carayne [dead body];
> The boxtre pipere, holm to whippes lashe;
> The saylynge fyr; the cipresse, deth to playne;
> The shetere ew; the asp for shaftes pleyne;
> The olyve of pes [peace], and eke the dronke vyne;
> The victor palm, the laurer to devyne [for prophecy].

Edmund Spenser imitates this:

> The sayling pine, the cedar proud and tall,
> The vine-propp elme, the poplar never dry,
> The builder oake, sole king of forrests all,
> The aspine good for staves, the cypresse funerall,
>
> The laurell, meed of mightie conquerours
> And poets sage, the firre that weepeth still,
> The willow worne of forlorne paramours,
> The eugh [yew] obedient to the benders will,
> The birch for shaftes, the sallow for the mill.

And then Chaucer borrows sixteen stanzas from Boccaccio,
to describe a garden "ful of blosmy bowes." It is a beautiful place, and you catch lines or phrases that Spenser in his
turn will take, and convert to sweeter melody. Here he
sees Cupid, with his bow and arrows, and various other persons, very much as in *The Romaunt of the Rose,* Pleasaunce,
Aray, Lust (good sense), Curtesie, Delyt, Gentilesse, and
so on, as well as Venus, and her servants. Then he walks
back to

> . . . wher that ther sat a queene
> That, as of lyght the somer sonne shene
> Passeth the sterre, right so over mesure
> She fayrer was than any creature.
>
> And in a launde, upon an hil of floures,
> Was set this noble goddesse Nature.

We have at last come to the main theme of the poem. As
in *The Book of the Duchess,* the prelude seems very long in
proportion to the whole, here three hundred lines out of
seven hundred; it is medieval, it reminds one of an ancient

church, where one traverses portico and narthex before reaching the door of the sanctuary itself. The day is Saint Valentine's Day, and all the birds are gathered together, each to choose its mate. Nature, "this noble emperesse," bids them take place according to their kind,

> That is to seyn, the foules of ravyne [prey]
> Weere hyest set, and thanne the foules smale
> That eten, as hem Nature wolde enclyne,
> As worm or thyng of whiche I telle no tale.

He then enumerates the various kinds of birds,

> The sparwe, Venus sone; the nyghtyngale,
> That clepeth forth the grene leves newe;
> The swalwe, mortherere of the foules smale
> That maken hony of floures freshe of hewe;
> The wedded turtil, with hire herte trewe;
> The pekok, with his aungels [angel's] fetheres bryghte;
> The fesaunt, skornere of the cok by nyghte.

Scholars say, that Chaucer takes his list of birds from Alain de Lille, *De Planctu Naturæ;* nevertheless, the reader feels a modern quality in the enumeration, a novel touch, a freshness of phrase, that indicate that the poet has set his face in a new direction.

> What shulde I seyn? Of foules every kynde
> That in this world han fetheres and stature
> Men myghten in that place assembled fynde
> Byfore the noble goddesse of Nature,
> And everich of hem dide his besy cure
> Benygnely to chese [choose] or for to take,
> By hire acord, his formel [female] or his make [mate].

[162]

Now, we are aware, the poet is approaching the gist of his subject:

> But to the poynt: Nature held on hire hond
> A formel egle, of shap the gentilleste
> That evere she among hire werkes fond,
> The most benygne and the goodlieste.
> In hire was everi vertu at his reste [home],
> So ferforth that Nature hireself hadde blysse
> To loke on hire, and ofte hire bek to kisse.

This admirable bird is, under the theory, the Princess Anne, waiting to be wooed. Nature then makes a little speech. The birds have come to choose their mates, let the worthiest begin. The allegory indicates young Richard:

> "The tersel [male] egle, as that ye knowe wel,
> The foul royal, above yow in degre,
> The wyse and worthi, secre, trewe as stel,
> Which I have formed, as ye may wel se,
> In every part as it best liketh me—
> It nedeth not his shap yow to devyse [tell]—
> He shal first chese [choose] and speken in his gyse [guise]."

Encouraged by Nature to speak first,

> With hed enclyned and with ful humble cheere [face]
> This royal tersel spak, and tariede noght [not]:—
> "Unto my soverayn lady, and not my fere [mate],
> I chese, and chese with wil, and herte, and thought,
> The formel on youre honde so wel iwrought,
> Whos I am al, and evere wol hire serve,
> Do what hire lest, to do me lyve or sterve [die] . . ."

And with that, he makes a very pretty profession of love.

[163]

Ryght as the freshe, rede rose newe
Ayeyn [opposite] the somer sonne coloured is,
Ryght so for shame al wexen gan the hewe
Of this formel, whan she herde al this;
She neyther answerde wel, ne seyde amys,
So sore abasht was she, tyl that Nature
Seyde, "Doughter, drede [fear] yow nought, I yow assure!"

I need not quote much more. Two other tercel egles, but
"of lower kinde," came forward also as wooers of the formel,
and commentators have theories as to who they are, foreign
princes of some sort, but that does not concern us. The
last lover makes a very long speech, and then the poet, our
Chaucer, as we know him from *The Canterbury Tales,*
shows himself at last. The birds (like the readers) get impatient; you hear cries "Have don, and lat us wende [go]!"
"Come of [off]!" "Allas!" "Whan shal youre cursede
pletynge have an ende?" And then the comic birds come
forth and bring merriment, until Nature breaks in, "Hold
your tonges there," and bids each species of bird elect a
spokesman to give the verdict of that species. The tercelet
of the falcons said:

"Me wolde thynke how that the worthieste
Of knyghthode, and lengest had used it,
Most of estat, of blode the gentilleste,
Were sittyngest [fittingest] for hire, if that hir leste [please];
And of these thre she wot hireself, I trowe,
Which that he be, for hit is light to knowe."

Then follow, in good Chaucerian style, the opinions of the
goose, the sparrowhawk, the turtle-dove, the duck, the
cuckoo, and the merlin (a small hawk). Nature, again, in-
terrupts and says that her decision is that the formel shall
choose the one she loves best, but she counsels her to take

[164]

the royal tercelet as "the gentilleste and most worthi." The formel asks for leave to consider till the year be done, and then she will choose. Nature grants the requests, and counsels the three suitors each to do his best to win her. And on this the poem ends with a roundel,

"Now welcome, somer, with thy sonne softe,
That hast this wintres wedres overshake,
And driven away the longe nyghtes blake!

"Saynt Valentyn, that art ful hy on-lofte,
Thus syngen smale foules for thy sake:
Now welcome, somer, with thy sonne softe,
That hast this wintres wedres overshake.

"Wel han they cause for to gladen ofte,
Seth ech of hem recovered hath hys make;
Ful blissful mowe [may] they synge when they wake:
Now welcome, somer, with thy sonne softe,
That hast this wintres wedres overshake,
And driven away the longe nyghtes blake."

At this the poet awoke.

There are difficulties as you see in applying this allegory to the young King. The falcon advises the formel to take the lover who has been knight the longest time—unless it can mean in the highest, noblest way—and length of time could hardly apply to Richard, but in all other respects what is said of the tercel eagle applies to him. The delay of a year in which to choose merely assigns the poem to the date when Sir Simon Burley starts on his embassy, or when the Bohemian envoy comes to England. The use of the conventional dream, garden and allegorical figures, certainly points to an allegory, and if the allegory does not apply to Richard, there seems to be very little point to it. Besides, a eulogy to a bride betrothed seems to prepare the way for the dedication of a book to that bride, when she has become a Queen, and in *The Legend of Good Women* (which Lydgate asserts was written at the Queen's request) Chaucer says,

> . . . whan this book ys maad, yive [give] it the quene,
> On my byhalf, at Eltham, or at Sheene.

On the whole the guess that the allegory does apply to King Richard and Queen Anne of Bohemia seems the most reasonable interpretation, but one hopes that it will be long before the truth is known, since commentators enjoy their rival hypotheses so keenly.

CHAPTER XX

On Poetry

I HAVE ventured to find *The Parlement of Foules* and *The House of Fame* lacking in the art of proportion and composition, that is often so happily displayed in the arts of building, sculpture and miniature, as well as in some Italian and French poems, of this period, and I also confess that, as a careless, pleasure-seeking reader, I find those two poems, on the whole, tedious as well as ill-constructed. And, as I shall be equally frank about Chaucer's later poems, whether to praise or to acknowledge my inability to appreciate, I think that the expressions I may use will be more intelligible, if I make some preliminary profession of faith, some exposition of my doctrine of poetic values. It would be more interesting if I were to abridge and recount what those poets have said who have deliberately given their opinions on poetry: Coleridge, for instance, Wordsworth, Shelley, Matthew Arnold, Francis Thompson, or Sir Philip Sidney; but so doing, I should not serve my purpose. You will not have a clear notion of what I mean by *good, delightful, melodious,* unless you first know my preconceptions and native bias. Circumstances push me, I think, to some definition of poetry, which I do reluctantly, because to my way of thinking poetry is the most personal of the arts and the pleasure of it dependent on the disposition, temperament, health, education and experiences of the reader.

Poetry, then, is a philosophy of experience interpreted by passion; it is the expression of the relation between the soul and that which has the power to stir it—woman, the waves of the sea, a child of seven, a galloping horse, an idea, a thunderstorm, a tree. It transmutes the material into the spiritual. It reaches out like the Almighty in Michelangelo's fresco to touch the outstretched finger of the Adam in us. It comes like the dawn over the mountaintops; like love to the young maid. It is a quickening of the spirit in the clutch of awe, of beauty, of voluptuousness, of pain; it is an intensity of life, an ennobling of the senses; it enables our eyes to see what they of themselves did not see, our ears to hear what they did not hear, and causes our hearts to beat at a hundred things which but for poetry we had not noticed. It is communion with souls greater than our own. And our English poetry holds out its arms to the highest and the lowest among us. Think of the range of English poetry from Blake to Pope, from Cowper to Byron, from George Herbert to Rochester.

And as you can not erect a pale around the subject-matter of poetry, you can not lay down any law for its expression; but from one's experience of the poetry that has moved one in the past, one may hazard certain inferences. Coleridge said that poetry consists in the arrangement of words in their best order, but, except by his practise, he does not tell us what that best order is. Any language adequate to express this relation of the soul to the quickening stimulus, I suppose is poetry; but under the constitution of human nature—for our pulses beat to stress and our senses are sensitive to waves of different lengths—the presence of rhythm, of rhyme, some element of music, is usually necessary for any such adequate expression. Words, that arranged in what we call prose would be inaudible to the soul, when arranged in their best order, in poetic form, knock importunately, and like the playing of the Pied Piper force us to listen. Meter renders an expression of the poet's feelings more intelligible to others, more readily communicates the passion of the quickened pulse, the glamour of the illuminating imagination; and so when we speak of poetry, we usually mean human speech in verse. There is no sharp line that divides poetry from prose. I can best indicate my idea of where poetry ends and prose begins by a metaphor. Listen to the dying notes of a church-bell, such as Dante describes in his perfect lines:

> *Era già l'ora che volge il disio*
> *Ai naviganti, e intenerisce il core,*
> *Lo dì che han detto ai dolci amici addio;*

> *E che lo nuovo peregrin d'amore*
> *Punge, se ode squilla di lontano*
> *Che paja il giorno pianger che si more:*

> It was already the hour when longing comes
> To those at sea, and mollifies the heart,
> The day they bade good-bye to their dear friends;

> And pricks the new-started traveler
> With love, if he hears a far-off bell
> That seems to bewail the dying day.

Listen to that bell, I repeat, and when you can say that among other noises you no longer hear its sweet echoes, then you have passed from poetry into prose. Don Quixote looks at the world and sees poetry, Mr. Babbitt looks and sees prose.

But I think I can best serve my purpose, best convey to you my scale of values, and also, as it were, sound a tuning-fork, if, in addition to the recital of my creed, I quote familiar models, in order that, with them fresh in your mind, you shall be able the more readily to judge for yourself what rank you will assign to Chaucer as a poet. For, always re-

[169]

member, what scholars are sometimes prone to forget, that the personal relation between you and Chaucer is the important matter; and, also, that convention provides, rightly enough, that there are three things for us to consider; there is the matter, there is the medium, and there is the marriage between matter and medium. In this chapter I have in mind the medium of expression, the verse; when I come to *The Canterbury Tales* I shall address myself primarily to the matter.

I assume that everybody will agree that these familiar citations bring their authority with them.

Spenser

A lovely Ladie rode him faire beside,
   Upon a lowly Asse more white then snow,
Yet she much whiter; but the same did hide
   Under a vele, that wimpled was full low;
And over all a blacke stole shee did throw:
   As one that inly mournd, so was she sad,
And heavie sat upon her palfrey slow:
   Seemed in heart some hidden care she had;
And by her in a line a milkewhite lambe she lad.

Shakespeare

There is a willow grows aslant a brook,
That shows his hoar leaves in the glassy stream;
There with fantastic garlands did she come
Of crow-flowers, nettles, daisies, and long purples,
         *   *   *   *   *
There, on the pendent boughs her coronet weeds
Clambering to hang, an envious sliver broke;
When down her weedy trophies and herself
Fell in the weeping brook. Her clothes spread wide,

And, mermaid-like, a while they bore her up;
Which time she chanted snatches of old tunes,
As one incapable of her own distress,
Or like a creature native and indued
Unto that element . . .

Milton

Weep no more, woful Shepherds, weep no more,
For Lycidas your sorrow is not dead,
Sunk though he be beneath the watry floar,
So sinks the day-star in the Ocean bed,
And yet anon repairs his drooping head,
And tricks his beams, and with new spangled Ore,
Flames in the forehead of the morning sky:
So Lycidas sunk low, but mounted high,
Through the dear might of him that walk'd the waves,
Where other groves, and other streams along,
With Nectar pure his oozy locks he laves,
And hears the unexpressive nuptiall song,
In the blest kingdoms meek of joy and love.
There entertain him all the Saints above,
In solemn troops, and sweet societies
That sing, and singing in their glory move,
And wipe the tears for ever from his eyes.

Earl of Rochester

Without thy light what light remains in me?
Thou art my life; my way, my light's in thee;
I live, I move, and by thy beams I see.

Thou art my life—if thou but turn away
My life's a thousand deaths. Thou are my way—
Without thee, Love, I travel not but stray.

My light thou art—without thy glorious sight
My eyes are darken'd with eternal night.
My Love, thou art my way, my life, my light.

Thou art my way; I wander if thou fly.
Thou art my light; if hid, how blind am I!
Thou art my life; if thou withdraw'st, I die.

Dissolve thy sunbeams, close thy wings and stay!
See, see how I am blind, and dead, and stray!
—O thou that art my life, my light, my way!

Dryden

Some of their chiefs were princes of the land;
In the first rank of these did Zimri stand;
A man so various that he seemed to be
Not one, but all mankind's epitome:
Stiff in opinions, always in the wrong,
Was everything by starts, and nothing long;
But in the course of one revolving moon
Was chymist, fiddler, statesman and buffoon;
Then all for women, painting, rhyming, drinking,
Besides the thousand freaks that died in thinking.
Blest madman, who could every hour employ
With something new to wish or to enjoy!
Railing and praising were his usual themes,
And both, to show his judgment, in extremes:
So over violent, or over civil,
That every man with him was God or Devil.
In squandering wealth was his peculiar art;
Nothing went unrewarded but desert.
Beggared by fools, whom still he found too late,
He had his jest and they had his estate.

[172]

Gray

Can storied urn or animated bust
    Back to its mansion call the fleeting breath?
Can Honour's voice provoke the silent dust,
    Or Flatt'ry soothe the dull cold ear of death?

Perhaps in this neglected spot is laid
    Some heart once pregnant with celestial fire;
Hands, that the rod of empire might have sway'd,
    Or waked to ecstasy the living lyre.

Coleridge

I look'd to heaven, and tried to pray;
    But or ever a prayer had gusht,
A wicked whisper came, and made
    My heart as dry as dust.

I closed my lids, and kept them close,
    And the balls like pulses beat;
But the sky and the sea, and the sea and the sky,
Lay like a load on my weary eye,
    And the dead were at my feet.

The cold sweat melted from their limbs,
    Nor rot nor reek did they:
The look with which they look'd on me
    Had never pass'd away.

An orphan's curse would drag to hell
    A spirit from on high;
But oh! more horrible than that
    Is the curse in a dead man's eye!
Seven days, seven nights, I saw that curse,
    And yet I could not die.

Wordsworth

Earth has not anything to show more fair:
    Dull would he be of soul who could pass by
    A sight so touching in its majesty:
This City now doth, like a garment, wear
The beauty of the morning; silent, bare,
    Ships, towers, domes, theatres, and temples lie
    Open unto the fields, and to the sky;
All bright and glittering in the smokeless air.
Never did sun more beautifully steep
    In his first splendour, valley, rock, or hill;
Ne'er saw I, never felt, a calm so deep!
    The river glideth at his own sweet will:
Dear God! the very houses seem asleep;
    And all that mighty heart is lying still!

Shelley

Make me thy lyre, even as the forest is:
    What if my leaves are falling like its own?
The tumult of thy mighty harmonies

    Will take from both a deep autumnal tone,
Sweet though in sadness. Be thou, Spirit fierce,
    My spirit! Be thou me, impetuous one!

Drive my dead thoughts over the universe,
    Like wither'd leaves, to quicken a new birth;
And, by the incantation of this verse,

    Scatter, as from an unextinguish'd hearth
Ashes and sparks, my words among mankind!
    Be through my lips to unawaken'd earth

The trumpet of a prophecy! O Wind,
If Winter comes, can Spring be far behind?

Keats

Thou wast not born for death, immortal Bird!
No hungry generations tread thee down;
The voice I hear this passing night was heard
In ancient days by emperor and clown:
Perhaps the self-same song that found a path
Through the sad heart of Ruth, when, sick for home,
She stood in tears amid the alien corn;
The same that oft-times hath
Charm'd magic casements opening on the foam
Of perilous seas, in faery lands forlorn.

Tennyson

There is sweet music here that softer falls
Than petals from blown roses on the grass,
Or night-dews on still waters between walls
Of shadowy granite, in a gleaming pass;
Music that gentlier on the spirit lies,
Than tired eyelids upon tired eyes;
Music that brings sweet sleep down from the blissful skies.
Here are cool mosses deep,
And thro' the moss the ivies creep,
And in the stream the long-leaved flowers weep,
And from the craggy ledge the poppy hangs in sleep.

Matthew Arnold

As some grave Tyrian trader, from the sea,
Descried at sunrise an emerging prow
Lifting the cool-hair'd creepers stealthily,
The fringes of a southward-facing brow
Among the Ægean isles;
And saw the merry Grecian coaster come,
Freighted with amber grapes, and Chian wine,
Green, bursting figs, and tunnies steep'd in brine—
And knew the intruders on his ancient home

The young light-hearted masters of the waves;
    And snatch'd his rudder, and shook out more sail,
    And day and night held on indignantly
O'er the blue Midland waters with the gale,
    Betwixt the Syrtes and soft Sicily,
        To where the Atlantic raves
    Outside the western straits, and unbent sails
        There where down cloudy cliffs, through sheets of
            foam,
        Shy traffickers, the dark Iberians come;
And on the beach undid his corded bales.

                    Francis Thompson

    Her beauty smoothed earth's furrowed face.
        She gave me tokens three:—
    A look, a word of her winsome mouth,
        And a wild raspberry,

    A berry red, a guileless look,
        A still word,—strings of sand!
    And yet they made my wild, wild heart
        Fly down to her little hand.

    For standing artless as the air,
        And candid as the skies,
    She took the berries with her hand,
        And the love with her sweet eyes.

    The fairest things have fleetest end,
        Their scent survives their close,
    But the rose's scent is bitterness
        To him that loved the rose.

    She looked a little wistfully,
        Then went her sunshine ways—:
    The sea's eyes had a mist on it,
        And the leaves fell from the day.

She went her unremembering way,
    She went, and left to me
The pangs of all the partings gone,
    And partings yet to be.

There! If you will bear these various samples of poetry in mind, I think you will be better fitted to establish a personal relation with Chaucer, the poet, than if you had read a dozen learned treatises about him.

CHAPTER XXI

Troilus and Criseyde

I quoted all those familiar poems, running down the centuries, because it seemed to me a fitting mode of approach to *Troilus and Criseyde,* for this poem, to my way of thinking, is far and away the best of Chaucer's poems, the most musical, the most moving, the most interesting, the poem that more than any other determines his rank among English poets. To *The Canterbury Tales,* on the other hand, the fitting mode of approach is by way of prose; for however much we may admire its chief excellencies, the portraits of the Wife of Bath, of the Host of the Tabard, of the Poor Parson, the essence of these excellencies is not founded in poetry, at least not as one, with the incomparable English lyrics in mind, conventionally defines poetry; that essence lies in Chaucer's admirable mastery of delineation, in his happy capture of traits, whether of speech, behavior or dress. These are the qualities that mark great novelists: Tolstoy, Balzac, Fielding. Natasha, la Cousine Bette, Mr. Micawber, Parson Adams, are great portraits, but their portraiture is not poetry; even in the case of Jeanie Deans or Tess of the D'Urbervilles, we call their pages prose. So, too, Chaucer's pilgrims, though described in verse, belong to the department of prose. *Troilus and Criseyde* is a poem, compact of poetical sentiment and imagery, and told in melodious verse. And the proper approach to it is by poetry, and therefore, as I say, I wished the reader to draw near with a mind and ear attuned to melody.

Chaucer took the story direct from Boccaccio, plot, structure, episodes, phrases, almost whole stanzas, word for word;

he expanded here, contracted there, omitted and interpolated; but though the two poems are like brothers, almost like brothers born at a birth, Chaucer has not made a copy, nor even a rearrangement, because he has suffused the story with his own personality, with English tenderness, beauty-lovingness and irony, in place of Boccaccio's specifically Italian qualities. *Troilus and Criseyde* is a beautiful poem, a great poem, English scholars say, and I think they are right. But, as I have suggested, the admiration of scholars is so readily enkindled by the poetry that is the object of their love, of their labors, of their *petits soins,* that consulting them as to merits is like asking Romeo what he thinks of Juliet. Indeed, I repeat, in every true scholar there is a touch of Romeo. And not only must the dilettante be on his guard against academic bias, but also against national bias. English-speaking scholars usually, if not invariably, ascribe a great superiority to Chaucer over Boccaccio, in their respective poems *Troilus and Criseyde* and *Filostrato,* and therefore, out of a regard to that golden mean in poetical judgments at which dilettanti aim, I quote the eminent French scholar, Emile Legouis. He says: "The *Filostrato* is undoubtedly a masterpiece. . . . [Chaucer] thought he could widen a work perfect in itself and still retain all its merits. [*Troilus* has, I believe, 8239 lines and *Filostrato* 5704]. Compared to Boccaccio's deftness and sureness of touch, revealing both mastery and national temperament, Chaucer's inexperience seems a little clumsy, one might almost say, if one dared, a little barbaric. . . . One hardly dares mention the word failure in connection with a poem admirable in so many respects, one so completely worked out. . . . A glorious failure indeed, but nevertheless the awkward and imperfectly realized conception of a man of genius." I quote this criticism of M. Legouis not because I agree with it, but as the opinion of a sympathetic scholar, who has a wide knowledge of English, French and Italian poetry. An earlier French writer, M. Gomont, speaking of this poem says (1847), *"Le mauvais goût et la bizarrerie y dominent."* Neither do I agree with M. Gomont. But I suppose that it is possible to overrate as well as to underrate.

But whatever the respective merits of the two poems, even the most Italianate among us must concede that they are two separate poems, not a poem and a translation; Chaucer has taken Boccaccio, but he has metamorphosed him into pure Chaucer. Boccaccio in his turn had taken the plot from Benoît de Sainte-Maure, a French poet attached to the court of Henry II, who wrote a *Roman de Troie,* and also some details from Guido delle Colonne, a thirteenth-century Sicilian, who had composed what he called a *Historia Trojana.* And what of it? As Chaucer says of a poet: "Him rekketh noght of what matere he take." In poetry the end justifies the means. Chaucer, also, had recourse, they say, to these two early poets; but what he took from Boccaccio, what from Guido, what from Benoît, are matters for scholars to expound and dispute over; our business with *Troilus and Criseyde* is to enjoy. Some people can not enjoy a man's society until they know who his father and mother are, where he was educated, what club he belongs to, whether he will interpose an adverb (like a slovenly unhandsome corse betwixt the wind and their nobility) to separate the *to* from an infinitive. Others take him as he is, and in this fashion I approach *Troilus and Criseyde.*

The opening stanza tells the plot:

> The double sorwe of Troilus to tellen,
> That was the kyng Priamus sone of Troye,
> In lovynge, how his aventures fellen
> Fro wo to wele, and after out of joie,
> My purpos is . . .

[180]

And the poet asks for his readers' sympathy:

> But ye loveres, that bathen in gladnesse,
> If any drope of pyte in yow be,
> Remembreth yow on passed hevynesse
> That ye han felt, and on the adversite
> Of othere folk, and thynketh [think] how that ye
> Han felt that Love dorste yow displese . . .

And, bidding them pray for sorrowful and also happy lovers, he says:

> For now wil I gon streght to my matere,
> In which ye may the double sorwes here
> Of Troilus in lovynge of Criseyde,
> And how that she forsook hym er she deyde.

You perceive at once how much Chaucer has learned from Boccaccio, how far superior this beginning is to the dreams and vision, and narthex-like prologues, that he had copied from French poets for his earlier poems. He then tells the situation, which is so different from the *Iliad* that the reader must put Homer quite out of his mind and accept the medieval substitution. Calchas, a Trojan lord, having learned from Apollo that Troy is doomed to destruction, stealthily slunk away to the Greeks. The Trojans in their first anger declared that the traitor's family deserved to be burned. Now Calchas had a widowed daughter,

> Criseyde was this lady name al right.
> As to my doom [opinion], in al Troies cite
> Nas non so fair, for passynge every wight
> So aungelik [angelic] was hir natif beaute,
> That lik a thing inmortal semed she,
> As doth an hevenyssh perfit creature,
> That down were sent in scornynge of nature.

When Criseyde heard of her father's treachery, she went and flung herself at Hector's feet for protection; he bade her be of good cheer as she should not be molested.

The author refrains from telling us of all the fighting between the Greeks and Trojans for, as he says, we may read that

> In Omer, or in Dares, or in Dite,

and proceeds to describe how the Trojans kept the feast of the Palladium:

> And so bifel, whan comen was the tyme
> Of Aperil, whan clothed is the mede
> With newe grene, of lusty Veer the pryme,
> And swote smellen floures white and rede,
> In sondry wises shewed, as I rede,
> The folk of Troie hire [their] observaunces olde,
> Palladiones feste for to holde.

The whole city trooped to the Temple:

> Among thise othere folk was Criseyda
> In widewes habit blak; but natheles,
> Right as oure firste lettre is now an A,
> In beaute first so stood she, makeles [peerless].
> Hire goodly lookyng gladed al [all] the prees.
> Nas nevere yet seyn thyng to ben preysed derre [dearer],
> Nor under cloude blak so bright a sterre.

The heroine is thus introduced, and she has all our sympathy,—her husband dead, her father a traitor, herself an object of undeserved suspicion to the townsfolk, and both beautiful and charming. Chaucer is not creating, he is taking Boccaccio's heroine and presenting her to English-

[182]

men under such guise as shall soonest touch their hearts and enable them to enjoy the sweet sorrows of tragedy. We shall now have the hero; for we arrive at the threshold of the plot with a speed that marks how great a distance he has traversed since the *Prologue to The House of Fame*. Criseyde was standing

> Byhynden other folk, in litel brede [space],
> And neigh the dore, ay undre shames drede,
> Simple of atir and debonaire of chere,
> With ful assured [feeling secure] lokyng and manere,

at the time when Troilus comes in. He is a sort of heroic Benedick, who has always mocked love and lovers; a dangerous thing to do,

> For kaught is proud, and kaught is debonaire.
> This Troilus is clomben on the staire,
> And litel weneth that he moot descenden; . . .
>   * * * * *
> For evere it was, and evere it shall byfalle,
> That love is he that alle thing may bynde . . .
>   * * * * *
> And trewelich [truly] it sit [suits] wel to be so.
> For alderwisest han therwith ben plesed;
> And they that han ben aldermost in wo,
> With love han ben comforted moost and esed;
> And ofte it hath the cruel herte apesed,
> And worthi folk maad worthier of name,
> And causeth moost to dreden vice and shame.

So Troilus fell head over heels in love; and even in his shame and confusion he thanked the god:

> "Yow thanke I, lord, that han me brought to this.
> But wheither goddesse or womman, iwis,
> She be, I not [I know not], which that ye do me serve;
> But as hire man I wol ay lyve and sterve [die]."

Poor Troilus, his heart is on fire, and he is a prey to mortification and desire. A friend of his, Pandarus, Criseyde's uncle, overhears him groaning and bewailing, asks what is the matter, and draws from him the admission that he is in love:

"Love, ayeins [against] the which whoso defendeth
Hymselven most, hym alderlest [all the less] avaylleth,
With disespeyr so sorwfulli me offendeth,
That streight unto the deth myn herte sailleth.
Therto desyr so brennyngly me assailleth,
That to ben slayn it were a gretter joie
To me than kyng of Greece ben [be] and Troye!"

Pandarus suggested that a friend can help him.

"A wheston is no kervyng [carving] instrument,
And yet it maketh sharppe kervyng-tolis [tools]."

Besides, he says, things are only known by their contraries,

"For how myghte evere sweetnesse han ben knowe
To him that nevere tasted bitternesse?"

Let Troilus tell who is the cause of his woe and Pandarus will do his best to help him.

"For this nys naught, certein, the nexte wyse
To wynnen love, as techen us the wyse,
To walve [wallow] and wepe as Nyobe the queene,
Whos teres yet in marble ben yseene."

Pandarus's counsels are worldly wise, and savor of Jean de Meung: they were probably heard before, and have certainly been heard since.—Shall I wasting in despair, die because a woman's fair?—

[184]

"What? sholde he therfore fallen in dispayr,
Or be recreant for his owne tene,
Or slen [slay] hymself, al be his lady fair?
Nay, nay . . ."

Pandarus has a bad reputation, but that is due to our Christian civilization and to Shakespeare. Troy was not a New England city; its people were pagans and Cupid was a god. Men and women were meant to fall in love with one another; love was recognized to be the crown of life. Monks and nuns had no place in their world. Lovers, whom our traditional conventions call immoral, were as innocent as wild animals in a wood. What made love sacred, was not an ecclesiastical rite, but depth and loyalty. Troilus was a true and loyal lover, and had no notion that what he was doing was wrong; love led to nobleness, to generosity, to courage and pity. The sense of evil creeps in because Chaucer can not help making Pandarus a humorous character, with a Mephistophelian touch, a man so laden with maxims of worldly wisdom that he perforce brings with him into Troilus's Garden of Eden an appetite for something that innocent love can not satisfy. Pandarus undoubtedly acts out of affection for Troilus, as Troilus says, from

Compassion, and felawship, and trist;

but he is by nature, by the Chaucerian nature imposed upon him, a little bored by innocence, and prefers a universe with the notion of sin in it to a universe without it. I think Socrates would say that Troilus did no wrong, that Criseyde did no wrong until she was false, and that Pandarus did no wrong other than to wish for the taste of sin. But I leave the reader to pass ethical judgments for himself and go back to the story.

[185]

Troilus rails on Fortune. Pandarus points out that her wheel sometimes turns from ill to good, and at last persuades Troilus to tell him his lady's name. Troilus names her, and Pandarus bursts into a eulogy of his niece, and says she has the kindest heart,

> "And forthy [therefore] loke of good comfort thou be;
> For certainly, the firste poynt is this
> Of noble corage and wel ordayné,
> A man to have pees [peace] with himself, ywis.
> So oughtest thou, for nought but good it is
> To loven wel, and in a worthy place;
> The oughte nat to clepe it hap, but grace."

And after reminding him of how he used to mock at love and lovers, bids him to be of good cheer:

> "For thilke grownd, that bereth the wedes wikke
> Bereth ek thise holsom herbes, as ful ofte
> Next the foule netle, rough and thikke,
> The rose waxeth swoote and smothe and softe;
> And next the valeye is the hil o-lofte;
> And next the derke nyght the glade morwe;
> And also joie is next the fyn [end] of sorwe."

Pandarus, I repeat, is no child of ascetic traditions, and knows no reason why true lovers should not meet; he thinks it but right to obey Nature and the God of Love. Each of the two lovers is worthy of the other, and altogether Pandarus is full of comfort:

> "Was nevere man ne womman yet bigete
> That was unapt to suffren loves hete,
> Celestial, or elles love of kynde . . ,"

[186]

You see, dramatic though he is, Chaucer can never refrain, or very seldom, from endowing his personages with touches of his own irony. You can see Pandarus's little smile of encouragement to the woebegone Troilus, as he pauses, longer than usual, on the comma after "celestial" and before "or elles love of kynde," that is, of one sex for the other. And he adds that Criseyde, confronted with the alternative of celestial or human love, is not suited to celestial love "as yet." One must remember that Pandarus is essentially romantic, that he completely accepts what scholars call the Courtly code, and believes that disobedience to the God of Love is "wikkedness."

Troilus wishes to know what Pandarus is going to do, but when Pandarus confidently bids him leave the whole matter to him, he consents, merely bidding Pandarus remember that he would rather die than that any wrong or rudeness be offered to Criseyde. So Pandarus goes off to devise a plan, and Troilus to fight the Greeks. Love casts its graces upon him,

> For he bicom the frendlieste wighte,
> The gentilest, and ek the mooste fre [generous],
> The thriftiest and oon [always] the beste knyght,
> That in his tyme was or myghte be.

Pandarus hies him to Criseyde and after long beating about the bush, tells her what the matter is and begs her to do no more than show a friendly face to Troilus; if she will not, Troilus will seek death on the battle-field, and if Troilus dies Pandarus will kill himself. In short, he depicts Troilus as so woebegone that Criseyde can not but be touched, and shortly afterward when she sees Troilus come back from the battle-field a conquering hero, his armor hacked in twenty places, and hears the people cry, "Troilus! Troilus!" she ponders over all her uncle has said, and love pushes open the door of her heart a little crack.

[187]

Let me quote here from a book on the psychology of love, *De l'amour,* by Stendhal, to show how, after four hundred years, the analysis of love has made little or no advance upon what Chaucer described except in the way of terminology (the millinery of science). "This," Stendhal says, "is what takes place in the soul. 1, Admiration; 2, The thought 'how delicious to kiss her and be kissed by her'; 3, Hope; . . . it needs but a very little bit of hope to cause the birth of love. . . . 4, Then love is born: to love means to derive pleasure from seeing, touching, feeling by every sense, and as close as possible, a lovable person who loves in return. 5, The first crystallization begins; the lover delights to endow the woman, of whom he feels sure, with a thousand perfections; he goes over and over his happiness in every detail with infinite satisfaction; he magnifies a glorious possession that has fallen to him like manna from heaven, that he does not comprehend, but which he is sure is his. . . . *Crystallization* is an operation of the mind, which discovers from every circumstance that the Beloved has new perfections . . . it comes from nature who bids us take pleasure and sends the blood to the head, and from the feeling that our happiness is increased by the Beloved's perfections, and also from the idea, She is mine, . . . and then the Beloved is decked out with jewelled perfections that the indifferent can not see, because she is not for them."

Here you have a man, with all the literature of the ages to draw upon, and his own experience to boot, far less delicate, subtle and true than Chaucer. But I will go back to the story.

How could Criseyde help falling in love? Troilus is abashed by the acclamations of the people, and drops his eyes in confusion, while she remembers how Pandarus has said that the hero will die unless she has pity on him. She feels what Stendhal calls the *crystallization;* "who yaf

[gave] me drinke?" she says to herself, as if she had drunk of the fatal chalice that Iseult gave to Tristram. Chaucer's analysis of Criseyde's emotions would have been very satisfactory to Stendhal, and one can not but regret that he probably never read the poem. That day Criseyde is long tossed by thoughts of love, until at last the sun set and the stars came out and she went to bed.

> A nyghtyngale, upon a cedir grene,
> Under the chambre wal ther as she ley,
> Ful loude song ayein the moone shene,
> Peraunter, in his briddes wise, a lay
> Of love, that made hire herte fressh and gay.
> That herkned she so longe in good entente,
> Til at the laste the dede slep hire hente.

Thus Pandarus plays his rôle skilfully. At his insistance Troilus writes a letter, Pandarus carries it; Criseyde, after much putting off, reads it and writes that she would like to please him "as his sister." Then, all having been arranged by Pandarus, Troilus rides by and humbly salutes her. A "thorn," hard to be pulled out, has pricked her deep.

> But fle we now prolixitee best is,
> For love of God, and lat us faste go
> Right to th' effect, withouten tales mo.

By a wholly successful but rather intricate contrivance Pandarus brings the two lovers together, and Criseyde seals her love with many vows; the sun should sooner fall from the sky, the eagle fear the dove, rocks leap from their base, than Troilus lose his place in her heart. By help of Pandarus the lovers meet frequently and life for a time was more full of joy than pen can tell. And love's effect was wholly good, for, in Troilus, desire to win his lady's praise caused him to increase in hardihood and might, made him pitiful toward wretchedness, reverential toward virtue, ready to succor all in distress, and glad to hear that other lovers were happy in their love. This blissful state lasted for three years. Then, alas, fickle Fortune turns her wheel. The Trojans were worsted in a battle, and one of their most important chiefs, Antenor, was captured. Calchas persuades the Greeks to offer to exchange him for his daughter Criseyde; they agree and the Trojans in their parliament override Hector's objections and accept. Poor Troilus!

> And as in wynter leves ben biraft,
> Ech after other, til the tree be bare,
> So that ther nys but bark and braunche ilaft,
> Lith Troilus, byraft of ech welfare,
> Ibounden in the blake bark of care.

Poor Troilus! He is a fine fellow and you have a great liking for him, especially when you find how deep and strong his love is, how true he is to the lordship of love. Even in his first grief he says:

> "O ye loveris, that heigh upon the whiel
> Ben set of Fortune, in good aventure,
> God leve that ye fynde ay love of stiel,
> And longe mote youre lif in joie endure!
> But whan ye comen by my sepulture,
> Remembreth that youre felawe resteth there;
> For I loved ek, though ich unworthi were."

The lovers must part, for though Troilus suggests that the two run away together, Criseyde rejects the plan as contrary to his honor and to her reputation, but she promises to find

[190]

a way to rejoin him in ten days. The fatal day comes and off she goes under the escort of Diomede. And so the tragedy stalks along. The ten days go by. Troilus is full of sorrow, though looking upward to a star of hope, but Criseyde is being wooed by Diomede. She believes that Troy will be destroyed, that not one Trojan will be left alive, and remembers that Diomede is a great prince and a gallant warrior, and she would sorely need protection. She is like Manon Lescaut, affectionate, tender, susceptible, but shallow, a lover of peace and comfort. The seeds of love had fallen where they had no deepness of earth, and sprang up fast, but when the sun of adversity shone, they were soon scorched. Poor Criseyde! Fame has treated her too harshly. She is but a woman, and "commanded by such poor passion as the maid that milks and does the meanest chares." But Troilus remains the true lover, and there are few passages in poetry more charming in sentiment than the account of his state of mind:

> Fro thennesforth he rideth up and down,
> And every thyng com hym to remembraunce
> As he rood forby places of the town
> In which he whilom hadde al his plesaunce.
> "Lo, yonder saugh ich last my lady daunce;
> And in that temple, with hire eyen cleere,
> Me kaughte first my righte lady dere.

> "And yonder have I herd ful lustyly
> My dere herte laugh; and yonder pleye
> Saugh ich hire ones ek ful blisfully.
> And yonder ones to me gan she seye,
> 'Now goode swete, love me wel, I preye;'
> And yond so goodly gan she me biholde,
> That to the deth myn herte is to hire holde.

"And at that corner, in the yonder hous,
Herde I myn alderlevest lady deere
So wommanly, with vois melodious,
Syngen so wel, so goodly, and so clere,
That in my soule yet me thynketh ich here
The blisful sown; and in that yonder place
My lady first me took unto hire grace."

And I add here, for the sake of those that know Italian,
Boccaccio's stanzas, to show how close Chaucer followed
his (closer even than Boccaccio followed Petrarch), and to
let English-speaking readers judge for themselves how
much, if it be so, Chaucer has improved upon him:

> *Quindi sen gì per Troia cavalcando,*
> *E ciascun luogo gliel tornava a mente;*
> *De' quai con seco giva ragionando:*
> *Quivi rider la vidi lietamente;*
> *Quivi la vidi verso me guardando:*
> *Quivi mi salutò benignamente;*
> *Quivi far festa e quivi star pensosa,*
> *Quivi la vidi a' miei sospir piatosa.*
>
> *Colà istava, quand' ella mi prese*
> *Con gli occhi belli e vaghi con amore;*
> *Colà istava, quando ella m'accese*
> *Con un sospir di maggio fuoco il core;*
> *Colà istava, quando condiscese*
> *Al mio piacere il donnesco valore;*
> *Colà la vidi altiera, e là umile*
> *Mi si mostrò la mia donna gentile.*

The poem, I repeat, is beautiful, delicate, subtle, psychological, and if it flows slowly, in linked sweetness long
drawn out, it is because it must do so in order to let us
enjoy the shifting hues of emotion, that follow one another
in delicate succession.

CHAPTER XXII

THE LEGEND OF GOOD WOMEN

IN *The Canterbury Tales* the Man of Law refers to this poem as "the Seintes Legende of Cupide," and personally I prefer that title, because it justifies the theory that the right frame of mind for reading *Troilus and Criseyde* is quite other than Puritanical; it reminds us that we are out of Jehovah's jurisdiction, that not Zion but Mount Olympus rises high on the horizon, that Aphrodite is "Seynt Venus," and that her worshipers and Cupide's are sanctified by their worship, and if any such worshipers hold true to love, and endure evil and persecution for love's sake to the end, they become saints. The Legend was written a little after *Troilus and Criseyde;* it refers to that poem, and I can not but think that Chaucer had some such thought as I suggest in the back of his mind.

The poem consists of a collection of lives of good women, good because they have been faithful to love, and of a prologue, or rather two versions of a prologue, one written, according to the most modern critics, in or about the year 1386, the other in 1395. The earlier prologue, denominated B-text by Skeat (who, however, believed that the A-text had come first), and Text F by Robinson, is that which I shall follow:

The poem begins in Chaucer's waggish manner:

> A thousand tymes have I herd men telle
> That ther ys joy in hevene and peyne in helle,
> And I acorde wel that it ys so;
> But, natheles, yet wot I wel also

That ther nis noon dwellyng in this contree,
That eyther hath in hevene or helle ybe,
Ne may of hit noon other weyes witen,
But as he hath herd seyd, or founde it writen;
For by assay ther may no man it preve.
But God forbede but men shulde leve [believe]
Wel more thing then men han seen with ye [eye]!
Men shal not wenen [deem] every thing a lye.
But yf himself yt seeth, or elles dooth;
For, God wot, thing is never the lasse sooth,
Thogh every wight ne may it nat ysee.
Bernard the monk ne saugh nat all, pardee!

The moral of this is that we should believe what old books say, and Chaucer is very ready to do so, as he loves reading better than any other pastime; except, however, in the month of May, when flowers spring and birds sing, then

Farewel my bok, and my devocioun!

The French poets I have named celebrated the Daisy, the *Marguerite,* as they call it, because of some great lady of that name. You remember how, two hundred years later, François Premier praises his sister Marguerite, herself a poet, as *la Marguerite des Marguerites;* for, as the word also means a pearl, it lends itself admirably to expressions of loyal admiration. Francis Thompson in his poem about the little girl he met on the Sussex hills from which I quoted, calls her the Daisy flower. Chaucer follows this fashion. The daisy is the flower of flowers, and excites the most ardent affection in his sad heart. When the month of May comes round he is up before daybreak, and walking in the meadows to see it unfurl its coronal to the sun, and again when evening comes on he runs out eagerly to see it fold itself to rest. He says that of himself he has not enough

English poetry or prose to praise the flower aright, and he appeals to all lovers that can compose love poetry to help him; they have reaped already and borne away the wheat, but he will glean after them, and hopes that they will not take it amiss that he repeats what their "fresshe songes" have said. Chaucer is never more sympathetic than in his love of flowers, of gardens, of outdoors; he seems to have introduced this floral affection—William James used to say that passion in English poetry was very largely a floral affair—into England, and there it has stayed. Most Englishmen and all English old maids, and many young maids, know far more than Americans do about the flowers of the field. This, I believe, they owe to Chaucer.

The poet then proceeds to tell how the Daisy, who seems to be metamorphosed into a great lady, is the light that guides him in this dark world; she is the mistress of his thoughts, and as a harper fingering his harp makes what sound he pleases, so she can make him laugh or weep. And then he openly apostrophizes her:

> Be ye my gide and lady sovereyne!
> As to myn erthly god to yow I calle,
> Bothe in this werk and in my sorwes alle.

He then tells how, on the first morning of May, his ardent devotion constrained him to rise betimes and see the Daisy unclose. He went to the meadow, knelt down, bade it good morrow, and then he eulogizes in charming verses the flower, the time of the year, and the little singing birds. The birds are as sensitive to the joy of it all as he is, and carol forth:

> "Blessed be Seynt Valentyn,
> For on this day I chees yow to be myn,
> Withouten repentyng, myn herte swete!"

Birds that had been unkind to others begged to be forgiven and swore by the blossoms about them never to offend again. The scene reminds one of the birds at the end of *The Parlement of Foules* who sang the roundel to Saint Valentine.

The breezes brought out all the fragrance of the flowers, and the happy union of Nature's pleasantnesses filled his heart with happy thoughts. He lay down and resting on his elbow gazed at

> The "dayesye," or elles the "ye [eye] of day,"
> The emperice and flour of floures alle.

In this fashion the day passed and when night came, he bade his servants make his bed in a little arbor, and strew flowers over it.

He fell asleep and dreamt a dream. This is his last employment of the vision in a dream, and, to my taste, far and away the most charming. His prologue, too, which I have been telling, is all borrowed from the French. When he called on poetic lovers to help him, and suffer him to glean after them, he was gleaning as he spoke, and more than gleaning. M. Legouis says: "No one would suspect that these flowing and apparently spontaneous lines are made up of reminiscences of Machaut, Froissart, Deschamps, from whom he borrowed the symbol of the daisy, even to the merest details." "An exquisitely woven texture of reminiscences," Mr. Lowes calls it. And why should not a poet take words from other poets, rather than from a dictionary? Well, then, he fell asleep and dreamed, and saw a vision, just as the French poets had done. But having sucked the honey of these medieval French poets he could hardly do otherwise; I think we should have been a little shocked if he had, for his state of mind naturally unfolds, like the daisy at dawn, into a dream and a vision. He dreams that he sees the

God of Love leading by the hand a Queen, whose coronal was fashioned like a daisy. The God looked at him so sternly that his heart turned cold; but the Queen was so womanly, so benign and meek that you might seek through the world and not find a creature half so lovely, and he was moved to sing a ballade in her praise:

Hyd, Absolon, thy gilte tresses clere;

a beautiful ballade which I quote elsewhere. He names a number of famous ladies in the ballade, but his lady, so good, so fair, so debonaire, surpasses them all as the sun's light surpasses that of a fire.

Behind the God of Love came nineteen ladies in a group, and after them a great multitude more; and every one of these women was true in love. This statement enables us to guess that fidelity in love is to be the subject of the poem. All these women fell on their knees before the Daisy and sang,

"Heel and honour
To trouthe of womanhede and to this flour."

Then all sat down, while Chaucer knelt as still as a stone beside the Daisy, not knowing what was going to happen. Nothing was said for a time, then the God spoke, "Who kneeleth there?" and Chaucer answered, "It is I." Then the God asks how he dare go so near his flower, says Chaucer is his enemy, and hinders people from worshiping, and then specifically denounces him for writing *The Romaunce of the Rose* and *Troilus and Criseyde,* both heresies against Cupid's law, and he vows that Chaucer shall repent. The poet's sins are, first, that he translated *The Romaunce of the Rose* with all of Jean de Meung's odious speeches against women, and, second, that in *Troilus and Criseyde* he had drawn the character of a false perjured woman. Fortunately for the erring bard the Queen comes to the rescue. She pleads that it is not a grievous offense to translate what old authors have written, not at all as if he himself had imagined disloyalty to Love, and she urges that the offender had done much to praise Love's name; he had written *The House of Fame,* the death of the Duchess Blanche, *The Parlement of Foules,* the love of Palamon and Arcite, and many a lyric for Love's festival days, ballades, roundels and virelays, also a prose translation of Boethius, a life of Saint Cecilia, a treatise of Pope Innocent III on the *Wretched Engendring of Mankind,* and another by Origen on Mary Magdelene, and had composed many a lay. She begs Cupid to forgive him. Cupid leaves the matter in her hands. Chaucer falls on his knees and thanks her, but avows that he has done no wrong, that no true lover should blame him for holding a false lover up to shame:

> Algate [at any rate], God woot, yt was myn entente
> To forthren trouthe in love and yt [it] cheryce,
> And to ben war fro falsnesse and fro vice
> By swich ensample; this was my menynge.

The Queen accepts his plea, but imposes as penance the task of writing a glorious Legend of Good Women, maidens and wives, that were always true in loving, and she adds:

> "And whan this book ys maad, yive it the quene,
> On my byhalf, at Eltham, or at Sheene."

The God of Love then asks Chaucer if he knows who the Queen is, and when Chaucer says no, asks if he has not a book that tells how Queen Alceste (Alcestis) chose to die and go to Hades in place of her husband, and was turned into a daisy; and then, bidding the poet write stories of the

[198]

nineteen ladies that have followed him, and of Alcestis, off he goes with all his company of ladies.

The *Prologue* is indeed charming, so light, so tripping, so full of pretty imagery, that many readers might rest content to go no farther, and perhaps they would not fare ill if they stopped here. The opening tale, somewhat to the reader's surprise (for our conception of this first "Good Woman," fashioned for us by Shakespeare, does not primarily picture her as a true lover), concerns Cleopatra, and tells us how she killed herself for love of Antony. The best passage in it is a description of a sea fight. The commentators say that Chaucer's sources, so far as he had any, were an old Latin historian, L. Annæus Florus, and Plutarch, but the account of this sea fight sounds as if he were repeating what some shipman had told him about the battle of Espagnols-sur-mer, where King Edward III had fought the Spanish Dons, and won a glorious victory, when Chaucer was a boy of eight or nine:

Up goth the trompe, and for to shoute and shete,
And peynen hem to sette on with the sunne.
With grysely soun out goth the grete gonne,
And heterly they hurtelen al atones,
And from the top doun come the grete stones.
In goth the grapenel so ful of crokes [hooks];
Among the ropes renne the sherynge-hokes.
In with the polax preseth he and he;
Byhynde the mast begynnyth he to fle,
And out ageyn, and dryveth hym over-bord;
He styngeth hym upon his speres ord [point];
He rent the seyl with hokes lyke a sithe;
He bryngeth the cuppe, and biddeth hem be blythe;
He poureth pesen [peas] upon the haches slidere [slippery];
With pottes ful of lyme [lime] they gon togidere;
And thus the longe day in fyght they spende . . .

[199]

The story of Thisbe is better. Chaucer does best when he stands wholly on his own feet, or where he clings close to his model. In *Cleopatra* the plot hindered rather than helped him. In *Thisbe* he follows Ovid's narrative in the *Metamorphoses* very closely, and converts the elegant concise hexameters into his own picturesque heroic couplets with considerable success. Ovid, one perceives, is an elegant city-bred fashionable poet, writing for sophisticated readers, but Chaucer, doubling the length of his model, expands an image, a thought, a sentence, with all the eagerness of a person telling a tale to simple uneducated readers, and if Romans, Italians, and M. Legouis prefer Ovid's tale, English readers will probably like Chaucer's better. If Ovid's

> *exhorruit aequoris instar,*
> *quod tremit, exigua cum summum stringitur aura,*

is poorly rendered by

> And lik the wawes quappe [heaving] gan hire herte;

Ovid's

> *amplexaque corpus amatum*
> . . . *et gelidis in vultibus oscula figens,*

is inferior to

> How clyppeth she the deede cors, allas!
> How kysseth she his frosty mouth so cold!

The third legend concerns Dido, and is taken from the *Æneid:*

Glorye and honour, Virgil Mantoan,
Be to thy name! and I shal, as I can,
Folwe thy lanterne, as thow gost byforn,
How Eneas to Dido was forsworn.

Still, I imagine that Mantuan Virgil would have been
astonished to read this transcription of his story, as for
example Chaucer's description of the luxury with which
Æneas was surrounded as the guest of Dido:

He nevere beter at ese was in his lyve.
Ful was the feste of deyntees and rychesse,
Of instruments, of song, and of gladnesse,
Of many an amorous lokyng and devys.
This Eneas is come to paradys
Out of the swolow of helle, and thus in joye
Remembreth hym of his estat in Troye.
To daunsynge chaumberes ful of paramentes [hangings],
Of riche beddes, and of ornementes
This Eneas is led . . .

The blame of the catastrophe is all laid upon Æneas, who
is represented as a heartless seducer. Virgil's *pius* Æneas is
hardly recognizable; but this was necessary in order to ap-
pease the God of Love and Queen Alceste and wipe out
the error of telling about Criseyde's disloyalty. This same
obligation of laying all the blame on the man obliges the
poet to castigate Jason, in *The Legend of Hypsipyle and
Medea,*

Have at thee, Jason! now thyn horn is blowe!

But methinks the poet doth protest too much, he overshoots
himself, and wearying a little of his brief on behalf of forsaken women, he lets now and again the shadow of irony
slip into his poems. He did this rather flagrantly in Dido:

[201]

She fledde hireself into a litel cave,
And with hire wente this Eneas also.
I not [know not], with hem if there wente any mo;
The autour maketh of it no mencioun.

Nevertheless, his denunciation of Jason for wooing and then abandoning first Hypsipyle and then Medea, sounds a little perfunctory. These two legends are assuredly dull. His sources were, I am told, Ovid and Guido delle Colonne. In the next story, *The Legend of Lucrece,* he follows Guido and Livy. This is a poor thing in comparison with Shakespeare. Chaucer's heart was not set on the proprieties, and he is becoming listless and bored by his undertaking. *The Legend of Ariadne* is also, they say, derived from Ovid and Plutarch in the main. Here Theseus is the villain, honey sweet of tongue, and shameless in asseveration. Ariadne agrees to save him from the Minotaur, and he is to marry her and take her sister and herself home with him. Theseus slays the Minotaur and escapes from the labyrinth by following the thread, and the three flee; but on their way back they put in at an island for the night and there Theseus leaves Ariadne sleeping and takes the sister who was fairer than she.

One would suppose that *The Legend of Bad Men* would have been a more appropriate title for this series. Theseus, Jason, Tarquin and Æneas are all depicted as cold-hearted voluptuaries. And now in *The Legend of Philomela,* which is taken from Ovid, there is a worse than Tarquin. Tereus, King of Thrace, has married Progne, daughter to the King of Athens; he ravishes her sister Philomela, cuts out the poor girl's tongue and shuts her up in a lonely castle. Philomela, however, weaves the story in embroidered cloth, and sends it to her sister. The horrible consequences Chaucer does not tell; he leaves the story at Tereus's wickedness and says nothing of the revenge taken by Progne and Philomela.

The story of Phyllis is that of Ariadne over again; Phyllis trusted Demophoon, Theseus's son. By this time Chaucer can not conceal that he is weary of his subject, and the reader is not surprised to find the last story, *The Legend of Hypermnestra,* left unfinished.

CHAPTER XXIII

From London to Kent

We have now come to a great change in Chaucer's life. He gave up London, left the Customs, and took up residence in the country. In October, 1386, a new tenant occupied Aldgate, and in December other men filled his two offices in the custom-house. And, in consequence, there has been much discussion as to whether he was obliged by a hostile political party to surrender his positions in the public service, or whether he resigned them voluntarily out of a wish for a quieter life and greater leisure for poetry. Personally, I believe that Chaucer resigned his offices voluntarily. I think that he was singularly free from party and partisan ties, and that whatever good fortune came to him, which he did not owe to his own character and abilities, was due directly to the friendship of John of Gaunt, or indirectly through the affection of Katharine Swynford for her sister and her brother-in-law, or, at times, to the kind interest of King Edward and Queen Philippa in early days, and of King Richard and Queen Anne in more recent years. But as I understand that others think differently, or are in doubt, I had better give a concise summary of politics at this time, and then such facts as we have concerning Chaucer, and leave the reader to draw his own conclusions.

During the reign of King Edward III parliament had been growing in power. The cost of the French war rendered the King dependent upon the good will of his people, and his people were well aware of it. In 1371, parliament compelled the King to dismiss ecclesiastics from the high offices of state and put laymen in their places; in 1376, it impeached the leading members of that party which Mr. Trevelyan stigmatized as the Duke of Lancaster's gang of rogues, and, in 1377, the Duke found it necessary to pack the House of Commons with members friendly to himself in order to undo what the hostile parliament had done. Control of parliament was, therefore, a matter of great political consequence. In 1383, King Richard was sixteen years old, and, elated by his own courage in dealing with Wat Tyler's rebels, desired to be master in his own house, for such he considered the Kingdom. He turned out the chancellor appointed by parliament, put in Michael de la Pole, a man of his own choosing, and gathered about him a group of counselors who profited by his reckless favoritism, and—so the people thought, perhaps unjustly—were no more honest than those whom the Duke of Lancaster had favored six or seven years before. There was Robert de Vere, Earl of Oxford, a swaggering, incompetent youth of ancient lineage, whom the King liked and rewarded most of all. There were Sir Simon Burley, Sir Nicholas Brembre, Sir Robert Tresilian, and others, including, though perhaps at a later period, those unfortunate gentlemen, Bushy, Bagot and Green, of whom Shakespeare speaks so slightingly. The King wasted his time with de Vere and other young spendthrifts, followed their advice in whatever he did, and disregarded the laws and customs of the realm. In *Henry IV*, Part I, Bolingbroke describes him unkindly, but from the point of view of an able and serious ruler not untruly:

> The skipping king, he ambled up and down
> With shallow jesters and rash bavin wits,
> Soon kindled and soon burnt: carded his state,
> Mingled his royalty with capering fools,
> Had his great name profaned with their scorns;

And gave his countenance, against his name,
To laugh at gibing boys and stand the push
Of every beardless vain comparative . . .

By his extravagance, his lavish gifts to favorites, his disregard of law and kingly dignity, Richard became very un-
popular with the mass of people, especially with Londoners,
and hateful to the proud nobles, who felt that they were
displaced by unworthy upstarts. These discontented nobles
rallied round the King's uncle, Thomas of Woodstock, and
constituted the party of opposition called the magnates or the
lords-appellant, because they stood ready to throw down
their gauntlets before the King's friends, and appeal to the
judgment of God by wager of battle. Thomas of Woodstock was, I take it, a mean, ungenerous, covetous, malicious
man, who, in the absence of his older brother, John of
Gaunt, and from the indifference of Edmund of York, believed that he had the best claim to direct the government.
Gaunt was busy with his projects upon the crown of Castile,
and actually out of the country from July, 1386, to November, 1389, and Edmund was a quiet, sluggish, amiable fellow. With Thomas of Woodstock sided the Earls of
Arundel and Warwick, the Archbishop of Canterbury, Lord
Cobham, Sir Richard Scrope and others, and with them
also, in course of time, went Henry Bolingbroke, Gaunt's
son, and Thomas Mowbray, afterward Duke of Norfolk.

The discord between these two parties grew great. It
seems as if the King made some effort of reconciliation,
for though he gave the title of Marquess of Dublin to his
favorite, Robert de Vere, and that of Earl of Suffolk to
Michael de la Pole, he created his Uncle Edmund Duke of
York, and his Uncle Thomas of Woodstock, Duke of
Gloucester, but he accomplished nothing thereby. For a time
fear of a French invasion prevented any open quarrel, for

Charles V had collected at Sluys an army and a great fleet, and the leaders of both parties were busy enough patrolling the English coast. The citizens of London were so frightened by the threatened invasion that they razed houses outside the walls, they ordered the bridge across the Medway at Rochester broken down, and, according to John Stow, "trembling like leverets, fearful as mice, seeke starting holes to hide themselves, even as if the city were now to be taken." Happily, adverse winds prevented the French fleet from leaving port. This was during the summer of 1386, while Chaucer was living at Kent, the seat of danger.

That autumn, when parliament met, an open quarrel between the King's party and the Duke of Gloucester's faction broke out. Since Chaucer was a member of this parliament, as knight of the shire for Kent, he was brought, if not into the thick of political strife, to the very edge of it; he must have heard the debates and could hardly have avoided casting his vote. Parliament opened on October first, and being under the domination of the Gloucester faction, demanded the dismissal of the Chancellor and of the Treasurer. The King replied that he would not dismiss the meanest valet in his kitchen at their bidding; and, after attempting to dissolve parliament, rode out to his palace at Eltham, and, to show his purpose to support his friends, he created de Vere Duke of Ireland. The Duke of Gloucester and the Earl of Arundel followed the King to Eltham, reminded him of the fate of his great-grandfather, Edward II, and by threats of their intention to follow that precedent, induced him to return to Westminster. Michael de la Pole was deposed, and Thomas Arundel, Bishop of Ely, brother to the Earl, appointed chancellor in his stead. Richard's friend, the Bishop of Durham, was removed from the treasury and the Bishop of Hereford substituted. And the reforming faction did not stop there; it charged Michael de la Pole with many crimes and committed him to prison in Windsor Castle; it banished de Vere to Ireland; and, in order to make its own power secure, appointed a council of eleven lords to have the oversight, "under the King," of the whole realm. To this council belonged the Duke of Gloucester, the Duke of York, the Archbishop of Canterbury, the Earl of Arundel, William of Wykeham, Bishop of Winchester, Lord Cobham, Sir Richard Scrope, and others; but the directing heads were the Duke of Gloucester and the Earl of Arundel.

The King was obliged to bow in outward guise, but his heart was not inclined to submission. It began to look as if the issue between him and the Gloucester faction must proceed to some tragic end. He did not abide by his promises. De la Pole was let out of prison, Robert de Vere did not go to Ireland, but lingered on the west coast of England; and rumor said that they and others of the King's friends were plotting the murder of Gloucester and Arundel. A private quarrel envenomed the enmity between Robert de Vere and the Duke of Gloucester. De Vere had married a niece of the Duke but he forsook her as he had fallen in love with a young Bohemian lady in the Queen's train, "called in the vulgar tongue of her country Lancecrona," at which the Duke and the lords of his faction, not inclining to leniency toward the misconduct of an enemy, were very indignant. There were meetings of the King's friends, and meetings of the Duke's faction. From Froissart's narration it seems that Gloucester and Arundel, realizing that the city of London, with its great power, controlled the situation, in an underhand way raised an alarm that the King intended a levy of heavy taxes, and stirred the citizens up to press inquiry as to what had become of the public moneys, of which the King's friends had had the handling. The Londoners applied to the Duke of Gloucester.

The Duke, according to Froissart, answered as follows:

"I alone can do nothing. I know you have well founded cause of complaint, as well as the rest of England; but notwithstanding I am son to a King of England, and uncle to the present King, if I were to interfere by speaking to him, he would not attend to me; for my nephew has counselors near his person in whom he confides more than in himself, and these counselors lead him as they please. If you wish to succeed in having your grievances redressed, you should enter into a confederacy with the principal towns, and with some of the nobles and prelates, and come before the King, where my brothers and myself will cheerfully meet you, and say to the King—'Most dear Lord, you were crowned when very young, and have hitherto been badly advised, nor have you attended to the affairs of your kingdom, because of the mean and weak counselors you have chosen. This has caused the mismanagement of affairs,' " and so on, counseling them to call a parliament to investigate the actions of the King's advisers, and, if anything were found contrary to good government, to provide the remedy. And he warned them not to let the King fob them off, but to insist on immediate action.

The Londoners said they would see the King at Windsor on Saint George's Day, and so they did. As the Duke had predicted, the King did try to dilly-dally. In vain, for the complainants were ready. Upward of seven broke into a sudden answer: "No time can be better than the present, we therefore unanimously declare that we will have an account, and very shortly, too, from those who have governed your Kingdom since your coronation, and know what is become of the great sums that have been raised in England for these last nine years."

Froissart's narrative is intended to please as well as to instruct, but he always tried to ascertain the facts, and his

[209]

errors of detail here are probably because he did not obtain his information until he came back to England ten years later. The substance of his story is correct enough; the two factions confronted each other, like boxers in a ring, each waiting to see which should lead first. The King returned to London, was welcomed by the Mayor, and took up his abode in the Tower (November, 10, 1387). Gloucester and Warwick were already in arms, and they were joined by Arundel. London, in spite of the Mayor's welcome, was unsympathetic to the King, and the Earl of Northumberland, when urged to take the field, said that he did not propose to have his head broken for the sake of the Duke of Ireland. In a vain attempt to come to a peaceable understanding, the King consented to meet the three rebellious leaders at Westminster. They denied that they were at fault and charged Robert de Vere, Michael de la Pole, Alexander Neville, Archbishop of York, Sir Robert Tresilian, the Chief Justice, and Sir Nicholas Brembre, with high treason, alleging that they were "traitorers, whisperers, flaterers, unprofitable people and should be removed." The King promised that these five should meet the charges at the next parliament, but in spite of his promise he let the accused go their ways. De Vere betook himself to the west, raised an army among the country gentlemen of Cheshire and Wales, and marched back through the midlands to join Richard who was in London. Gloucester, Warwick and Arundel, reenforced by Henry Bolingbroke and Thomas Mowbray, hurried with far superior forces to intercept de Vere. The two armies came near each other at Radcot Bridge, near Faringdon, not four miles from Chipping Norton in the Cotswolds. According to John Stow, when Robert de Vere beheld the host of the lords-appellant "his heart straightways failed." He said, "Friends, I must fly, for a greater puissance seemeth to be yonder; against you they have no quarrel, so that I being shifted away, yee shall escape well ynough," and setting spurs to his horse he galloped off. The others took to their heels, and the lords-appellant found themselves masters of the Kingdom (December 20, 1387).

The day after Christmas, the victors reached London, and the mob compelled the Mayor to open the gates. Resistance was useless. The keys of the Tower were surrendered and Gloucester, Warwick and Arundel entered, as I understand, in imitation of the principle of a round-robin, arm-in-arm. The King attempted to deny any responsibility for de Vere's army, but the lords-appellant showed him his own letters to the contrary, and the Duke of Gloucester, to give weight to his requests, pointed to the troops on Tower Hill and said that there were ten times more ready to join them. He proceeded bluntly to threats of deposition, and the King consented to the imprisonment of those persons, whom the lords-appellant had accused of treason, until parliament should pass upon the charge. Gloucester, Warwick and Arundel wished to go further and depose the King, but Bolingbroke and Mowbray would not consent.

Parliament met again on February 3, 1388, and earned the title of the Merciless Parliament according to some, and of the Parliament of Wonders according to others. The five persons accused were found guilty, and all except Alexander Neville, the Archbishop of York, were condemned to death. Pole, Neville and de Vere escaped to the continent. Sir Robert Tresilian, Sir Nicholas Brembre, Sir Simon Burley, Thomas Uske, Under Sheriff of London, John Beauchamp of Holt, Lord Stewart of the King's household, Sir John Bernes, Knight of the King's court, "a lustie young man," and Sir John Salisbury were all beheaded. And the lords-appellant voted themselves twenty thousand pounds. The King again bowed to the storm, and did not stir for a year, and, then, on May 3, 1389, claimed the right that, as he said, every Englishman of full age enjoyed, to manage that which belonged to him. Arundel was deposed from the chancellorship and the wise old William of Wykeham put in; otherwise few changes were made. John of Gaunt came back in November, and used his good offices and apparently to happy effect, for in December, Gloucester, Arundel and Warwick were restored to the council. But Richard treasured up these doings in his heart.

There you have an outline of the political situation during the years 1385-1389. Let us now see what Chaucer's relation to all this is. In February, 1385, at his own request he was allowed to keep a permanent deputy. From this request the only natural inference is that he proposed to absent himself from London; and, judging by what happened afterward, the next inference is that he also intended to establish himself in the country. He had reached the age of forty-five, or nearly, an advanced age as men reckoned in those days, and if he wished to leave a noble memorial of himself in poetry, as Dante and Boccaccio had done, it was high time to set to work; he must choose between the custom-house and a more leisurely life. That he settled at Kent is certain, because, on October twelfth, he was appointed a justice of the peace for that shire in association with Sir Simon Burley, John de Cobham and others, and eight months later on June 28, 1386, he received a full commission. The office of a justice of the peace was purely local. A justice's duties were "to cause the Statutes of Winchester, Northampton and Westminster to be observed; to take sureties from any persons using threats of bodily injury against others, or of burning their houses; and to inquire and adjudge in respect of felonies, trespasses, forestallers, regraters, extortions, unlawful meetings, persons going or riding about armed, or lying in wait to maim or kill, the giving of liveries, innkeepers, victuallers, abuses of weights and measures, and defaulting workmen, artificers, and servants, who were to be fined or to be submitted to corporal punishment."

And in August of the same year Chaucer was elected a knight of the shire, together with one William Betenham, to represent Kent in the coming parliament. He attended parliament at Westminster during the two months of its session, October and November, and the two knights received twenty-four pounds nine shillings (say thirty-six hundred dollars) for going, staying and returning during a period of sixty-one days.

The lords-appellant did not come into power until this session of parliament, and could not before that time have issued an order depriving Chaucer of his offices in the custom-house, as they must have done according to the theory of dismissal. On the other hand the theory of voluntary resignation has all the indications in its favor; Chaucer's request for a deputy, his appointment as justice of the peace for Kent, his election as a knight of the shire for Kent, all hang together and constitute very strong evidence that from the beginning of 1385, he intended to abandon his residence in London and go to live in the country. The motive of literary work is a sufficient explanation; but wherever knowledge can not enter, guesses squeeze in. Perhaps Mrs. Chaucer was not very well, and needed country air, for indeed she did not live long after this; or, it may be that their son, Thomas, who must have been about twenty, had left home and so rendered them free to go. The only facts that give color to the theory that Chaucer was dismissed, are that his friend John of Gaunt was away at the time he left office, and that on September first a royal commission was appointed to inquire as to abuses of customs and subsidies, but this commission may merely have represented the King's desire to get a larger revenue.

My own view is that Chaucer was not a partisan, that he inclined to the King's party because of his personal regard for the King and Queen, and yet that he saw how much right the lords-appellant had on their side. He followed here, as in other decisions in life, in accordance with his character, the midway path, keeping himself free from the violence and injustice of both sides. Clear evidence of this is, to my thinking, that he wrote in 1385-1386, at least so the commentators say, the charming, unconstrained *Legend of Good Women* with its praise of the month of May and in 1388, while hanging, drawing and quartering was going on upon Tyburn Hill, the joyous, care-free *Prologue to The Canterbury Tales,* which in every verse seems to chaunt aloud the author's belief in sympathy, tolerance and good-fellowship.

There is a record in July, 1387, that he was granted protection for a year to go to Calais in the retinue of Sir William Beauchamp. There is no further information concerning this journey and my guess would be that it was prevented by political events.

CHAPTER XXIV

CHAUCER'S FAMILY

IN THIS same stirring year, 1387, Philippa Chaucer died. This seems certain for her annuity was paid in June and not again; and her death brings us to the question of what was the relation between her and her husband, whether of affection and good companionship, or of mutual irritation and annoyance. The qualities that make a good husband do not of necessity make a good poet. Byron and Burns were poor hands at matrimony, whereas Wordsworth (barring certain peculiarities of temper), Tennyson, Browning, Matthew Arnold were exemplary. But one likes Chaucer so much as a man, that one would like to think that the large tolerance and generous sympathy, which he shows to all the outside world, did not leave him when he entered Aldgate, or crossed the threshold of his house in Kent. Let us first see what little there is to be known of Philippa.

She was a lady. Her father was a Fleming, her mother also, as I understand, and as she was probably named after the Queen, it is likely that she was born in England. The Queen liked her, John of Gaunt liked her, the Duchess Blanche liked her. Her sister, Katharine, was very pretty and held Gaunt's affection all her life. Philippa was accustomed to aristocratical society; and the court recognized that she belonged to it, more, one may imagine, from her personal traits than from her father's position or her husband's, and it gave marked evidence of its recognition. On February 19, 1386, after the Chaucers had moved into the country, she received an honor bestowed upon persons of the highest rank. She was received as a sister into the Fraternity of Lincoln Cathedral, at the same time with Henry Bolingbroke, Gaunt's eldest son, the future Henry IV, Sir Thomas de Swynford (Katharine's son, I believe) and six others. The Duke of Lancaster, Katharine's lover, was present at the ceremony. He was a member of the Fraternity; the Black Prince had been a member, so had Prince Lionel, and the year following, King Richard and Queen Anne were admitted. Members took an oath of fidelity and love to the church and chapter, and to assist and maintain the minster; and, thereupon, they were admitted to participate in "all prayers, fastings, pilgrimages, alms-deeds, and works of mercy," connected therewith. It was, you see, a fashionable *œuvre de charité*. I know no more about Philippa, unless there be some confirmation of our theory that she was very much of a lady—wrought, to be sure, of unsubstantial inferences—some confirmation, to be found in her son Thomas's marriage into a family of the first rank and fashion.

As to Philippa's relations with her husband, I have quoted Mr. Masefield's unsympathetic suggestion, that she might be like the Wife of Bath. As far as manners and language are concerned, I think we may certainly reject that suggestion, for though a woman may be of high rank and not be a lady or behave like a lady, such a woman would not have been a favorite with Queen Philippa and the Duchess Blanche. The commentators take a very different view from Masefield, but they are happy married men, amiable at home, thoughtful and serene, who believe in the family, the hearth, the sanctity of marriage, and the solid virtues that make the bourgeoisie so unbohemian a class, and do not approach the matter free from bias.

It can not be denied that there are many passages in Chaucer that treat marriage as a sort of purgatory and wives as if they were shrews, vain, fickle, wayward, or worse. The Wyf of Bathe takes the lead in narrating connubial infelicities with a wealth and fulness of detail, and with sparkling vivacity of manner; the Miller, the Manciple, the Shipman, tell stories in which the wives' conduct is reprehensible; the Pardoner is apprehensive; and the Merchant utters a sad ejaculation upon his wife's "cursedness"; and introduces his tale with a long ironical homily on wives, beginning with the creation of Eve:

Heere may ye se, and heerby may ye preve,
That wyf is mannes helpe and his comfort,
His paradys terrestre and his disport.
So buxom [obedient] and so vertuous is she,
They moste nedes lyve in unitee.
O [one] flessh they been, and o flesh, as I gesse,
Hath but oon [one] herte, in wele and in distresse.
   A wyf! a, Seinte Marie, *benedicite!*
How myghte a man han any adversitee
That hath a wyf? Certes, I kan nat seye [see].
The blisse which that is bitwixte hem [them] tweye
Ther may no tonge telle, or herte thynke.
If he be povre, she helpeth hym to swynke;
She kepeth his good, and wasteth never a deel [bit];
All that hire housbonde lust [husband wishes], hire liketh
      weel;
She seith nat ones [once] "nay," whan he seith "ye" [yea].
"Do this," seith he; "Al redy, sire," seith she.

And Harry Bailly, in his usual hearty, boisterous manner, dwells upon his own wife's impatience and pictures her behavior when she is not pleased with him. But in these cases, we may say that Chaucer has been speaking dramatically, and, wishing to make his characters both true to life and humorous, has drawn rather heavily on one of the two

[217]

medieval treasuries of humor, the frailty of women, the other being the knavery of friars. It would have been impossible for any medieval story-teller not to try to raise a laugh at the expense of husbands, ill-used by light or shrewish wives. Chaucer's readers expected this, and demanded it, they would not have understood humor that expressed itself in other terms. Older men can still remember how in American humor a mother-in-law used to serve for a vulgar audience in much the same way, and one must remember that among these pilgrims to Canterbury the majority were vulgar.

On the other hand, there are a number of passages that speak well of matrimony. At the end of *The Knight's Tale,* when Palamon has married Emily, the poet says:

> For now is Palamon in alle wele,
> Lyvynge in blisse, in richesse, and in heele [health],
> And Emelye hym loveth so tendrely,
> And he hire serveth al so gentilly,
> That nevere was ther no word hem bitwene
> Of jalousie or any other teene.

And in *The Man of Law's Tale,* King Alla and his wife Custance, so long as evil fate permits, live in joy and quiet; and poor Griselda, in *The Clerk's Tale,* after her unusual proof, was happy with her wayward husband,

> Ful many a yeer in heigh prosperitee
> Lyven thise two in concord and in reste . . .

And Griselda's son was "fortunate in marriage," and again, in *The Franklin's Tale,* the wife loved her husband "as her herte's life," though he was almost as peculiar in his behavior as Griselda's husband. And when Chaucer in *The Book of the Duchess* speaks of the married life of Blanche and her knight, he describes perfect happiness.

[218]

If there was nothing more to go on, Mr. Masefield's
opinion might be dismissed without ceremony. But there
are other passages which may be autobiographical, and no
doubt it is upon these that Masefield bases his opinion. One,
in *The Parlement of Foules* which I have quoted, where the
poet says that he was awaked from sleep by the eagle, in
the same voice as one that he could name, only the eagle
spoke kindly and the other's voice was never wont to be kindly. This must certainly be a comic reference to his wife.
The other is in *Lenvoy to Bukton,* presumably written when
Bukton was about to be married. The poet begins by saying
that when Christ was asked what truth is He answered
nothing, by which the poet thought he meant that no man is
wholly true,

And therfore, though I highte [promised] to expresse
The sorwe and wo that is in mariage,
I dar not writen of it no wikkednesse,
Lest I myself falle eft [again] in swich dotage.

I wol nat seyn [say] how that yt is the cheyne
Of Sathanas, on which he gnaweth evere;
But I dar seyn, were he out of his peyne,
As by his wille he wolde be bounde nevere.
But thilke [that] doted fool that eft [again] hath levere
Ycheyned be than out of prison crepe,
God lete him never fro his wo dissevere,
Ne no man him bewayle, though he wepe!

But yet, lest thow do worse, tak a wyf;
Bet ys to wedde than brenne in worse wise.
But thow shal have sorwe on thy flessh, thy lyf,
And ben thy wives thral, as seyn these wise;
And yf that hooly writ may nat suffyse,
Experience shal the teche, so may happe,
That the were lever to be take in Frise
Than eft to falle of weddynge in the trappe.

[219]

The last line but one "You had better be taken prisoner in Friesland," refers to a military expedition in which English forces took part.

Envoy

This lytel writ, proverbes, or figure
I sende yow, tak kepe of yt, I rede [advise];
Unwys is he that kan no wele [happiness] endure.
If thow be siker [safe], put the nat in drede [uncertainty].
The Wyf of Bathe I pray yow that ye rede.
Of this matere that we have on honde.
God graunte yow your lyf frely to lede
In fredam; for ful hard is to be bonde.

This poem really contains the whole case against Chaucer's married happiness. The reference to Friesland is said to date it between 1393 and 1396, from six to nine years after his wife's death. It seems to be a bachelor's merry poem on the occasion of a friend's wedding. It is rather elaborate fooling. But I think that the reference to the Wyf of Bathe shows that the poem is not to be taken as a deduction from Chaucer's own experience; if he had been serious, he would have referred more specifically to his own marriage. He evidently had made a great hit with the Wyf of Bathe, and wrote these verses in the strain of medieval humor.

If Chaucer had been unkind to his wife, or even if the two were unhappy together with no fault on either side, it is not likely that his wife's sister, Katharine Swynford, would have continued to use her influence with the Duke of Lancaster to further Chaucer's worldly interests, as I believe she did. But that is bolstering up one guess by another. The happiness of the Chaucer household must be left to conjecture. He seems to me too good a fellow not to have been kind, courteous and constant to his wife, too much of a gentleman. His code was strict:

[220]

Looke who that is moost vertuous alway,
Pryvee and apert [open], and moost entendeth ay
To do the gentil dedes that he kan;
Taak hym for the grettest gentil man.

He is very clear that a gentleman can "do no villainy or vice."

Geoffrey and Philippa had one son, perhaps two, Thomas and Lewis. Of Lewis, all that is known is this. In 1391 Chaucer wrote a treatise on the astrolabe, an instrument used to determine the altitude of the sun and the stars, and other astronomical matters; in this treatise he follows very closely the book of an old Arabian astronomer of the eighth century, at least as he found it in the Latin translation, *Compositio et Operatio Astrolabie*. Chaucer's treatise begins, "Litel Lowis, my sone, I aperceive wel by certeyne evidences thyn abilite to lerne sciences touchinge noumbres [numbers] and proporciouns; and as wel considre I thy bisy preyer in special to lerne the Tretis of the Astrolabie. Than, for as mechel [much] as a philosofre seith, 'he wrappeth him in his frend, that condescendeth to the rightful preyers of his frend,' therfore have I geven thee a suffisaunt Astrolabie as for oure orizonte, compowned after the latitude of Oxenford." He says that he writes in English "for Latin ne canstow [thou knowest] yit but smal, my lyte [little] sone," and he writes simply for the sake of "swich a child." It used to be assumed that by *sone,* Chaucer meant son by nature, but as the treatise is evidently meant for many, there seems much likelihood in Professor Kittredge's theory that Lewis was the son of a friend. Personally, even though the name Lewis Chaucer appears in some record, my guess would have been that the "Litel Lowis my sone" of the "Prologue" is a mere fiction to serve for an introduction and to justify the simplicity of the author's exposition—his "ful lighte rewles and naked wordes in English." The treatise is obviously meant for publication, and the suggestion that it was written for a little boy might tempt readers, who otherwise would be fearful of a dry and tedious disquisition, as indeed it seems to me to be. Besides, even simply expressed "the general rewles of theorik in astrologie" seem pretty hard for a "litel sone" readily to understand. The treatise was never finished; I don't know what inferences scholars draw from that. Altogether little Lewis is a very ghostly figure, and, I think, may be disregarded.

Of the other son, Thomas, the only mention as a son occurs in the middle of the next century. Thomas Gascoigne, at one time Chancellor of Oxford University, compiled a Theological Dictionary, in which he says: *"Fuit idem Chawserus pater Thomae Chawserus, armigeri, qui Thomas sepelitur in Nuhelm juxta Oxoniam."* (This same Chaucer was father of Thomas Chaucer, knight, which Thomas is buried in Ewelme near Oxford.) Thomas Chaucer had held the manor of Ewelme, not a dozen miles from Oxford, till his death, in 1434, and as Thomas was a man of wealth and position, and married into the very distinguished Burghersh family, the Chancellor of Oxford would be likely to know. Besides, the assumption that Thomas was Geoffrey's son fits in with the facts, to make a strong chain of circumstantial evidence, each link helping the other. If Thomas was the son of Philippa, and nephew of Katharine, Duchess of Lancaster, it is not surprising that he married a lady of high rank, and that his grandson, John de la Pole, Duke of Suffolk, should marry Elizabeth Plantagenet, a great-granddaughter to John of Gaunt's brother, the Duke of York. This lady's ashes also lie in the church at Ewelme, and her effigy wears the Order of the Garter on her left arm. And other evidence is very strong. Thomas Chaucer used Geoffrey Chaucer's seal; the arms of Roet, Philippa's family, adorn his tomb, and there was a stained-glass window in the parish church at Woodstock in which the arms of Geoffrey Chaucer impaled those of Burghersh.

Besides this, as we shall see, Geoffrey Chaucer was forester of North Petherton Forest for seven years or more, and Thomas Chaucer, long years afterward to be sure, then a very rich man, took a lease of the bailiwick of the Forests of Somerset, including that of North Petherton; and also, eleven years after Geoffrey's death, Thomas is found paying rent for the house in Westminster in which Geoffrey died. To an ignorant layman the evidence that Thomas was Geoffrey's son seems strong.

There is another theory, more romantic and more in accordance with modern theories of proper relations between the sexes, that Thomas was the son of Philippa by John of Gaunt, but in spite of ingenious arguments it does not commend itself to the Victorian-minded. That Chaucer should accept such a situation seems inconsistent with one's notion of him derived from his poetry.

CHAPTER XXV

The Canterbury Tales

CHAUCER had now come, as I have said, to an age which his contemporaries felt to be oldish, and young men deemed time-honored; an age when he began to reckon up probabilities and reflect that, if he cherished an ambition of any great reach in his heart, he had better set about achieving it. He had practised his craft as poet a long time, he had made, as he says,

> Bookys, songes, dytees,
> In ryme, or elles in cadence,

ballades, roundels, virelays, he had written *The Book of the Duchess, The House of Fame, The Parlement of Foules,* the story of Palamon and Arcite, and many another poem. He had translated part of *De Contemptu Mundi,* written by the great Pope Innocent III, and the *De Consolatione Philosophiæ* by Boethius. He had studied the art of versification as practised by the chief French and Italian poets, and was no longer an apprentice. Indeed, he knew very well that he was a master, and, as a bold aeronaut craves to sail in some uncharted region of the sky, he wished to write a book, of which men would say, not, this is borrowed from Boccaccio or Machaut, nor, this is imitated from Dante or Jean de Meung, but this is our Chaucer's own handiwork, it bears his effigy and superscription. Besides, he recognized that the work he had already done belonged to an older generation, a generation by which tradition and convention were too piously respected; he was aware of a new spirit stirring, that concerned itself more with the actual world, with the actual life of the day. He had traveled abroad and met the new influences in France and Italy. Things are changed, he said to himself, a new spirit is come to birth.

I should go too far afield, if I were to try to narrate the advent of this new spirit in Europe. There had been a nativity, and magi were gathering about. Literature had shown this in Italy, and other arts were also showing it in Flanders and in France. Let me quote what Lord Conway says of the work of Claas Sluter, the sculptor from the Low Countries, who entered the Duke of Burgundy's service in this very year, 1385, of which we are talking. Substitute literature for sculpture, and you would think Lord Conway was writing of *The Canterbury Tales*. "Few mediaeval forms—and almost nothing of the mediaeval spirit are here discoverable. We are in the presence of a new ideal, a new art epoch, and the essentials of the Renaissance are plainly manifest. It has often been said that Michelangelo would not have disdained these figures. . . . The spirit that animates them is the spirit of the new day—the spirit that discovered new continents, that plunged joyously into the romance of an adventurous life and of adventurous thinking. Here too is the love of life expressed in stone—the love of this earthly human life of ours such as it is, for better or worse, without much regard for another in some ideal regions of time and space. These folks are all immensely, transcendently human." Substitute, I say, language for stone, Shakespeare for Michelangelo, and you have any competent critic's opinion on Chaucer and *The Canterbury Tales*.

Now turn to the sister art of drawing; and let me quote what Mr. Roger Fry says of sketches which he attributes to Jacquemart de Hesdin, the painter, do you remember, who, as I conjectured, might when a lad have seen Chaucer

[225]

and the English army march through his native town. Jacquemart was in the service of the Duke of Berri in this year, 1385, and some critics have thought that it was he who painted the famous portrait of Richard II in the presbytery of Westminster Abbey. "The author of these designs shows himself not only as a supreme master of that linear design which had been till now the basis of the miniaturist's art, but as having a sense of plastic relief treated pictorially, which was altogether new to the artist of the fourteenth century. He has, moreover, an extraordinary sense of what that new relief can express in the rendering of character and mood in the human face. Character and dramatic purpose had, indeed, long before been marvelously conveyed by pose and gesture of the body as a whole, but in this sketch-book we see a predilection for the elaborate treatment of the head, which surprises us. When we look at the subtlety of gradation, at the *sfumato* of these heads, and appreciate the psychological imagination revealed in them, we can scarcely believe we are looking at the work of an artist who died between 1402 and 1413." Might not Mr. Fry be talking of the Wife of Bath, of Harry Bailly, of the Prioress, or of the Monk, or any of the Canterbury pilgrims? Claas Sluter died in 1404; Jacquemart a little later, Chaucer in 1400. The three were swept along by the new inspiration emanating from the living of life.

Chaucer acknowledged the authority of this new spirit of realism, and showed himself the greatest master of them all. He obeyed the precept, "know thyself," and knew that studying from life, not from old models, was his particular talent. Youth was the time for roundels and virelays, and he had tried his hand at them, but he was well aware that he had written no lyrics, that could be compared to Dante's *canzoni* or to Petrarch's sonnets. Besides, as he could see when he looked back, he was not primarily a lyrical poet,

[226]

he had never been passionately in love with any woman, never with such love as that, for instance, which Clerk Saunders felt for Margaret,

> And deep and heavy was the love
> That fell thir twa between,

never like Romeo, never like Paolo Malatesta. And, now, he realized that what interested him most was this brave world about him, this theater, in which he beheld his countrymen playing their English parts. One muses what he would have written had he lived in Queen Elizabeth's time, when William Johnson was host of the Mermaid Tavern, instead of when Harry Bailly was Host of the Tabard, or in the eighteenth century when Henry Fielding had his chambers in Pump Court and was intercalating between his briefs and conveyances sketches of Thwackum and Square, of Squire Western and Lady Bellaston.

Chaucer's age was very much an age of story-telling, and in *The Legend of Good Women* he had done something in the way of stringing stories together on a connecting thread; and, already, though with no definite plan in his mind, he had several stories in his desk, *The Lyf of Seynt Cecyle, Palamon and Arcite,* and minor fragments, and as soon as the pressure of the daily round at the custom-house was removed, he gave himself seriously to thinking out a project.

As a poet, to my thinking, Chaucer has been surpassed in various ways by a number of Englishmen, but as a story-teller in verse, or rather I should say as the story-teller of *The Prologue to the Canterbury Tales,* he is, if not the best, neck-and-neck with the nearest competitors. And, for that reason, if one were put to a choice in the road of approach to *The Canterbury Tales,* whether it should be by

[227]

poetry, or by prose, I should say by prose. And in asserting that prose is the proper road of approach, I mean no depreciation; consider, for instance, the scenes between Prince Hal and Falstaff, or between Sir John and Justices Shallow and Silence, or chapters in *Joseph Andrews* or *Tom Jones,* or passages in Dickens. Sometimes in reading Trollope I am reminded of Chaucer. Do you remember Archdeacon Grantley in his judgment upon the poor parson, Mr. Crawley?

Archdeacon Grantley's son, Henry, against his father's wish, has proposed to the charming daughter of this indigent clergyman, the incumbent at Hogglestock, a very worthy, proud man, who has been accused, owing to an untoward train of circumstances, of stealing. Mrs. Grantley, who adores her son, pleads with her husband. "I understand it all," the Archdeacon said at last, "I've nothing to do with the girl, I don't care whether she be good or bad."

"Oh, my dear!"

"I care not at all,—with reference to my own concern. Of course, I would wish that the daughter of a neighboring clergyman,—that the daughter of any neighbor,—that the daughter of any one whatsoever,—should be good rather than bad, but as regards Henry and me, and our mutual relation, her goodness can make no difference."

If young people come to *The Canterbury Tales* by way of Keats and Shelley, of Coleridge or Tennyson, they will experience a sense of incongruity, of alien atmosphere, but if they go via *The Vicar of Wakefield,* or Smollett, or by any of what are known as the robust novelists of the eighteenth century, redolent of what Ruskin called the Englishman's "earthly instincts," they will feel but slight change of altitude or air. Henry Fielding, with his love of irony and the Rabelaisian in life, is the nearest to Chaucer here. Do

[228]

you recall the scene in *Joseph Andrews* where two young bucks come into an inn together?

A coach and six, with a numerous attendance, drove into the inn. There alighted from the coach a young fellow, and a brace of pointers, after which another young fellow leaped from the box, and shook the former by the hand; and both, together with the dogs, were instantly conducted by Mr. Tow-wouse (the innkeeper) into an apartment; whither as they passed, they entertained themselves with the following short facetious dialogue:

"You are a pretty fellow for a coachman, Jack!" says he from (the inside of) the coach; "you had almost overturned us just now." "Pox take you!" says the coachman; "if I had only broke your neck, it would have been saving somebody else the trouble, but I should have been sorry for the pointers." "Why, you son of a b——," answered the other, "if nobody could shoot better than you, the pointers would be of no use." "D—n me," says the coachman, "I will shoot with you five guineas a shot." "You be hang'd," says the other, "for five guineas you shall shoot at my a——." "Done," says the coachman, "I'll pepper you better than——" "Pepper your grandmother," says the other. "Here's Tow-wouse will let you shoot at him for a shilling a time." "I know his honour better," cries Tow-wouse, "I never saw a surer shot at a partridge. Every man misses now and then; but if I could shoot half as well as his honour, I would desire no better livelihood than I could get by my gun." "Pox on you," said the coachman, "you demolish more game now than your head's worth. There's a bitch, Tow-wouse: by G—— she never blinked a bird in her life." "I have a puppy, not a year old, shall hunt with her for a hundred," cries the other gentleman. "Done," says the coachman, "but you will be poxed before you make the bet." "If you have a mind for a bet," cries the coachman, "I

[229]

will match my spotted dog with your white bitch for a hundred, play or pay." "Done," says the other, "and I'll run Baldface against Slouch with you for another. "No," cries he from the box, "but I'll venture Miss Jenny against Baldface, or Hannibal either." "Go to the devil," cries he from the coach, "I will make every bet your own way, to be sure. I will match Hannibal with Slouch for a thousand, if you dare; and I say done first." (*Joseph Andrews,* Chapter XVI.)

I do not forget the poetry, the tale of Arcite and Palamon, of the little Christian Martyr, of Constance, of Patient Grissel, nor do I forget the prolixities of Melibeus and the Parson's homily, but the dominant note in *The Canterbury Tales* is given by mine Host and Alice of Bath, well supported by the Miller, the Reeve, the Summoner, the Friar and others. It is the note of our "earthly instincts."

Let us then approach *The Canterbury Tales* by a path that takes us via Squire Western and Parson Adams, rather than one by Endymion and the Red Cross Knight. Chaucer confronted two questions: how should he obtain variety, and how should he bind the stories together into one bundle. The question, I think, was thrust upon him because he did not know what to do with the stories he had on hand,—a romantic poem, a saint's life, and a collection of brief biographies of famous men who had been the sport of malign fortune. As he pondered what to do, he came to see that the primary question was not variety, but the binding rope, the setting, the frame. What sort of setting, what sort of frame, had he better devise? There were plenty of collections of stories, but the frames that held them together, were for one reason or another unsatisfactory, they were monotonous, artificial, unimaginative, dull. One frame alone, fresh and brilliant, stands out as superior to the tales within it. Nevertheless, many scholars declare that Chaucer never saw the *Decameron*. Tyrwhitt, to be sure, believed that Chaucer had grouped his tales together in imitation of Boccaccio; but modern scholarship, as I understand, inclines as a rule to think not. This judgment is based on negative testimony; Chaucer never names Boccaccio, and he has taken no plot directly from the *Decameron*. To be sure, he shows himself to have known most of Boccaccio's works, *Il Filostrato, De Casibus Virorum, De Claris Mulieribus* and the *Teseide;* nevertheless, many scholars are positive that he never saw the *Decameron*. The resemblances in *The Miller's Tale, The Reeve's Tale, The Shipman's Tale* and *The Franklin's Tale,* to stories in the *Decameron,* are slight and may be traced to use of the same sources.

This denial that Chaucer saw the *Decameron* puzzles the layman, and also some scholars. Signor Rajna, for instance says: "Such an opinion is an *inescusable balordaggine* [inexcusably silly]." The argument that because a writer does not name, or borrow, therefore he does not know the work of a famous predecessor, might be applied to a good many distinguished men of letters with unsatisfactory results. I do not recall that Fielding mentions Robinson Crusoe, or that Dickens speaks of the Bible. It seems easier to believe that Chaucer deliberately rejected Boccaccio's plots, as not suitable for some reason or other, than that, when he was in Florence, among the bourgeois society for which the *Decameron* was written, among literati who told him of so many other works of their distinguished fellow citizen, nobody ever mentioned the *Decameron* to him. Somebody told him that Petrarch had composed in Latin the story of Patient Grissel, and that person must have known that Petrarch had merely translated Boccaccio. As Chaucer strolled about Florence, in 1373, as he walked to Fiesole, or to Settignano, would not somebody have pointed out the *dilettevole* Villa Poggio Gherardi, the *piacevole* Villa de

[231]

Schifanoja, as the house and garden where the young people of the *Decameron* had fled from the plague and had told their stories? Or, in Milan, in 1378, would he not have asked about the illustrious Petrarch, who had been an honored guest in that city, would he not have mentioned that he had read Petrarch's story, and would he not have been told, "But you know that that tale is a translation from Boccaccio"?

Is the fact that Chaucer does not mention Boccaccio by name a sound argument that he never heard of the *Decameron?* It does not make against his having heard of Boccaccio's other works. And, being no scholar, I do not know, but I do not think Chaucer mentions the name of Guillaume de Deguilleville, whose *Pèlerinage de l'Ame,* scholars say, is the source of his *A. B. C.;* nor do I think that he mentions Guillaume de Machaut by name, nor Froissart, nor Eustache Deschamps, from all of whom, scholars say, he borrowed; nor am I sure that he ever names Guillaume de Lorris or Jean de Meung, though he translated part of the *Roman de la Rose.* Had Chaucer not borrowed from these poets, it might have been argued that he did not know them.

At all events, the *Decameron,* had he known it, would have shown him how important a frame is to a picture, how it enhances the beauty, emphasizes the composition, pulls details into place, adds luster to the high lights and may in itself be a charming work of art. Personally, I can not imagine any one but a youth of eighteen or nineteen reading the *novelle* in the *Decameron,* but Boccaccio's description of the plague, of the garden, of the party of pleasure, is charming, and interesting to every reader. And, to my thinking, the same holds true for *The Canterbury Tales,* the frame— I mean the *Prologue* and the connecting conversations between the tales—is far more interesting than the tales themselves. Might it not be that the same spirit of emulation and proud triumph, that made Turner hang his pictures

[232]

next those by Claude, crept into Chaucer's heart, and urged him to resolve that as he had written a *Troilus and Criseyde* more poetic, more touching, more true, and better told than the *Filostrato,* he would also gather scattered tales into a setting that should outdo the *Decameron,* and for that very reason, to conceal his debt, he never mentions Boccaccio nor openly borrows. But I am not qualified to discuss the question, and I retire.

When Chaucer got the idea of a comedy for the frame, then all he had to do was to make a plot, hardly more than a scenario, which should provide him with as many characters as he might deem necessary to obtain the variety he sought. His *dramatis personæ* should tell the stories; the stories they were to tell should be in keeping with their characters; and his task would then consist of casting about and getting together the appropriate stories. He never thought of inventing a plot, his habit was to look about for one suitable to his needs. He was acquainted with the French fabliaux, with stories of all sorts from France and Italy, and with others, that had drifted in from the obscurity of the East.

The *dramatis personæ* of his comedy must be chosen with care, so that the stories should have variety: those that he had were a little high-brow, and most people preferred subjects that bordered upon our "earthly instincts." Jack Falstaff, Sir Toby Belch, Mercutio, Gratiano, and care-burdened merchants, would rather have a rollicking story to make them laugh. Chaucer decided to have enough of those, and therefore his comedy must have churls of some kind to tell them; but variety must be procured,—there were plenty of subjects to choose from,—he might take something magical, something pious, something perhaps that would expose fraudulent alchemists, and there was Petrarch's story of Patient Grissel. These ideas lay in solution, waiting for happy chance to crystallize.

[233]

CHAPTER XXVI

THE TABARD INN

AFTER all, that dispute concerning the *Decameron* is of no great matter. The real source of the setting in which Chaucer places *The Canterbury Tales* is to be found in his journeys from London to Kent. His duties as guardian to young Edmund Staplegate for a year or two must have obliged him to visit Staplegate properties in Kent, and later he probably went there familiarly upon similar errands with respect to the heir of John Solys; and now in 1385, when he was giving up his house in London and establishing himself in Kent, he must have been a frequent traveler on the road. The regular way was by Dartford, Rochester and Ospringe to Canterbury. The pilgrims started from the Tabard Inn in Southwark, took their way eastward, passing within sight of Deptford where two hundred years later Kit Marlow was killed in a tavern brawl, and then crossing Blackheath where the rebels had camped on their way to London, rode within sight of Greenwich where the Duke of Lancaster's great-great-great-grandson, Henry VIII, and his great-great-great-great-granddaughters, Bloody Mary and Queen Elizabeth, were to be born, and on to Dartford, the place where in Jack Straw's time the tiler beat out the tax-collector's brains for insolence to his daughter. Here travelers were wont to pass the night, having come a stage of fifteen miles. A farther stage of fifteen miles carried them across the wooden bridge over the Medway and into Rochester, notable for its castle and cathedral. It was Bishop Ernulf of Rochester Cathedral, according to Lawrence Sterne, who composed the glorious curse that is recorded in *Tristram Shandy*.—Doctor Slop read it aloud to Mr. Shandy, while Uncle Toby whistled *Lillabullero*. "May the Holy and Eternal Virgin Mary, Mother of God, curse him, may St. Michael, the advocate of holy souls curse him!—May all the angels, archangels, principalities and powers, and all the heavenly armies curse him. (Our armies swore terribly in *Flanders* cried my Uncle Toby—but nothing to this)."—From Rochester the road runs ten miles to Sittingbourne, which in its way is a seaport; and, here, travelers might dine—oysters were a *spécialité*—and thence on to Ospringe, making this day's stage sixteen miles. Canterbury lies ten miles farther.

Chaucer going to and fro along this road, stopping at Harry Bailly's tavern to wet his whistle, before starting forth, must have met a wide range of travelers, franklins, friars, monks, bailiffs, knights, priests, pilgrims of all classes high and low, and heard them tell yarns in the hostelries along the road over their wine, or, may be, at some ale-stake by the wayside. He had already on hand, as I have said, one story suitable for a gentleman to tell, a second for a nun, and a third that might probably be arranged for a monk. The idea of a pilgrimage as the framework for his stories must have come to him from actually seeing a company of pilgrims start from Harry Bailly's tavern. There was Harry Bailly himself, shouting out jokes and good-byes in his jovial commanding manner. To see him was to know that he was specially designed by Providence as the central figure to group other characters about. His name would be an excellent advertisement in itself; everybody knew Harry Bailly. He had sat in parliament for the borough of Southwark ten years before, and the Tabard was as familiar to persons going down from London to Kent as the tower of Saint Paul's. The hostelry must have been excellent, for Bailly was a competent man; and the same qualities that induced his fellow-citizens to elect him to parliament, must have rendered him popular with his guests—his bluff boisterous good-humor, his ready adaptability to the rank and bearing of his patrons, his courtesy to ladies, his quick wit, his rude backhand repartees to boorish carters. The moment that Chaucer had grasped the idea of the Host of the Tabard as his central figure, all the other pilgrims presented themselves; there had to be a gentleman to tell the tale of Palamon and Arcite, a nun that of Saint Cecilia's life, a monk to recount the doleful revolutions of Fortune, and a group of churls to recount stories taken from fabliaux, and so on.

The scheme must have come upon him like a vision; characters and tales almost hand in hand. The plot was perfect, it gave scope for all Chaucer's talents and qualities, his genial disposition, his gift for drawing characters—better than Jacquemart de Hesdin with line, or Claas Sluter with chisel—his mastery of prosody, his power of story-telling. So, one blithe morning in spring, when the birds were singing, when the hawthorn was in blossom, the sun shining royally, and lazy white clouds slept in the soft air, he dipped his pen in his inkhorn and wrote:

> Whan that Aprille with his shoures soote
> The droghte of Marche hath perced to the roote,
> And bathed every veyne in swich licour
> Of which vertu engendred is the flour;
> Whan Zephirus eek with his sweete breeth
> Inspired hath in every holt and heeth
> The tendre croppes, and the yonge sonne
> Hath in the Ram his halve cours yronne,
> And smale foweles maken melodye,
> That slepen al the nyght with open ye [eye]
> (So priketh hem nature in hir corages):
> Thanne longen folk to goon on pilgrimages . . .

He is off! And what a happy start! Success often lies in the take-off. How brilliantly the *Iliad* begins, and the imitative *Æneid*! *Hamlet* opens well; the sudden words, "Who's there?" make the heart beat quicker. And in *Antony and Cleopatra*, "Nay but this dotage of our general's" announces the tragedy. By Chaucer's opening you know that life is sweet, that the world is a happy place, that the flowers, the young crops, and the little birds, have done well to come forth and rejoice, and you understand exactly why folk want to go traveling by field and stream, by croft and castle, through villages and towered cities, even across the seas, to Rome, may be, to Santiago di Compostella, or even to Jerusalem, and most of all through England's countryside to Canterbury.

So the company assembled at the Tabard in Southwark on the sixteenth of April, 1387, twenty-nine in all. We shall make their better acquaintance as they come to tell their tales, but I will tell those of you who do not already know that some of the pilgrims are sympathetic, and some not.

Sympathetic	*Unsympathetic*
The Knight	The Miller
The Squire	The Reeve
The Prioress	The Friar
The Clerk	The Summoner
The Parson	The Pardoner
The Plowman	The Franklin
Dan Chaucer	The Shipman
The Host	The Manciple
The Monk	The Sergeant at Law
The Second Nun	The Physician
The Nun's Priest	The Cook
	The Merchant

The Wife of Bath stands in a category by herself. Before he starts to tell his story of how the pilgrimage began, Chaucer warns his readers that his tales will not be fit for ears polite, he begs them not to impute to lack of good breeding his plainness of speech, for as an honest man he is obliged to tell the tales in the very language in which they were told, no matter how rude or liberal the tongue. And he adds, rather audaciously, and possibly to let us know at the beginning that he is no Lollard,

> Crist spak hymself ful brode in hooly writ,
> And wel ye woot no vileynye is it.
> Eek Plato seith, whoso that kan hym rede,
> The wordes moote be cosyn to the dede.

This is, as you will have guessed, Chaucer's way of letting the less strait-laced know that there will be something that journalism to-day calls "snappy" and that they must not be discouraged by any tale of romantic poetry that may come first, for "snappiness" will surely follow. At any rate, the strait-laced are warned and know what to expect from the unsympathetic persons. That done, the poet starts in to say that they had a good supper, and describes the Host. As Harry Bailly may properly be deemed the hero of the epic I will quote his description:

> A semely man Oure Hooste was withalle
> For to han been a marchal in an halle.
> A large man he was with eyen stepe [prominent]—
> A fairer burgeys is ther noon in Chepe—
> Boold of his speche, and wys, and wel ytaught,
> And of manhod hym lakkede right naught.
> Eek thereto he was right a myrie man,
> And after soper pleyen he bigan,
> And spak of myrthe amonges othere thynges,
> Whan that we hadde maad our rekenynges . . .

What an excellent portrait of an Englishman—one remembers that he had sat in the Good Parliament of 1376—and the crowning trait in the last line! Then Bailly makes the proposal that, for the sake of passing the time pleasantly, each pilgrim shall tell two stories on the way to Canterbury and two on the way back, and whoever does best shall have a supper at the general cost, and adds that he will go with them at his own expense and be their guide, and whoever gainsays what he commands shall pay for all they spend by the way. To this all heartily agree, and beg him to be not only governor but the judge and reporter of the tales told.

CHAPTER XXVII

The Pilgrims

Amorwe, whan that day bigan to sprynge,
Up roos oure Hoost, and was oure aller cok [cock],
And gadrede us togidre, alle in a flok,
And forth we riden . . .

But first I had better enumerate the company, one by one. Chaucer, himself, you remember is of the party. The Knight, as the person of highest social rank, is introduced first. He is the portrait of an English gentleman. He brings with him an atmosphere of quiet, courtly dignity, and his modesty, in spite of all his adventures in foreign lands, bears, as it were, if one may anticipate, the stamp of Eton and Cambridge;

And though that he were worthy, he was wys,
And of his port as meeke as is a mayde.
He nevere yet no vileynye ne sayde
In al his lyf unto no maner wight.
He was a verray, parfit gentil knyght.

In this last line, I am told, *verray* is not an adverb qualifying *parfit,* but an adjective meaning true; and, what a felicitous verse by which to sum up his character, no wonder it is proverbial. And, how well the poet, even after that verse, adds to the effect of the description, by telling how careless the Knight is of his appearance, his *gypon* (doublet) all *bismotered* (besmutted) by his armor. Next him rides his

[240]

He was a manly man, with "many a dainty horse" in his
stables. He happened now to be riding a palfrey as brown
as a berry. He was in excellent shape—"in good poynt"—
and so was his horse. As you surmise he was not over
pious:

The reule of seint Maure or of seint Beneit [Benedict],
By cause that it was old and somedel streit [strict]
This ilke Monk leet olde thynges pace [go by],
And heeld after the newe world the space [course].
He yaf nat of [for] that text a pulled [plucked] hen,
That seith that hunters ben nat holy men . . .
What [why] sholde he studie and make hymselven wood
    [mad],
Upon a book in cloystre alwey to poure [pore],
Or swynken with his handes, and laboure,
As Austyn [Augustine] bit [bade]? How shal the world be
    served?
Lat Austyn have his swynk [toil] to hym reserved!

The contrast between his neat and fashionable dress, and
the Knight's negligence, is its own comment; and the single
line devoted to his palate,

A fat swan loved he best of any roost [roast],

conjures up a cheerful picture of the monastic offices, with
buttery, dairy, chicken-run, duck pond and kitchen. The
monk is nearly a gentleman, and takes the Host's coarse
raillery just as he should, without resentment and with a
little condescending disregard.

The Friar, one knows immediately, is to be an object of
satire; the literary tradition of the fourteenth century demanded it. The itinerant orders had outlived their spiritual
passion for non-worldliness; they had become in great meas-

[243]

ure mere implements in the hands of the Papacy for
political or pecuniary purposes, and to the eyes of the ordinary layman fully justified the literary tradition.   And
Chaucer's description is satirical.   This is why I quoted
Dryden's portrait of Zimri, for Chaucer's descriptions of
the Friar and of the Pardoner belong to the same category,
and (if we include Pope's lines on Addison) stand at the
top:

> A Frere ther was, a wantowne and a merye,
> A lymytour, a ful solempne man.
> In alle the ordres foure is noon that kan [knows]
> So muchel of daliaunce and fair langage.

A *lymytour* was a friar to whom a definite district was
assigned in which to go the rounds on his quest for alms,
and of course the brother, who had the best gift for dal-
liance, that is, for standing about to pass the time of day
and exchange news, or speculations about the weather and
neighbors' doings, was selected for the job.   Just what
Chaucer means by *solempne* I don't know.   Skeat says the
word here means *cheerful,* but as Chaucer has already called
him *wantowne* and *merye* that would seem an anticlimax.   I
think it means a man that could rise to the dignity of any
occasion, fitting his face to mirth or sorrow, one that could
express compassion or reprobation, and though inclined to
laugh would take certain duties seriously;

> He hadde maad ful many a mariage
> Of yonge wommen, at his owene cost.

For though Chaucer loved satire, he loved real life much
more.   He does not take a vice, as Molière for instance did
with Tartuffe, dress it up and call it a man; he mixes qualities, as Nature does, good, bad, pleasant, disagreeable, hasty,

[244]

slow, hot and cold, and creates an individual person. You understand exactly why Friar Hubert was chosen among his fellows to be lymytour; he was so comfortable and such cozy company, he enjoyed singing—

> And in his harpyng, whan that he hadde songe,
> His eyen twynkled in his heed aryght,
> As doon the sterres in the frosty nyght—

or loitering at a tavern and drinking healths with host or tapster; but the popular notion of a friar asserts itself, and satire is the dominant note:

> He was an esy man to yeve penaunce,
> Ther as he wiste to have a good pitaunce
> [Where he knew he would receive a good portion].
> For unto a povre ordre for to yive
> Is signe that a man is wel yshryve [shriven];
> For if he yaf, he [the friar] dorste make avaunt [boast],
> He wiste [knew] that a man was repentaunt;
> For many a man so hard is of his herte,
> He may [can] nat wepe, althogh hym soore smerte.
> Therfor, in stede of wepynge and preyeres
> Men moote [should] yeve silver to the povre freres.

This passage, though it is akin to the *Roman de la Rose,* is Chaucerian in every line, and shows how Chaucer had loosed himself from his French model, and can now express his own ideas in his own way; the touch of Jean de Meung is merely the nice agreement between their points of view.

The Merchant is a narrow-minded conventional man, with nothing I think to recommend him. He was shy, and dressed and talked like a rich man, in order to produce the impression of being such. His forked beard and his Flanderish beaver hat have nothing large or generous behind them; and one is not surprised later on, to learn that,

[245]

though he has been married but two months, he and his wife are on bad terms. His lack of wit is apparent when he tells his tale, for though it is meant to show how untrustworthy a young wife is, the old husband is the butt of the story. One is glad to leave him gravely riding his tall horse, and pass on to the lean Clerk of Oxford who is mounted on a Rosinante. This Clerk is a real scholar, and a most worthy person. His clothes are as shabby as his steed, for he had no benefice and did nothing to get one. He cared not for raiment, or for the light gaiety that goes with fiddles and psalteries; he would far rather have had twenty volumes of philosophy than all such stuff. Whatever money he got he spent on books; and he repaid the kindness of those that give him means to study by praying for the welfare of their souls. His speech was brief, full of dignity and to the point and his manner befitted his words:

> Sownynge [sounding] in moral vertu was his speche,
> And gladly wolde he lerne and gladly teche.

When it becomes his turn to tell a tale, Harry Bailly jollies him:

> "Sire Clerk of Oxenford . . .
> Ye ryde as coy and stille as dooth a mayde
> Were newe spoused, sittynge at the bord;
> This day ne herde I of youre tonge a word. . . .
>   For Goddes sake, as beth [be] of bettre cheere!
> It is no tyme for to studien heere."

And bids him not to preach, or make the pilgrims weep for their past sins, nor send them to sleep, but to tell a merry tale, and not to employ a high style, suitable for writing to a King, but to speak simply so that the others could understand.

[246]

This worthy clerk benignely answerde:
"Hooste," quod he, "I am under youre yerde [rod];
Ye han [have] of us as now the governance,
And therfore wol I do yow obeisance,
As fer as resoun axeth, hardily."

Then he tells the strange tale of Patient Grissel, which
Petrarch translated into Latin from Boccaccio's *Decameron*.
He says he had it from Petrarch, and it is this statement of
the Clerk's that gave rise to the belief that Chaucer and
Petrarch had met.

A Sergeant at Law is next in order. Sergeants were
great personages at the bar, and perhaps Chaucer remembered his young days at the inns of Court when the big-wigs
were scandalized to hear that one of their students had
beaten a friar on Fleet Street; at any rate he takes a fling
at this sergeant, for after speaking of his excellence and
discretion, of his wise words, of his appointments as justice,
of his fees and high renown, he adds,

Nowher so bisy a man as he ther nas,
And yet he semed bisier than he was.

And when the Host calls upon him, and reminds him of the
agreement to tell stories at his behest, he answers pompously
in legal terms,

"Hooste . . . *depardieux* ich assente;
To breke forward [promise] is not myn entente."

Before beginning, however, the Sergeant remarks by way
of preface that he knows no profitable tale to tell just now,
but that Chaucer had written some in English that were
popular. And then he refers to *The Book of the Duchess*

[247]

and to *The Legend of Good Women,* and takes occasion to make a kindly gibe at Gower, who had just published two incestuous tales, by saying that Chaucer would never do that. To me this reference seems to violate ordinary canons of art, and I see no object in it, unless it be to call attention to his other poems. It is awkward to praise oneself to one's face. The commentators say that the Sergeant does not know that Chaucer is one of the company, and in fact it appears later on that Harry Bailly does not recognize him. This ignorance on Bailly's part is postulated, I take it, for the sake of the general plot, for if Harry Bailly was still living and Host of the Tabard in 1387, he must have seen Chaucer, Comptroller of Customs, knight of the shire, stopping on his way to or from Kent, hitching his horse in the Tabard yard and calling for a mug of ale.

Now for the Frankeleyn. A franklin was a sort of country gentleman, a well-to-do farmer, such as lived in Chaucer's neighborhood while he was knight of the shire for Kent. This franklin had been knight of the shire himself, also sheriff, and county magistrate, but his most distinguished trait is that of *bon vivant.* He had all the appetites attributed to the Saxons, enhanced and refined by the taste for luxuries that had come in from France; he was a true Epicurean, and very hospitable. He always kept open table, and made everybody welcome. He was proud of his bread and ale, of his excellent cellar, of his baked meats, and their abundance.

It snewed [snowed] in his hous of mete and drynke,

and every season had its appropriate sort of fish or game;

Wo was his cook but if his sauce were
Poynaunt and sharp . . .

[248]

He showed his love of gormandizing in his face which was sanguine, and the more conspicuously so because

Whit was his berd [beard] as is the dayesye [daisy].

This touch which seems to the casual reader so Chaucerian is also one of his happy borrowings; at least in the *Chanson de Roland* an emir has a beard white as the blossom of a thorn.

CHAPTER XXVIII

THE PILGRIMS (Continued)

THE more worshipful persons, at least in a worldly sense, unless we except the Doctor, have been introduced, and we now proceed to those of a lower class. First come several mute personages, who not merely say nothing, but are not even mentioned again, a Haberdasher, a Carpenter, a Weaver, a Dyer, a Tapicer (weaver of tapestry). You conceive them, men unaccustomed to society outside that of their daily routine, shy, conscious of their lack of breeding, but proud withal and self-content, tradesmen that had made their own way, men used to sitting on the dais in the guild hall, with well-filled purses, husbands of wives who were socially ambitious. With them, but not of them, for he would never be invited to sit on a dais, a Cook, whom they had brought for the journey, so that they should not have to trust to the bungling of country mar-dishes. This man was master of his art, he could roast, seethe, broil, fry, make *mortrewes,* and blanc manger, at which he equaled the best. Skeat says that blanc manger is a compound of minced capon with cream, sugar and flour; no wonder that the prosperous tradesfolk would not travel without him. Unfortunately he had a *mormal,* some kind of sore, on his shin; unfortunately I say, I mean for him, because there are scholars who take delight in studying medieval medicine in order to discover what this mormal was, or, perhaps, how it should have been treated. He seems to have been a good-natured fellow, for Harry Bailly rallies him as if he were, on the pies in his cook shop, which had been prepared twice hot and twice cold,

[250]

and on the curses pilgrims had laid on him for his fly-blown food. The Cook laughed merrily and answered back. His name was Hodge, and he came from Ware.

After him comes the Shipman, interesting like the yeoman archer, for he was one of the seamen, precursors of the Devon pirates in Queen Elizabeth's time, who had defeated French, Spanish and Flemings at sea, in spite of their bigger ships, and established English supremacy in the Channel. He was not only piratical—

> Of nyce conscience took he no keep.
> If that he faught, and hadde the hyer hond,
> By water he sente hem [them] hoom to every lond,

in other words to Davy Jones's locker—but he was also thievish toward the Bordeaux merchants who had entrusted their wines to his ship, the *Magdelene,* named for that damsel, I should suppose, before her days of repentance; but *Magdalene* was also the name of the Genoese ship stolen by English pirates, a rape complained of and paid for, you remember, shortly before Chaucer went on his first Italian mission. The supremacy of the English at sea, however, did not depend upon the knavery of these mariners, but on their seamanship, which was excellent; this Shipman knew all about currents, tides, shoals, headlands and harbors, along the channel and down the French and Spanish coasts. Though on a pilgrimage, perhaps because sailors are superstitious, he was not pious, and when something is said that leads him to think the Parson will deliver a sermon (you will remember that I quoted this before) he bursts out:

> Nay, by my fader [father] soule, that schal he nat!
> . . . heer he schal nat preche;
> He schal no gospel glosen here ne teche.

Then fearing that he had spoken too sincerely, he hastens to add,

> We leven [believe] alle in the grete God,

and explains that his fear was lest the Parson, whom the Host suggested was inclined to Lollardry, might sow "cokkel in our clene corn." Probably no parson had ever set foot on the *Magdelene*. Anyhow, the Shipman does not propose to be overawed by the Clerk of Oxford, or by the Doctor of Physic, or even by the solemn Sergeant at Law, for when he starts to tell his tale, he says that there will be no philosophy in it, nor physic, nor any quaint terms of law.

The Doctor of Physic was a very learned man, well up on his Æsculapius, Dioscorides, Rufus, Hippocrates, Hali, Galen, Avicenna, Averroes, and so on; you might think you were reading Molière or Bernard Shaw.

> In al this world ne was ther noon hym lik,
> To speke of phisik and of surgerye,
> For he was grounded in astronomye.

And he was careful of his own body, moderate in diet, and what he ate was both nourishing and digestible. But he had his weaknesses; he read the Bible but little, he was on too good terms with the apothecaries,

> For ech of hem made oother for to wynne,

and he took good care not to spend recklessly the gold he had got during the pestilence,

> For gold in phisik is a cordial,
> Therfore he lovede gold in special.

Alice, the Wife of Bath, should be the next in order, but as I shall give her a chapter to herself, I will proceed to the finest fellow in the company, not even excepting the perfect Knight. Yeats, and other lyrical poets, who set their ideal in terms of beauty and joy, and whose theology represents angels, as in Botticelli's celestial circle, dancing round the throne of a God who is playing the fiddle for them, will think the Poor Parson busies himself too much with the somberer, more puritanical, aspects of existence, takes this single chance of ours to be gay and merry too seriously, that he regards life too much as a means instead of an end in itself; but Yeats, and such, look upon the Poor Parson's life as a separate unit, whereas Chaucer and the rest of us usually look upon an individual as one strand in the web of the cloth of life, without which that cloth would lose not only much of its strength, but also much of its beauty. You can not find a more delightful description of what you would wish the parson of your town to be, rich in holy thought and work, learned, a preacher and a teacher of what Christ said, benign, diligent, patient in adversity, living on little, generous, not seeking his own, and though his parish was wide and his parishioners lived far apart, kept by no inclemency of weather from ministering to them, and he went on foot, staff in hand.

> This noble ensample to his sheep he yaf [gave],
> That first he wroghte, and afterward he taughte.

For he believed that the weightiest obligation lying on a priest is to set an example of purity of life, and duty done, to his people. He was the shepherd of his sheep, full of compassion for them that erred and strayed, but if he deemed it his duty he would rebuke the sinner, whether high or low, and he did not perplex with subtle casuistry,

> But Cristes loore and his apostles twelve
> He taughte, but first he folwed it hymselve.

[253]

With this Christian Parson came his brother, a Plowman, the same sort of man, "living in peace and perfect charity," loving God with all his heart and his neighbor as himself, and for Christ's sake, wherever he could, he would thresh and ditch and delve for every poor neighbor without taking pay for it.

We now come to those, whom for want of a better generic name I shall call the churls. First the Miller, a stout carl, all brawn and bone, broad-shouldered, with a head that could batter down a door, a great wrestler, with a red beard, and a wart on his nose, and mouth wide as a furnace, a dishonest fellow, with his talk running on indecencies. Next a Manciple, a purveyor for the Inner or Middle Temple, and it is possible that this *gentil Maunciple* is one of the memories of Chaucer's youth. In the Temple (the poet says) there were more than thirty masters "of law expert and curious," and out of these a full dozen worthy to be stewards of any lord in England, and yet this Manciple was able to trick them all. But he was a good man in his place, very provident, always beforehand,

> Now is nat that of God a ful fair grace
> That swich a lewed mannes wit shal pace [outstep]
> The wisdom of an heep of lerned men?

The Reeve, the superintendent of a great estate, was "a slender choleric man" close-shaven, crop-headed, with long lean legs, very competent and businesslike, knowing all about drought and rain, sowing and reaping, about sheep, cattle, pigs, horses, poultry, about the dairy and the storehouse. He managed it all and kept the laborers and employees under him in constant fear; there was no way to hoodwink him. As a lad he had been bred a carpenter, but he had risen, and now by deftly lending and selling to his lord the

[254]

lord's own property, and getting thanks as well, he had laid by a comfortable sum, and owned a house pleasantly situated on a heath and shaded by green trees. He came from a town called Baldeswell in Norfolk, and rode hindermost, perhaps in order to avoid the Miller whom he did not like, who rode first blowing his bagpipe, or perhaps the Reeve rode last merely in order to avoid the bagpipe.

The Summoner, whose business it was to serve summonses upon persons directing them to appear before ecclesiastical courts, is another of the churls. He, with the Miller, the Reeve, the Friar, and the Pardoner make five. Perhaps the Summoner is the most unpleasant of them all, even more than the drunken Miller, for the Miller is merely a sot, but the Summoner is all rogue. He had a red face, covered with pimples, black eyebrows and scanty beard, so horrid-looking a creature that his face frightened children. He ate garlic, onions, leaks, and drank strong red wine, and then he would talk and shout as if he were mad, gabbling the few Latin words that he had learned from some legal document. He was a low ribald fellow, and would sell his concubine for a year in return for a quart of wine. If he found a man to his liking, "a good felawe," he would tell him that he need not mind the archdeacon's curse, unless indeed he had money in his purse and then he had better be careful. He kept his eye on the young people of the diocese, and learned their secrets, so that he might have them in his power. Before the start he seems to have been drinking too much, for he wore a great garland on his head, and carried a cake for a buckler.

By the side of the Summoner rode his comrade, the Pardoner, who had just come back from the Papal Curia. This fellow was in high spirits, and sang, "Come hither, love, to me," while the Summoner sang the bass. His most noticeable characteristics were his glaring eyes, like a hare's, his yellow hair that hung down smooth like flax all over his shoulders in thin untidy shreds, and a small voice like a goat's. He carried with him all that was necessary for his trade, a cloth sewed on his cap, with a picture of Christ like that of Saint Veronica's, a wallet cramfull of pardons all hot from Rome, and a bagful of relics, a pillow-case that he said was our Lady's veil, a bit of the sail of Saint Peter's fishing boat, a latten cross studded with stones, and a glass containing pig's bones. With these he was wont to trick poor country parsons out of two months' salary. But in church he was a noble ecclesiast, and sang the offertory best of all, and sharpened his tongue for the sermon that should unloose purses.

CHAPTER XXIX

The Wife of Bath

The Wife of Bath is, I believe, generally admitted to be
Chaucer's masterpiece, though for my part, I think Harry
Bailly even better. There lurks but one doubt in a lay-
man's mind, is this poetry?

> A good Wif was ther of biside Bathe,
> But she was somdel deef, and that was scathe [too bad].
> Of clooth-makyng she hadde swich an haunt,
> She passed hem of Ypres and of Gaunt.
> In al the parisshe wif ne was ther noon
> That to the offrynge bifore hire sholde goon;
> And if ther dide, certeyn so wrooth was she,
> That she was out of alle charitee.

> * * * * *

> Boold was hir face, and fair, and reed of hewe.
> She was a worthy womman al hir lyve;
> Housbondes at chirche dore she hadde fyve,
> Withouten [not counting] oother compaignye in youthe . . .

Already we know that she is well in middle age, that she is
competent, and that she exacted what she deemed was due
her. We also learn that she dressed smartly and that
she had been on far pilgrimages to Jerusalem, to Rome, to
Compostella, and altogether knew a thing or two.

> In felaweshipe wel koude she laughe and carpe [talk].

[257]

But still she remains in the background a vague figure till it comes her time to tell a story. In Skeat's canon she begins her prologue immediately after the Pardoner has told his tale and exchanged scurrilities with Harry Bailly. There is no connecting link, no introduction by the Host, no "By your leave"; she starts speaking of her own accord, bold as her face indicated:

> "Experience, though noon auctoritee
> Were in this world, is right ynogh for me
> To speke of wo that is in mariage."

She asserts at once that since she was twelve years old she has had five husbands, and, quoting Scripture, she thought herself justified,

> "But wel I woot [know], expres, withoute lye,
> God bad us for to wexe and multiplye;
> That gentil text kan I wel understonde."

Solomon had more wives than one,

> "Yblessed be God that I have wedded fyve!
> Welcome the sixte, whan that evere he shal."

And she continued to call upon the Bible to support her in her advocacy of the wedded state, and depreciation of virginity,

> "For hadde God comanded maydenhede,
> Thanne hadde he dampned weddyng with the dede.
> And certes, if ther were no seed ysowe,
> Virginitee, thanne wherof sholde it growe?"

She has evidently argued her points before, for she cites Saint Paul and the Gospels very appositely, and she proceeds, warming to her argument, to where I shall not follow her, until she becomes so eloquent in her exposition that she frightens the Pardoner:

> Up stirte the Pardoner, and that anon:
> "Now, dame," quod he, "by God and by seint John!
> Ye been a noble prechour in this cas.
> I was aboute to wedde a wyf; allas!"

But she has no intention of being interrupted,

> "Abyde," quod she, "my tale is nat bigonne."

And she starts in to narrate her own experiences with her five husbands, of whom two were bad, and three were good men and rich and old. She has a great gift of animated narration, and being quite free from any Puritanical or courtly conventions, rattles on in a manner one would hardly have expected from a woman so addicted to pilgrimages to holy places. Nothing, perhaps, gives one a better idea of the ebb of the Christian religion at this epoch than this evidence that a trip to Jerusalem was a mere jaunt to see strange lands. The Wife of Bath is, I repeat, usually deemed Chaucer's masterpiece. With whom shall we compare her? The two great comic characters in modern European literature are Sir John Falstaff and Sancho Panza. It is usual to put Don Quixote as comic, but he is a hero, and heroism is the antithesis of the comic.

Falstaff and Sancho Panza, and to these I should add Alceste of *Le Misanthrope,* are dramatic creations of the greatest genius. Is the Wife of Bath entitled to be placed in their company? Read once again those rapturous scenes in the First Part of *King Henry IV,* where Jack Falstaff recounts his adventures with the men in buckram at Gadshill, and then enacts the anticipated meeting between Prince Hal and his father, the King; or in the Second Part where he visits Justice Shallow. Or, read Sancho's conversations with his master, where credulity, shrewdness and doglike devotion unite to touch deep chords of tenderness as well as to provoke laughter. The medieval mystical reverence that Sancho has for Don Quixote makes him, perhaps, the greatest of comic characters, for the ridiculous merely ripples the surface of our feelings, but when the comic is bound up with the noble, it gives to laughter a poignancy akin to pain, that purifies the soul. But Falstaff's triumphant wit is nonpareil. Alceste, also, by his constant perversity and his perverse constancy brings the comic into alliance with tragedy. Now, there is nothing tragic about the Wife of Bath, she is the embodiment of ribald wit roaming about where no angels of tragedy, of pity, ever tread. Let me make another comparison, the Nurse in *Romeo and Juliet,* although I am not sure that she does not depend somewhat upon the tragic beauty of the drama that sheds its dark and dazzling radiance over her. You remember how she first comes in, attendant upon Lady Capulet, who is speaking of Juliet as old enough to be married:

> NURSE. Even or odd, of all days in the year,
> Come Lammas-eve at night shall she be fourteen.
> Susan and she—God rest all Christian souls!—
> Were of an age: well, Susan is with God;
> She was too good for me:—but, as I said,
> On Lammas-eve at night shall she be fourteen.

And she recalls an incident when she was nursing Juliet, and her husband—"A' was a merry man"—made a broad jest, which lodged in the Nurse's mind. Her next scene is when she is sent, accompanied by Peter, upon an errand to

Romeo, and meets him and Mercutio in the street. Mercutio is very free in his greeting to her, and then departs saying "Farewell, ancient lady, farewell!"

NURSE, *to Romeo:* I pray you, sir, what saucy merchant was this? . . . Scurvy knave! I am none of his flirt-gills; I am none of his skains-mates.—*(To Peter.)* And thou must stand by, too, and suffer every knave to use me at his pleasure. . . . Now, afore God, I am so vexed, that every part about me quivers. Scurvy knave! (And then she talks to Romeo of Juliet): Well, sir; my mistress is the sweetest lady—Lord, Lord! when 'twas a little prating thing—O! there's a nobleman in town, one Paris, that would fain lay knife aboard; but she, good soul, had as lieve see a toad, a very toad, as see him. I anger her sometimes, and tell her that Paris is the properer man; but, I'll warrant you, when I say so, she looks pale as any clout in the versal world. Doth not rosemary and Romeo begin both with a letter?

ROMEO: Ay, nurse; what of that? both with an R.

NURSE: Ah! mocker! that's the dog's name; R is for the——No; I know it begins with some other letter—and she hath the prettiest sententious of it, of you and rosemary, that it would do you good to hear it.

ROMEO: Commend me to thy lady.

NURSE: Ay, a thousand times.

And when she gets back to the impatient Juliet:

JULIET: O honey nurse, what news? Hast thou met with him? Send thy man away.

* * * * *

NURSE: I am aweary; give me leave awhile. Fie, how my bones ache! What a jaunt have I had!

[261]

JULIET: I would thou hadst my bones, and I thy news.
  Nay, come, I pray thee, speak; good, good nurse, speak.
NURSE: Jesu! what haste? can you not stay awhile?
  Do you not see that I am out of breath?
              * * * * *
JULIET: Is thy news good or bad? Answer to that.
              * * * * *
NURSE: Well, you have made a simple choice; you know
  not how to choose a man. Romeo! no, not he; though
  his face be better than any man's, yet his leg excels all
  men's; and for a hand, and a foot, and a body, though
  they be not to be talked on, yet they are past compare.
  He is not the flower of courtesy, but, I'll warrant him,
  as gentle as a lamb. Go thy ways, wench; serve God.
  What, have you dined at home?

  (Poor Juliet, she can draw forth no answer.)

NURSE: Lord! how my head aches! what a head have I!

Thus having teased Juliet enough the old Nurse, who adores
her, bids her go to Friar Lawrence's cell to find a husband.
  There is also the scene wherein the Nurse, harbinger of
woe, tells Juliet how Romeo killed Tybalt. Poor old Nurse,
caught up in the toils of tragedy! And, again, when she
takes a ring from her mistress to Romeo,

      Ah, sir! ah, sir! Well, death's the end of all.

And, when she counsels Juliet to wed the County Paris,

          O! he's a lovely gentleman;
          Romeo's a dish clout to him.

  But I have quoted more than enough. The concernancy
of this digression is to support my former statement that

[262]

it is wrong to praise a great poet too much, or for excellencies that he has not got. *The Wife of Bath's Prologue* is on a single note, it presents a ribald, jocose view of marriage, of man and wife, it is gay, witty, boisterous, rampageous, but from first to last it befits an ale-house. The Wife does not run through an octave, as the Nurse does, touching the stops of tenderness, susceptibility, egotism, devotion and inconstancy—vulgarity cheek by jowl with poetry. The lesser to the greater poet, is as Hogarth to Rembrandt. And yet, the Nurse has two hundred and seventy lines, whereas the Wife of Bath has eight hundred and fifty-nine, apart from the story she tells. Shakespeare presents his character with so many more planes and contours than Chaucer does, each caused by the pressure of a separate force, inward or outward; he makes comedy and tragedy interplay, like light and shade, where wind and sun romp together in a thick forest; he explains each character by its relations to others. Besides, it may be said that *The Wife of Bath's Prologue* is out of all proportion, not only to her story, for it is more than twice as long, but also to the other intercalated links between story and story, for it is longer than all the others put together. Might it not have been more effective had it been shorter, for the better parts are admirable:

> "But, Lord Crist! whan that it remembreth me
> Upon my yowthe, and on my jolitee,
> It tikleth me aboute myn herte roote.
> Unto this day it dooth myn herte boote
> That I have had my world as in my tyme.
> But age, allas, that al wole envenyme,
> Hath me biraft my beautee and my pith;
> Lat go, farewel; the devel go therwith!"

She tells the story of her wedded life with her three good, old, rich husbands and her two bad husbands, with a frankness hardly reached by our most advanced modern novelists, but her experiences with the fifth were most dramatic. At the funeral of her fourth husband she had noticed what a handsome pair of legs Jankyn, their clerk, had, and though he was but twenty and she forty, they were married by the end of the month. Jankyn, "joly clerk" though he had been, proved an exasperating husband. Every night he would read in a "book of wicked wives," a great compilation collected from the writings of various detractors of women. He would sit before the fire and read aloud of Delilah, of Xantippe, of Phasiphae, of Clytemnestra.

> "Thanne tolde he me how oon [one] Latumyus
> Compleyned to his felawe Arrius,
> That in his gardyn growed swich a tree
> On which he seyde how that his wyves thre
> Hanged hemself [themselves] for herte despitus.
> 'O leeve [dear] brother,' quod this Arrius,
> 'Yif me a plante of thilke blissed tree,
> And in my gardyn planted shal it bee.' "

And so on, about wives who had driven nails into their husbands, who had poisoned their husbands, until Alice could bear it no longer:

> "I with my fest so took hym on the cheke
> That in oure fyr he fil bakward adoun."

Jankyn jumped up like a crazed lion and smote her such a blow that he thought he had killed her; she made full use of her advantage, and the episode ended in her complete victory:

[264]

"But atte laste, with muchel care and wo,
We fille acorded by us selven two.
He yaf me al the bridel in myn hond,
To han the governance of hous and lond,
And of his tonge, and of his hond also;
And made hym brenne his book anon right tho [then]."

And having uttered a prayer for Jankyn's soul, she is ready to tell her tale.

Commentators tell us that in *The Wife of Bath's Prologue* Chaucer has drawn upon Jean de Meung, Saint Jerome, and from some Latin work, *Epistola de non ducenda uxore,* a letter against marriage. But, as I have said, dilettanti care very little where Chaucer got his materials, and very much as to how he used them.

CHAPTER XXX

WILLIAM BLAKE'S DESCRIPTION

BLAKE made a famous picture of the Canterbury pilgrims riding on their way, and wrote the following description of them, published in Gilchrist's *Life of William Blake,* which I give in full, partly because Charles Lamb, though not blind to a mystical element, pronounced it the best criticism of the pilgrims that he knew, and also because the opinion of a man of genius is always the most interesting criticism that one can have.

"The Knight and Squire with the Squire's Yeoman lead the procession, as Chaucer has also placed them first in his prologue. The Knight is a true Hero, a good, great, and wise man; his whole-length portrait on horseback, as written by Chaucer, cannot be surpassed. He spent his life in the field, has ever been a conqueror, and is that species of character which in every age stands as the guardian of man against the oppressor. His son is like him, with the germ of perhaps greater perfection still, as he blends literature and arts with his warlike studies. Their dress and their horses are of the first rate, without ostentation, and with all the true grandeur that unaffected simplicity when in high rank always displays. The Squire's Yeoman is also a great character, a man perfectly knowing in his profession:

" 'And in his hand he bare a mighty bow.'

Chaucer describes here a mighty man, one who in war is the worthy attendant on noble heroes.

"The Prioress follows these with her female chaplain:

> " 'Another Nonne also with her had she,
> That was her Chapelaine, and Priestes three.'

This Lady is described also as of the first rank, rich and honoured. She has certain peculiarities and little delicate affectations, not unbecoming in her, being accompanied with what is truly grand and really polite; her person and face Chaucer has described with minuteness; it is very elegant, and was the beauty of our ancestors till after Elizabeth's time, when voluptuousness and folly began to be accounted beautiful.

"Her companion and her three priests were no doubt all perfectly delineated in those parts of Chaucer's work which are now lost; we ought to suppose them suitable attendants on rank and fashion.

"The Monk follows these with the Friar. The Painter has also grouped with these the Pardoner and the Sompnour and the Manciple, and has here also introduced one of the rich citizens of London;—characters likely to ride in company, all being above the common rank in life, or attendants on those who were so.

"For the Monk is described by Chaucer, as a man of the first rank in society, noble, rich, and expensively attended: he is a leader of the age, with certain humorous accompaniments in his character, that do not degrade, but render him an object of dignified mirth, but also with other accompaniments not so respectable.

"The Friar is a character also of a mixed kind:

> " 'A friar there was, a wanton and a merry';

but in his office he is said to be a 'full solemn man': eloquent, amorous, witty, and satirical; young, handsome, and

[267]

rich; he is a complete rogue; with constitutional gaiety enough to make him a master of all the pleasures of the world:

> " 'His neck was white as the fleur de lis,
> Thereto strong he was as a champioun.'

"It is necessary here to speak of Chaucer's own character, that I may set certain mistaken critics right in their conception of the humour and fun that occur on the journey. Chaucer is himself the great poetical observer of men, who in every age is born to record and eternize its acts. This he does as a master, as a father and superior, who looks down on their little follies from the Emperor to the Miller: sometimes with severity, oftener with joke and sport.

"Accordingly Chaucer has made his Monk a great tragedian, one who studied poetical art. So much so that the generous Knight is, in the compassionate dictates of his soul, compelled to cry out:

> " 'Ho,' quoth the Knyght, 'good Sir, no more of this;
> That ye have said is right ynough, I wis,
> And mokell more; for little heaviness
> Is right enough for much folk, as I guess.
> I say, for me, it is a great disease,
> Whereas men have been in wealth and ease,
> To heare of their sudden fall, alas!
> And the contrary is joy and solas.'

The Monk's definition of tragedy in the proem to his tale is worth repeating:

> " 'Tragedy is to tell a certain story,
> As olde books us maken memory,
> Of hem that stood in great prosperity,
> And be fallen out of high degree,
> Into misery, and ended wretchedly.'

[268]

"Though a man of luxury, pride, and pleasure, he is a master of art and learning, though affecting to despise it. Those who can think that the proud Huntsman and noble Housekeeper, Chaucer's Monk, is intended for a buffoon or burlesque character, know little of Chaucer.

"For the Host who follows this group, and holds the center of the cavalcade, is a first-rate character, and his jokes are no trifles; they are always, though uttered with audacity, equally free with the Lord and the Peasant; they are always substantially and weightily expressive of knowledge and experience; Henry Baillie, the keeper of the greatest Inn of the greatest City; for such was the Tabarde Inn in Southwark, near London: our Host was also a leader of the age.

"By way of illustration, I instance Shakespeare's Witches in Macbeth. Those who dress them for the stage, consider them as wretched old women, and not, as Shakespeare intended, the Goddesses of Destiny; this shows how Chaucer has been misunderstood in *his* sublime work. Shakespeare's Fairies also are the rulers of the vegetable world, and so are Chaucer's; let them be so considered, and then the poet will be understood, and not else.

"But I have omitted to speak of a very prominent character, the Pardoner, the Age's Knave, who always commands and domineers over the high and low vulgar. This man is sent in every age for a rod and scourge and for a blight, for a trial of men, to divide the classes of men; he is in the most holy sanctuary, and he is suffered by Providence for wise ends, and has also his great use, and his grand leading destiny.

"His companion, the Sompnour is also a Devil of the first magnitude, grand, terrific, rich, and honoured in the rank of which he holds the destiny. The uses to society are perhaps equal of the Devil and of the Angel; their sublimity, who can dispute?

> " 'In daunger had he at his owne gise,
> The younge girles of his diocese,
> And he knew well their counsel,' &c.

"The principal figure in the next group is the Good Parson: an Apostle, a real Messenger of Heaven, sent in every age for its light and its warmth. This man is beloved and venerated by all, and neglected by all: he serves all, and is served by none. He is, according to Christ's definition, the greatest of his age: yet he is a Poor Parson of a town. Read Chaucer's description of the Good Parson, and bow the head and knee to Him, Who, in every age, sends us such a burning and a shining light. Search, O ye rich and powerful, for these men and obey their counsel; then shall the golden age return. But alas! you will not easily distinguish him from the Friar or the Pardoner; they also are 'full solemn men,' and *their* counsel you will continue to follow.

"I have placed by his side the Sergeant-at-Lawe, who appears delighted to ride in his company, and between him and his brother the Ploughman; as I wish men of Law would always ride with them, and take their counsel, especially in all difficult points. Chaucer's Lawyer is a character of great venerableness, a Judge, and a real master of the jurisprudence of his age.

"The Doctor of Physic is in this group, and the Franklin, the voluptuous country gentleman; contrasted with the Physician, and, on his other hand, with two Citizens of London. Chaucer's characters live age after age. Every age is a Canterbury Pilgrimage; we all pass on, each sustaining one or other of these characters; nor can a child be born who is not one of these characters of Chaucer. The Doctor of Physic is described as the first of his profession: perfect, learned, completely Master and Doctor in his art. Thus the reader will observe that Chaucer makes every one of his characters perfect in his kind; every one is an Antique Statue, the image of a class, and not of an imperfect individual.

"This group also would furnish substantial matter, on which volumes might be written. The Franklin is one who keeps open table, who is the genius of eating and drinking, the Bacchus; as the Doctor of Physic is the Æsculapius, the Host is the Silenus, the Squire is the Apollo, the Miller is the Hercules, &c. Chaucer's characters are a description of the eternal Principles that exist in all ages. The Franklin is voluptuousness itself most nobly portrayed:

" 'It snewèd in his house of meat and drink.'

"The Ploughman is simplicity itself, with wisdom and strength for its stamina. Chaucer has divided the ancient character of Hercules between his Miller and his Ploughman. Benevolence is the Ploughman's great characteristic; he is thin with excessive labour, and not with old age, as some have supposed:

" 'He woulde thresh, and thereto dike and delve,
For Christe's sake, for every poore wight,
Withouten hire, if it lay in his might.'

"Visions of these eternal principles or characters of human life appear to poets in all ages; the Grecian gods were the ancient Cherubim of Phœnicia; but the Greeks, and since them the Moderns, have neglected to subdue the gods of Priam. These Gods are visions of the eternal

[271]

attributes, or divine names, which, when erected into gods, become destructive to humanity. They ought to be the servants, and not the masters, of man or of society. They ought to be made to sacrifice to Man, and not man compelled to sacrifice to them; for, when separated from man or humanity who is Jesus the Saviour, the vine of eternity? They are thieves and rebels, they are destroyers.

"The Ploughman of Chaucer is Hercules in his supreme eternal state, divested of his spectrous shadow; which is the Miller, a terrible fellow, such as exists in all times and places, for the trial of men, to astonish every neighborhood with brutal strength and courage, to get rich and powerful, to curb the pride of Man.

"The Reeve and the Manciple are two characters of the most consummate worldly wisdom. The Shipman, or Sailor, is a similar genius of Ulyssean art, but with the highest courage superadded.

"The Citizens and their Cook are each leaders of a class. Chaucer has been somehow made to number four citizens, which would make his whole company, himself included, thirty-one. But he says there were but nine-and-twenty in his company:

" 'Full nine-and-twenty in a company.'

"The Webbe, or Weaver, and the Tapiser or Tapestry Weaver, appear to me to be the same person; but this is only an opinion for full nine-and-twenty may signify one more or less. But I daresay that Chaucer wrote 'A Webbe Dyer,' that is a Cloth Dyer:

" 'Webbe Dyer and a Tapiser.'

[272]

"The Merchant cannot be one of the Three Citizens, as his dress is different, and his character is more marked, whereas Chaucer says of his rich citizens:

"'All were yclothèd in one liverie.'

"The Characters of Women Chaucer has divided into two classes, the Lady Prioress and the Wife of Bath. Are not these leaders of the ages of men? The Lady Prioress in some ages predominates, and in some the Wife of Bath, in whose character Chaucer has been equally minute and exact; because she is also a scourge and a blight. I shall say no more of her, nor expose what Chaucer has left hidden; let the young reader study what he has said of her; it is useful as a scarecrow. There are of such characters born too many for the peace of the world.

"I come at length to the Clerk of Oxenford. This character varies from that of Chaucer, as the contemplative philosopher varies from the poetical genius. There are always these two classes of learned sages, the poetical and the philosophical. The Painter has put them side by side, as if the youthful clerk had put himself under the tuition of the mature poet. Let the Philosopher always be the servant and scholar of Inspiration, and all will be happy."

CHAPTER XXXI

The Tales

On April seventeenth, the day after the meeting you remember, the Host, like Chantecleer, had waked the Pilgrims and gathered them together, and they had ridden forth to Saint-Thomas-a-Waterin, where the Host reined in, and said that the company should draw lots to see who was to tell the first tale. The lot fell to the Knight. He assented at once, and as they rode along he told his tale of Palamon and Arcite. It seems that Chaucer had written this poem before this, for it is referred to in *The Prologue to the Legend of Good Women,* but whether in our present form or not, nobody knows, and it makes no matter. The story is this:

Theseus, the Duke of Athens, with whom we are acquainted in *A Midsummer-Night's Dream*, having conquered the Amazons and married Hippolyte, returns to Athens with her and her young sister, Emily. Shortly before reaching the town, a company of mourning ladies kneel in his way and beseech his help. They are from Thebes. Their husbands have been killed in battle there, but the tyrannical Creon, Lord of Thebes, will not allow their bodies to be buried or burned, but has left them to the dogs. Theseus at once marched on Thebes, slew Creon, and gave the bodies of the dead husbands to their wailing widows for burial. In the battle necessary to accomplish this, many warriors had been killed, and pillagers stripping the harness from the dead, found two young knights, Palamon and Arcite, still half alive, and recognized them as sons of sisters and of the

blood royal. They are made captive, and Theseus sends
them to Athens for perpetual imprisonment. The two
young men are locked in a tower, and years pass,

> Til it fil ones, in a morwe of May,
> That Emelye, that fairer was to sene
> Than is the lylie upon his stalke grene,
> And fressher than the May with floures newe—
> For with the rose colour stroof hire hewe,
> I noot which was the fyner of hem two—

walks abroad in the garden before it was daylight, "for
May wole have no slogardie a-nyght," and gathered roses,
and sang as the angels sing. You guess the plot. Palamon,
pacing his prison cell, sees her

> . . . and cride, "A!"
> As though he stongen were unto the herte.

Arcite, startled by his cry, starts up and asks what ails him.
Palamon says that his cry was caused by the beauty of a
lady, woman or goddess, Venus surely, who was walking in
the garden. Arcite looks, and he is hurt as much as Palamon. Palamon says he loved first, and that Arcite is a
traitor to him. Arcite replies that Palamon did not know
whether the lady was a woman or a goddess, that his is an
"affeccioun of hoolynesse, and myn is love, as to a creature." So they strove together.

It happened that a friend of Theseus, Duke Perithous,
came, and begged him to let Arcite go free. Theseus grants
the boon, upon condition that if Arcite shall be found in
Athenian land he shall surely lose his head. So, the two
young men are separated now, one in prison but with a
sight of Emily, the other at large and far away.

[275]

A year or two passed. Then Arcite, unable to bear longer absence from Emily, disguised as a poor laborer, and also disfigured by love's woe, risks his neck, and goes to Athens and gets work of hewing wood and drawing water at the palace, where his merits are discovered and he becomes a squire. Seven years are now gone by, and Palamon breaks loose from prison, hides in a grove where he intends to stay until he shall find a means to escape to Thebes. At this juncture Arcite, a prosperous squire, but unrecognized, rides out from town:

> The bisy larke, messager of day,
> Salueth in hir song the morwe gray,
> And firy Phebus riseth up so bright
> That al the orient laugheth of the light,
> And with his stremes dryeth in the greves [groves]
> The silver dropes, hangynge on the leves.

It is a beautiful May day, and Arcite means to gather a garland. He roams about and sings, and then

> Into a studie he fil sodeynly,
> As doon thise loveres in hir [their] queynte geres [ways],
> Now in the crope, now doun in the breres,
> Now up, now doun, as boket in a welle.

Of course, Palamon sees him, and it is agreed between them that Arcite shall bring weapons for both the next day and one shall die. But it chances that, while they are fighting, Theseus, who is going a-hunting, comes upon them and after a first hasty purpose to have them pay the punishment incurred, decides that each shall bring a hundred knights to the lists, and that the winner shall have Emily. There is

[276]

great preparation, and among other things, the three persons mainly interested pray to the three divinities whose statues are set up in the lists. Palamon prays to Venus, asking that he may have his beloved, and her statue shook as if she granted what he asked. Arcite prays to Mars for victory, and the rings of the doors clattered. Emily prays to Diana that she may live and die a maid, but Diana appears and says that she must marry one of the two lovers. The great tournament takes place; Palamon in spite of prodigies of valor is dragged out of the lists and Arcite wins the victory, but by divine intervention his horse leaps for fear of an apparition, and Arcite is thrown and hurt fatally. The wounded knight bids good-bye:

> "Allas, the deeth! allas, myn Emelye!
> Allas, departynge of oure compaignye!
> Allas, myn hertes queene! allas, my wyf!
> Myn hertes lady, endere of my lyf!
> What is this world? what asketh men to have?
> Now with his love, now in his colde grave
> Allone, withouten any compaignye.
> Fare wel, my sweete foo, myn Emelye!
> And softe taak me in your armes tweye,
> For love of God, and herkneth what I seye."

Then he talks to her of Palamon,

> "And if that evere ye shul ben [be] a wyf,
> Foryet nat Palamon, the gentil man."

And so he died and Palamon wedded Emily.

It is a noble poem, admirably told, in sweet smooth verse. The personages are not very human, rather they are like figures in early Flemish tapestry, lovely in design and color, set against a background of love, of war, of gardens and marvelous temples. The poem, as I have said, was written before Chaucer had the idea of *The Canterbury Tales* in his mind. The commentators assign the composition of it to the years, 1382 to 1385, near the time when Chaucer was writing *Troilus and Criseyde*. Like that, it is taken from Boccaccio. Chaucer follows the plot of the *Teseide* (a poem about Theseus) with pious steps, he omits a great deal, and shapes his material to suit himself, but always with deference to the original. As I say, dilettanti do not care much about the model, the source, the material, they concern themselves with the work of art as the artist presents it to them. Chaucer is certainly still in the Italianate period, but there are touches here and there to indicate in what direction his muse must travel in order to achieve his masterpiece, as for instance, the talk of the populace just before the tournament begins:

The paleys ful of peples up and doun,
Heere thre, ther ten, holdynge hir [their] questioun,
Dyvynynge of thise Theban Knyghtes two.
Somme seyden thus, somme seyde "it shal be so";
Somme helden with hym with the blake berd,
Somme with the balled, some with the thikke herd [haired];
Somme sayde he looked grymme, and he wolde fighte;
"He hath a sparth [ax] of twenty pound of wighte."

After the Knight had finished, everybody said his was a noble story; and Harry Bailly, delighted with the success of his program, cried out; "This gooth aright," and asked the Monk, perhaps out of deference to his gentility, to tell the next story, "to quite with the Knyghtes tale." It was still well before nine o'clock, but the Miller had drunk too much ale and began in a terrific voice to swear and say that

[278]

he could tell a noble tale and "quite the Knyghtes tale." The Host bids him wait, but the Miller insisted,

> "By Goddes soul [quod he], that wol nat I,"

and said that if he misspeaks, they must put the blame on the Southwark ale, and that he will tell a story of a carpenter and his wife, and of a clerk who tricked the husband. The choleric Reeve, who you remember was a carpenter by trade, suspected what was coming and cried out,

> . . . "Stynt thy clappe!
> Lat be thy lewed dronken harlotrye [ribaldry]."

The Miller answers him with drunken levity,

> "Leve [dear] brother, Osewold,
> Who hath no wyf, he is no cokewold.
> But I sey nat therfore that thou are oon [one];
> Ther been ful goode wyves many oon,
> * * * * *
> Why artow [art thou] angry with my tale now?"

He's not so very drunk; that final *now* indicates a certain clearness of wit. And so he told "his churle's tale," Chaucer repeats his warning to the strait-laced:

> M'athynketh that I shal reherce it heere.
> And therfore every gentil wight I preye,
> For Goddes love, demeth nat that I seye
> Of yvel entente, but for I moot reherce
> Hir tales alle, be they bettre or werse,
> Or elles falsen som of my mateere.
> And therfore, whoso list it nat yheere,
> Turne over the leef . . .
> * * * * *

Blameth [blame] nat me . . .
The Millere is a cherl, ye knowe wel this;
So was the Reve, and othere manye mo,
And harlotrie [ribaldry] they tolden bothe two.

The reader at least is warned; and to tell the truth this medieval humor, that animates the fabliaux and was, I suppose, the stuff that furnished forth the yarns that Chaucer heard at tavern and ale-house when he journeyed through the country, is tedious and distasteful enough. It would take many a mug of good pale ale to wash it down now. But there are old men who, not having reread these stories for fifty years, associate them with their own boyhood, with rum-and-ginger, with Pontet Canet, Veuve Clicquot and laughter, with the pruriency of inconsiderate youth, and all the boisterous jollity of the young animal, and say, mixing all their golden memories in inextricable confusion, "What delightful tales! What wit! What humor!" "No, my dear fellow, Mr. Justice Shallow,—no, my good Slender!" The Miller's tale, in spite of Chaucer's skill as a raconteur, is, in spite of its wit, as muddy as ditch water, and very like ditch water in oderiferousness. Let us take the Miller's advice and turn over leaf.

The company received the tale diversely; "the moore part" laughed. The others, I presume the ladies, the Knight, and perhaps the Monk, seem to have been politely silent; they knew that there were churls in their company and no one made a fuss. Osewold the Reve, however, became angry because a carpenter was the butt of the story, and started up:

". . . ful wel koud I yow quite
With bleryng of a proud millere's ye· [eye],
If that me liste to speke of ribaudye.
But ik [I] am old . . ."

[280]

And then he forgets the company and wanders off moralizing about old age, and becomes admirable sententious,

"Gras tyme is doon [done], my fodder is now forage;"

the fresh green grass is dry in the hayloft, the only sins left to old men are boasting, lying, anger and covetousness; and then he proceeds,

> ". . . whan I was bore, anon
> Deeth drough the tappe of lyf and leet it gon [run];
> And ever sithe hath so the tappe yronne
> Til that almoost al empty is the tonne.
> The streem of lyf now droppeth on the chymbe [the rim
>   of a barrel]."

You begin to suspect that the Reeve has frequented the camp-meetings of Wycliffe's poor preachers; at least the Host does, and shouts out, lordly as a king,

> . . . "What amounteth al this wit?
> What shul we speke alday of hooly writ?
> The devel made a reve for to preche . . ."

and bids him get to his story. And so the Reeve, protesting he has a right to shove back force with force, begins:

> "This dronke Millere hath ytoold us heer
> How that bigyled was a carpenteer,
> Paraventure in scorn, for I am oon.
> And, by youre leve, I shal hym quite anoon;
> Right in his cherles termes wol I speke.
> I pray to God his nekke mote [might] to-breke;
> He kan wel in myn eye seen a stalke,
> But in his owene he kan nat seen a balke [beam]."

Then, having eased his spleen, he gets to his tale;

> At Trumpyngtoun, nat fer fro Cantebrigge,
> There gooth a brook, and over that a brigge,
> Upon the whiche brook ther stant a melle [mill].

Of course, at mention of a mill, the company knew at once that the Reeve would take his revenge up to the hilt. The story belongs to the same genus as the last, but to my mind it is better. The Reeve draws a choice picture of a Miller,

> As any pecok he was proud and gay,

and of his wife, who being a parson's daughter was socially his superior,

> And she was proud, and peert as is a pye.

The Miller cheats two Cambridge students, John and Alan, north country lads, who take revenge in the best fabliaux manner. If you think you should read one of these churlish stories, I advise this.

How the others received this story, Chaucer does not say, but the Cook, Roger Hodge of Ware, was so delighted with it that for joy he clapped the Reeve on the back, and offers to tell of a trick played in his town. Harry Bailly rallies him on what he sells in his cook shop, and so on, adding that he is only joking. The Cook says that they shall be quits before they part, and starts upon a tale of an idle apprentice who was on his way to the dogs, but he broke off and the tale remains a brief fragment.

CHAPTER XXXII

THE TALES (Continued)

THE Sergeant at Law came next. It is now the eighteenth of April, and ten o'clock in the morning. The plot of the Sergeant's story is taken from the poem of an English Dominican monk, written in French, some sixty years before. It is this:

The Emperor of Rome sent his daughter Constance (Custance) to Syria to marry the Soldan, who is ready to turn Christian for her sake. The Soldan's mother can not endure this apostasy; she poisons her son, and sends Constance adrift in a rudderless boat. The voyage lasts for years, but Constance arrives safely in Northumberland, thanks to God's care, and after various vicissitudes marries King Alla, who becomes a Christian, and they have a child. The King's mother is as staunch in her opinion as the Soudan's mother in hers, and, by wicked wiles, causes Constance to be cast adrift a second time. Constance takes her baby with her. Marvels happen. She gets back to Rome, and after long years is restored to both father and husband.

It is not a plot that would hold a vagabond attention today; and so, perhaps, even the casual reader should dip into Saintsbury, or some other scholar, who writes about pre-Chaucerian literature, in order to understand, without going so far as to take the books down from their shelves, why a story such as this should really be interesting to Chaucer's contemporaries. It is written in what is called rhyme-royal, stanzas of seven lines, rhyming a b a b b c c, with ten syllables or eleven, and five beats. As the other tales were in the heroic couplet, the change of meter makes a pleasant variety to the ear.

The Shipman comes next in Skeat's canon. You remember that the Shipman pushed the Parson aside in his fear lest he should be obliged to listen to a sermon. His story, which concerns a wife and a monk, seems to me one of the less interesting. If the fo'c'sle of the *Magdelene* heard no better yarns than that, I marvel that so many stout fellows went to sea. The genial Host, however, praised it; any jest at a monk's expense had its flavor especially a jest at a smartly dressed, sporting monk, such as they had in their company. But he felt that after it something quite different would be acceptable, so he called upon Madame Eglantine,

> As curteisly as it had been a mayde,
> "My lady Prioresse, by youre leve . . ."

And the Prioress tells the sweet story of a little Christian boy, who had learned to sing *O Alma Redemptoris,* and for that was by cruel Jews murdered, and by a miracle continued to sing after death.

She apostrophizes him thus:

> O martir, sowded to virginitee,
> Now maystow syngen, folwynge evere in oon [always]
> The white Lamb celestial—quod she—
> Of which the grete evaungelist, Seint John,
> In Pathmos wroot, which seith that they that goon
> Biforn this Lamb, and synge a song al newe,
> That nevere, flesshly, wommen they ne knewe.

You will remember Matthew Arnold's criticism of Chaucer in his essay, *The Study of Poetry:* "I feel disposed [he

says] to say that a single line is enough to show the charm
of Chaucer's verse; that merely one line like this,

'O martyr souded in virginitee!'

has a virtue of manner and movement such as we shall not
find in all the verse of romance-poetry. . . . Virtue such
as we shall not find, perhaps, in all English poetry, outside
the poets whom I have named as the special inheritors of
Chaucer's tradition—Spenser, Shakespeare, Milton, Keats."
    That is all very well. A rosebush may be beautiful, and
one bud may convey a sense of its beauty, and sometimes
one petal may convey the color and fragrance of a rose, and
the analogy is often true as to a single line of poetry; but
this particular line does not depend so much upon its "liquid
diction"—that is the quality Arnold is praising—as for the
pathos of the innocent child cut off before love opens its
wings. Take this other verse, from *The Man of Law's Tale*,
and you will find the same liquid diction:

O messager, fulfild of dronkenesse,

but these words, though heralding tragedy, merely call up
a grotesque image to the mind. Liquid diction is but a ve-
hicle of thought, and in praising poetry, however much the
melody of verse may unlock our hearts, we must remember
that the essence of great poetry lies in the significance of its
thought, of what we call, a little rhetorically, its spiritual
truth, that is, its intellectual content regarded as sacred because of inherent truth or beauty.
    I go back to the pilgrims:

Whan seyd was al this miracle, every man
As sobre was, that wonder was to se,

[285]

Til that oure hooste japen [jest] tho [then] bigan,
And thanne at erst he looked upon me,
And seyde thus, "What man artow?" quod he;
"Thou lookest as thou woldest fynde an hare,
For evere upon the ground I se thee stare.

"Approche neer, and looke up murily.
Now war [room] yow, sires, and lat this man have place!
He in the waast is shape as wel as I;
This were a popet in an arm t'enbrace
For any womman, smal and fair of face.
He semeth elvyssh by his contenaunce,
For unto no wight dooth he daliaunce."

As this is the only account, so far as I know, of Chaucer's appearance made in his lifetime, I will interpolate here a description of a picture painted by the poet Hoccleve on a manuscript. It was written by one Thomas Hearne (in his diary April 28, 1711) and is as follows: "Chaucer was a Man of an even Stature, neither too high nor too low, his Complection sanguine, His Face fleshie, but pale, his Forehead broad, but comly smooth and even. His eyes rather little than great, cast most part downward, with a grave Aspect, His Lipps plump and ruddy and both of an equal thickness, the hair on the upper being thin and sort of a wheat Colour, on his chin 2 thin forked Tuffs. His Cheeks of like coller with the rest of her Face being either shaved or wanting Hair. All which considered together with his Witt and Education in Ye Cort, and his Favour among Great Ladys one of whose Women he married: it was his Modesty made him speak of his Unlikeliness to be a Lover."

I go back to the Tales.
The Host continues:

[286]

"Sey now somwhat, syn oother folk han sayd;
Telle us a tale of myrthe, and that anon."
"Hooste," quod I, "ne beth [be] nat yvele apayd,
For oother tale certes kan I noon,
But of a rym I lerned longe agoon."
"Ye [verily], that is good," quod he; "now shul we heere
Som deyntee thyng, me thynketh by his cheere [look]."

Chaucer then recites the *Tale of Sir Thopas,* which is a
burlesque on popular rhymed romance. It is a sort of ballad, and the commentators say that it is a very clever and
amusing imitation, and incidentally shows his mastery of
meter for he has half a dozen different arrangements of
verse in the several stanzas. But the novice in Chaucerian
literature will agree with Harry Bailly,

"Namoore of this, for Goddes dignitee,"
Quod our Hooste, . . .

* * * * *

"Myne eres aken [ache] of thy drasty [rotten] speche."

So Chaucer instead tells a tale in prose, *The Tale of Melibee.* But this tale is far worse; it is medieval and tedious
beyond the measure of any but a genius. It occupies sixty
pages in Tyrwhitt's edition. A young man, Melibeus, rich
and mighty, has a wife, Prudence, and a daughter, Sophie.
One day his foes burst into his house and wounded his
daughter in her feet, her hands, her ears, her nose and her
mouth. The whole tale is taken up by discourses by Dame
Prudence, advising her husband not to take a violent revenge. Melibeus, persuaded by his wife's good sense, for-
gave his enemies.

Commentators have nothing good to say for the story.

[287]

It is literally unreadable. But Harry Bailly sees an element
in it that he can commend:

> ... "As I am feithful man,
> And by that precious corpus Madrian [St. Mathurin],
> I hadde levere than a barel ale
> That Goodelief, my wyf, hadde herd this tale!
> For she nys no thyng of swich pacience
> As was this Melibeus wyf Prudence."

And then he tells something of Mrs. Bailly's disposition.
Having finished, he turns to the Monk in his rough, jovial
way, and rallies him a little indelicately upon his celibate
condition. "This worthy Monk took it in all patience,"
which was very good of him, for Bailly had certainly
pushed his genial familiarity to the border of rudeness, and
starts off upon his tale, prefacing that it will deal with
personages who have fallen from high prosperity into misery. He then narrates the ill fortunes of Lucifer, Adam,
Samson, Hercules, Nebuchadnezzar, Belshazzer, Zenobia,
Peter the Cruel of Spain, Peter of Cyprus, Bernabò Visconti, Ugolino, Nero, Holofernes, King Antiochus, Alexander the Great, Julius Cæsar and Crœsus. I have spoken
of the most celebrated episode, that of Ugolino; as to the
rest, I leave the Knight to speak,

> "Hoo!" quod the Knyght, "good sire, namoore of this!"

He does not like to hear of misfortunes, but rather of rising from low estate to high prosperity. Thus encouraged
the Host heartily agrees:

> "Ye," quod our Hooste, "by seint Poules [Paul's] belle!
> Ye seye right sooth; this Monk he clappeth lowde.

* * * * *

"Sire Monk, namoore of this, so God yow blesse!
Youre tale anoyeth al this compaignye.
Swich talkyng is nat worth a boterflye . . .

* * * * *

For sikerly, nere clynkyng of youre belles,
That on youre bridel hange on every syde,
By hevene kyng, that for us alle dyde,
I sholde er this han fallen doun for sleep."

He then calls on the Nun's Priest, who tells the tale of
Chauntecleer and Pertelote, the cock and the hen, and of
the col-fox full of sly iniquity, with the joyful ending of the
glorious hullabaloo after the fox and the rescue of Chauntecleer. The characters of Chauntecleer and of Dame Pertelote are far better drawn than those of Palamon, Arcite and
Emily, and the whole story is gay as a lark, and dances as
it goes.

The Host compliments the Priest on his merry tale, and
chaffs him in very much the same liberal, raffish, fashion as
he had done to the Monk, and calls on the next man. According to Skeat's canon, the next man is the Physician;
the brief prologue given by Tyrwhitt being omitted as spuri-
ous. The tale is the classical story of Virginius and his
daughter and Appius Claudius, originally told by Livy, very
much changed by the time Jean de Meung retold it in the
Roman de la Rose, and still different in Chaucer's hands.
Being tragic it seems to find its proper place after a comic
tale. The Host, as usual, plays the chorus; he comments
on the story, blames the villains in it, prays God to keep the
Physician in sound health, jollies him, and then turning to
the Pardoner, says:

"Thou beel amy, thou Pardoner . . .
Telle us som myrthe or japes [jokes] right anon."

[289]

The *beel amy* says that he must first have something to eat and drink. The pilgrims, at least the "gentils" among them, cry out for a moral story, that will teach them something, and no ribaldry. But the Pardoner must have drunk too many draughts of "corny ale," for he starts off by describing his practise as a pardoner, which he never would have done had he been quite sober, and then he proceeds to tell the story of the three Robbers who meet Death. It is a very ancient plot, and very good, and, I think, makes the best story in the book. Old plots that come down through many generations are usually the best. The adventitious, the irrelevant, the local, are rubbed away by multitudinous criticisms and disapprovals, and the essential is left, shaped, molded and polished, until it becomes a tale of primary human interest. This plot, scholars have traced back to India.

When the Pardoner has finished his tale, he continues to talk, mindful of his trade, asking the others to buy his pardons, and requests the Host to step forward and kiss his holy relics. To this offer Harry Bailly responds in a jocose but unseemly manner, and angers the Pardoner. The Pardoner's anger in turn irritates Bailly, who says

"Now . . . I wol no lenger pleye
With thee, ne with noon oother angry man."

The worthy Knight interposes, and persuades them to make it up. Then comes *The Wife of Bath's Tale*. As I have said, I follow Skeat's order, though others disagree, for the manuscripts leave the sequence undetermined; probably Chaucer had not come to a final decision himself. As to *The Wife of Bath's Tale*, if one is in the critical spirit one asks oneself if this is a tale that she, being what she is, would be likely to tell.

It begins with fairies, and then goes on in a style that is
Chaucer's own:

> I speke of manye hundred yeres ago.
> But now kan no man se none elves mo,
> For now the grete charitee and prayeres
> Of lymytours and othere hooly freres,
> That serchen every lond and every streem,
> As thikke as motes in the sonne-beem,
> Blessynge halles, chambres, kichenes, boures,
> Citees, burghes, castels, hye toures,
> Thropes, bernes, shipnes, dayeryes—
> This maketh that ther been no fayeryes.
> For ther [where] as wont to walken was an elf,
> Ther walketh now the lymytour hymself
> In undermeles [afternoons] and in morwenynges,
> And seyth his matyns and his hooly thynges
> As he gooth in his lymytacioun.
> Wommen may go now saufly up and doun
> In every bussh and under every tree;
> There is noon oother incubus but he,
> And he ne wol doon hem but dishonour.

After this gibe at the expense of the Friar, who you remember is a lymytour, the Wife proceeds to her tale: A
knight has committed a trespass for which under the law
he must die, but the King leaves the matter to his Queen
and she gives the knight a chance for his life. If he can tell

> What thyng it is that wommen moost desiren . . .

he shall be pardoned, and a twelvemonth is given him to
discover the answer. The knight travels about inquiring, but
no two people agree as to the right answer, one says this,
one that, and the poor knight is still wholly at a loss at the

[291]

end of his twelvemonth. Then he chances to meet a most
singularly repellent woman,

> A fouler wight ther may no man devyse.

This horrid woman asks him what is the matter; he tells
her and she says that, if he will promise to do what she
asks, she will tell him. He pledges his word and she whis-
pers in his ear. So he goes back to the Queen, who is sitting as judge, attended by maidens, wives, and widows, all
come to hear his answer.

> "My lige lady, generally," quod he,
> "Wommen desiren have sovereynetee
> As wel over hir housbond as hir love,
> And for to been in maistrie hym above.
> This is youre mooste desir . . ."

All the women present agree that he has answered right, and
then the foul woman starts forth and demands that he
should marry her. So he does; but she is so loathly and so
old that he wishes his heart would break. She, with no
great pertinence, describes, in the words I have already
quoted, the essentials of a gentleman, and then bids him
choose whether he had rather have her foul and old and a
true humble wife, or young and fair and take his chances.
He leaves the decision to her,

> "I put me in youre wise governance,"

* * * * *

> "Thanne have I gete of yow maistrie," quod she,

and bids him kiss her, for she will become both fair and

[292]

good, and behold she does become both young and beautiful, and his heart is bathed in bliss.

> And she obeyed hym in every thyng
> That myghte doon hym plesance or likyng.
> And thus they lyve unto hir lyves ende
> In parfit joye . . .

And then the Wife terminates with a few words in her own
character; nevertheless, the story itself is hardly in keeping
with what we know of her.

Commentators find that the central idea of the plot goes
way back and has wandered into many literatures, Icelandic,
Gaelic, Turkish, Sanscrit and Kaffir; the proof to which
the honest Knight is put and the reward of his submissive
loyalty, please all the world. The Friar applauds with the
rest of us:

> "Dame . . .
> Ye han seyd muche thyng right wel . . ."

but he adds that he thinks merry stories more suitable for
the pilgrimage; and then, to gratify his displeasure with
the Summoner, he tells a tale at the expense of Summoners.
It is a tale of *ribaudye,* and tedious as those horse-play medieval stories usually are. However, the Friar is completely
successful in his purpose to anger the Summoner, who, as
the phrase goes, was mad as hops, and proceeds to tell his
tale and give the Friar as good as he gave. This, too, is
another of those stable-boy stories, impossible except to ex-
treme youth, and yet there are admirable Chaucerian lines in
it.

Then the Clerk of Oxenford follows with the tale of
Patient Grissel. After him comes the Merchant, who tells

another story of ribaldry, concerning old January and his young wife *fresshe* May. There is much wit to flavor the indecency, but the plot is suited to Hottentots. The infirmities of our animal nature were an endless treasure-house of mirth to the Middle Ages; one thinks how appalling life must have been at Warwick Castle or Château Gaillard, or among the bourgeoisie of Rouen or Nottingham, in order to render such stories popular. But the Host, who is tender on the subject of matrimony, is full of interest, and rambles off again to his own personal matrimonial miseries. He then calls on the Squire, who tells the unfinished story to which Milton refers in the oft-quoted words:

"Or call up him that left half told
The story of Cambuscan bold,
Of Camball, and of Algarsife,
And who had Canace to wife,
That own'd the vertuous Ring and Glass,
And of the wondrous Hors of Brass,
On which the Tartar King did ride; . . ."

It is a tale of magic and romance, suited to this charming young Englishman. The Franklin is pleased, and praises the Squire's wit, saying that he is more eloquent than any of them, and wishes that his own son had such good sense and intelligence, and would incline to "lerne gentillesse [to be a gentleman] aright"

"Straw for youre gentillesse!" quod oure Hoost . . .

who, one suspects, may have harbored some sympathy for Wat Tyler's followers, and bade the Franklin tell his tale without more words. This tale has a plot as impossible as that of Patient Grissel. A young man of Brittany falls in love with a gentleman's wife, and plagues her so much that she promises to yield, if he will remove all the rocks along the coast from the mouth of the Gironde to that of the Seine. A necromancer does the impossible. The wife in despair tells her husband, who says that she must be true to her word:

Trouthe is the hyeste thyng that man may kepe,

but the young lover is magnanimous and all turns out well. One of Boccaccio's stories has the same plot, but the setting is wholly different. As always, in Chaucer's stories, whether courtly or churlish, there are some sweet pathetic verses. Here for instance, this young man, a former student at the University of Orléans, goes back and meets a resident scholar:

This Briton clerk hym asked of felawes
The whiche that he had knowe in olde dawes;
And he answerede hym that they dede were,
For which he weep ful ofte many a teere.

After this the Second Nun tells her pious tale of Saint Cecilia and Christian martyrdom in pagan times, and no sooner had she finished than the party is joined by a Canon and his Yeoman, who have ridden hard to overtake them. It is now April twentieth, and they are at Boughton-under-Blean, near Canterbury. The Yeoman confides to the Host that his master is a wonderful man, able to pave the road with gold. The Master, overhearing his man reveal such secrets, slinks away; and then the Yeoman tells a tale of alchemy. The tale is more interesting to students of medieval science than to us dilettanti; but it is so full of indignation that it is fair to surmise that Chaucer had somehow come into contact with alchemists, to the detriment of himself, or of some friend.

The pilgrims have now come very near Canterbury.

> Woot ye nat where ther stant [stands] a litel toun
> Which that ycleped is Bobbe-up-and-doun,
> Under the Blee, in Caunterbury weye?

Wherever that is, the Cook was so tipsy that he fell off his horse, and another tale from him was impossible. The Manciple took his place, and told a story of mild ribaudye. It is of slender interest, but Chaucer is always better than his matter. To illustrate his thesis that human nature will not be constrained, he cites the cat:

> Lat take a cat, and fostre hym wel with milk
> And tendre flessh, and make his couche of silk,
> And lat hym see a mous go by the wal,
> Anon he weyveth [forsakes] milk and flessh and al,
> And every deyntee that is in that hous,
> Swich appetit hath he to ete a mous.

But the afternoon sun is hastening on. The commentators here have a great deal of trouble. Chaucer, it seems, never put the stories in their final order. Two, the Cook's and the Squire's, were never finished; and the plan for each pilgrim to tell two stories on the journey to Canterbury and two more on the journey back, was dropped. But the poet, deterred for some unknown reason from carrying out his original scheme for the whole series of tales, puts in an unexpected ending, or at least what he meant perhaps to be a temporary ending. The dear and well beloved Parson tells his tale, and brings the series as we have it to a conclusion, by preaching a sermon in prose that in Tyrwhitt's edition fills one hundred and ten pages. God bless us all! It is quite as medieval in its way as the churls' stories. I have not read very much of it; I presume that none but scholars ever read either *Melibee* or the beloved *Parson's Tale* all through.

CHAPTER XXXIII

CLERK OF THE WORKS

COMMENTATORS, as well as you and I, find several of the tales inferior, much inferior, to the others—*Melibee,* that intolerable homily in the form of a story delivered by Prudence to an unwise husband, the tales told by the Physician and the Manciple, and the Poor Parson's wearisome discourse. Nobody but a serious student would or should read them. To excuse Chaucer, the commentators surmise that these stories were written while he was very busy with a new public office; the theory is plausible enough.

On July 12, 1389, Chaucer was appointed clerk of the King's works. The appointment concerned Westminster, the Tower of London, the castle of Berkhampstead, the manors of Kennington, Eltham, Clarendon, Shene, Byfleet, Chiltern Langley, and Feckenham, with the park-lodge of Hathebergh in the New Forest, and the royal mews near Charing Cross. The office must have kept him busy; there was hiring of laborers, impressing (like a crimp) the unwilling, buying materials, inspecting, renewing, repairing, in short doing all sorts of things. Apparently kitchen utensils came under his charge—bowls, trays, ladles, frying-pans, andirons, and—what is more interesting, for one would like to connect Chaucer's realism with the same new spirit in other arts—bronze and stone statues, some of them statues of kings, and so forth. The castle of Berkhampstead, where the Black Prince had been used to stay, lies twenty-eight miles northwest of London, Eltham seven miles to the southeast, Clarendon, sixty or seventy west, Byfleet twenty-five miles southwest, Chiltern Langley forty miles west, and, while Shene is near Richmond, the New Forest is a hundred miles away, or more. How far he rode in a day, one can only guess. The Canterbury pilgrims riding leisurely traversed about fifteen miles a day, and though the Clerk of the King's Works probably made better progress than that, not very much better when, as commonly happened, the roads were bad. Such a life would explain inferior work. If Chaucer had been riding all day, and usually, it being England, riding in the rain, his horse's hoofs in mud up to the fetlocks, and found himself at the end of weary afternoon in a smoky hostelry, and obliged to dine with fellows like Osewald the Reeve, Roger Hodge, the Cook, with millers and summoners, and no choice but to listen to their "harlotry" tales and to put up with their bad manners, it is excusable that he turned for relief to transposing *Le Livre de Melibée et de Dame Prudence* into his tale of Melibeus, or Dominican sermons into the Parson's prolixity. No doubt he had much to think of besides poetry—endless trouble with careless workmen, contrary counsels as to what guild he should apply to for the reparation of damaged statues, or what would be the best andirons for the King's bedchamber in Eltham Palace, and so on.

In addition to this work, a little later, he was charged with repairs upon Saint George's Chapel, at Windsor, and also with building a scaffolding for the spectators at a tournament at Smithfield. Here for a moment his career and pictured history meet. It is recorded that on the tenth, eleventh and twelfth of October of this year the King held a great jousting in Smithfield, to which many knights from France, Germany, Holland and other foreign countries came; and that at these jousts the King's badge of the White Hart with golden chains and crowns was given for the first time. This was his personal badge. There is at Wilton House a picture of him as a youth, painted perhaps in honor of his birthday, for he was born on Twelfth Night, the feast of the Epiphany, offering his Kingdom to the Virgin. He is depicted, on his knees, one of three Kings, while two other Kings, Saint Edward the Confessor, and Saint Edmund, stand behind him. The badge of the White Hart hangs about his neck on a chain, and similar badges are fastened to the garments of the eleven angels that attend the Virgin.

Froissart gives a long account of these tournaments held at Smithfield. The days set for it were Sunday and following days. There were great preparations. "You would have seen [he says] on the ensuing morning, Monday, squires and varlets busily employed in different parts of London, furbishing armor and horses for their masters who were to engage in the jousts." The like scene is told in *The Knight's Tale:*

> And on the morwe, whan that day gan sprynge,
> Of hors and harneys, noyse and claterynge
> Ther was in hostelryes al aboute;
> And to the paleys rood ther many a route
> Of lordes upon steedes and palfreys.
> Ther maystow seen devisynge of harneys
> So unkouth and so riche, and wroght so weel
> Of goldsmythrye, of browdynge, and of steel;
> The sheeldes brighte, testeres, and trappures,
> Gold-hewen helmes, hauberkes, cote-armures,
> Lordes in parementz on hir [their] courseres,
> Knyghtes of retenue, and eek squieres
> Nailynge the speres, and helmes bokelynge;
> Giggynge of sheeldes, with layneres [straps] lacynge
> (There as nede is they weren no thyng ydel);
> The fomy steedes on the golden brydel
> Gnawynge, and faste the armurers also

[300]

With fyle and hamer, prikynge to and fro;
Yeman on foote, and communes many oon
With shorte staves, thikke as they may goon.

You can see the populace, the whole town taking a holiday, pressing their noses against the barricades, and pushing one another to get a glimpse of their favorite champions all in panoply:

Pypes, trompes, nakers, clariounes,
That in the bataille blowen blody sounes;
The paleys ful of peples up and doun,
Heere thre, ther ten, holdynge hir [their] questioun.

On that Sunday about three o'clock in the afternoon, sixty squires mounted on barded horses, all ornamented for the tournament, paraded out of the Tower of London at a foot-pace. Then came sixty ladies most elegantly and beautifully dressed, mounted on palfreys, one after the other in long sequence, each leading by a silver chain a knight in complete armor ready for tilting. Minstrels and trumpeters attended them; and the procession wound slowly through the streets and out beyond the walls to Smithfield, where the King and Queen and her ladies-in-waiting were already arrived and seated in boxes handsomely decorated. These boxes must have been Chaucer's work. When the procession reached the lists, servants assisted the ladies to dismount from their palfreys and ushered them into their respective boxes, while squires of honor fetched the tilting coursers and the knights got off their hackneys, had their helmets laced, mounted their coursers, and made ready for the tilt. The Count of Saint Pol, a French nobleman, who had married a half-sister of King Richard, led to foreign knights. He and his companions rode first into the lists, all handsomely armed, and the tilting began. Then followed individual jousts, in which the English knights, as tenants, held the field against all opponents until evening set in. The prize to the best knight among the opponents was awarded to the Count of Saint Pol, and among the tenants to the Earl of Huntington, the King's half-brother. That night there was a banquet in the Bishop of London's palace near Saint Paul's church, and dancing. The next day, also, the beauty and fashion of England again repaired to Smithfield and the tilting began once more. Many riders were unhorsed, many lost their helmets, but it was well fought, and champions came forward till the sun set. Another banquet that night, and more dancing. On Tuesday the squires had their chance to show off their prowess before King, Queen, ladies and knights. More feasting, and dancing till daybreak. On Wednesday, any knight or squire, indiscriminately, who desired rode into the lists and tilted. On Thursday the King gave a great supper to all the foreign knights and squires; the Duke of Lancaster another on Friday. On Saturday the King went to Windsor Castle, and invited all the foreign knights. There were more dinners and suppers, and in Saint George's Chapel, which Chaucer had repaired a month or two before, the King conferred the Order of the Garter on his cousin, Count William of Hainaut. With such junketings going on, the office of clerk of the works was no sinecure.

Another record of that year concerns Chaucer, as clerk of the works, for on Saint Edward's day—it would seem that the King held the royal saints of England in great honor—the King observed the festival at his palace at Kennington, glittering in all his regalia, and the Queen, too; even at mass the King wore his crown and held his scepter, and both King and Queen wore their crowns at table. It might seem that this ostentatious wearing of the crown was a sign that the King meant to be his own master and defy the Duke of Gloucester and the magnates, who had bullied him into submission, and indeed only the year before, he had asserted himself and removed several of the rebellious lords from office; he took the great seal from Thomas Arundel, Archbishop of York, and entrusted it to William of Wykeham, Bishop of Winchester, an old and experienced statesman; he dismissed the Bishop of Hereford, another of the Gloucester faction, from the treasury and appointed the Bishop of Exeter; he removed the Duke of Gloucester, himself, the Earl of Warwick, and others of their faction from the Council, and put in their places such as pleased him. This was not long before the government appointed Chaucer, clerk of the works; and therefore one may draw the inference that the King's party was favorably inclined to the poet, and indeed, whether due to chance or not, the two years that the poet was out of office were while the Duke of Gloucester and his faction held the upper hand.

Another proof of the King's favor, or rather perhaps that the Duke of Lancaster had recovered his place among the King's advisers, is that in March, 1390, the year of the celebrations I have referred to, Chaucer and Sir Richard Stury, were appointed on a commission of what one might call the Thames Conservancy, to survey the walls, ditches, sewers and bridges along the banks of the Thames, between Greenwich and Woolwich. Sir Richard Stury, you remember, was one of the members of what Trevelyan denounced as the Duke of Lancaster's corrupt ring, so it is likely that the appointment of these two gentlemen was due to the Duke. At all events, the more one finds how much Chaucer had to do, the more one excuses those dreadful medieval discourses, *Melibee* and the Parson's homily.

One other incident, or rather set of incidents in the year 1390, remains to be recorded. It reminds one so much of

Falstaff and his disreputable friends that I quote Shakespeare again:

Scene: Rochester. An Inn-Yard

Chamberlain: Good morrow, Master Gadshill. It holds current what I told you yesternight; there's a franklin in the wild of Kent hath brought three hundred marks with him in gold. . . .

Gadshill: Sirrah, if they meet not with Saint Nicholas clerks [thieves], I'll give thee this neck.

Scene: The Road by Gadshill

First Traveller: Come, neighbor: the boy shall lead our horses down the hill; we'll walk afoot awhile, and ease our legs.

Thieves: Stand!

Travellers: Jesu bless us!

Falstaff: Strike; down with them; cut the villains' throats. Ah! whoreson caterpillars! bacon-fed knaves! they hate us youth; down with them; fleece them.

Travellers: O, we are undone, both we and ours for ever.

Falstaff: Hang ye, gorbellied knaves, are ye undone? No, ye fat chuffs . . . What! ye knaves, young men must live, you are grandjurors, are ye? we'll jure ye, i' faith.

Here they rob and bind them.

Except that Prince Hal had no part in this robbery, for he was but a baby at the time, Chaucer's experience was very like that of the Shakespearian franklins from the wild of Kent. In September, 1390, he was stopped two or three times by robbers, at Westminster, at Hatcham, Surrey, and at the Fowle Oak, in Kent, places not far apart, and

[304]

relieved of twenty pounds; his horse and *autres moebels* (removables) were taken from him. Chaucer was excused for the loss of the twenty pounds, but for a man near fifty, an old man as men reckoned then, it was a very alarming experience.

At any rate Chaucer gave up his clerkship of the works on June 17, 1391. As the Duke of Lancaster was in England, and seems to have possessed much political influence at this time, this relinquishment of office was probably voluntary, and made because he had the offer of another office of less pecuniary responsibility. In the fourteenth year of Richard II, which may mean 1390 or 1391, he and one Richard Brittle were appointed by Sir Peter Courtenay, foresters of North Petherton Park in Somersetshire. Seven years later, Courtenay reappointed Chaucer as sole forester. Sir Peter had been master of the King's falcons when Chaucer as clerk of the works had charge of the Royal Mews for falcons next Charing Cross, and constable of Windsor Castle at the time when Chaucer was repairing St. George's Chapel there. The two, therefore, must have been friends, or at least acquaintances.

CHAPTER XXXIV

Politics

THE commentators suggest that, during the years 1392-1394, after he had given up his appointment as clerk of the works and was forester in Somersetshire with no importunate duties, Chaucer put his leisure time to good purpose and wrote many of the tales—those of the Pardoner, the Friar, the Summoner, the Wife of Bath, the Clerk, the Merchant, the Franklin and the Squire. After this period his fertility diminished. Some think that in the following years he was poor and troubled for money. As to that I shall speak in the next chapter; but my own idea is that political uncertainty and the possible danger of civil war are more likely than poverty to have distraught his thoughts from poetry. At all events, the notices concerning him during these years are very meager, and if we wish to learn anything about him it is necessary to refer to the general history of politics, for then, at least, we shall know the background of the stage on which he played his part.

You remember that in 1388 the Merciless Parliament, under the domination of the Gloucester faction, had put many of the King's friends to death, and had appointed a council to guide and control the King. For a year the King submitted, for submit he must, but in May, 1389, he had felt strong enough to remove Archbishop Arundel from the chancellorship, and replace him by a man more to his liking, but not, however, one of his clique, the famous William of Wykeham; and in other matters he acted as master but with moderation and self-restraint. In 1394, his wife, Anne, died, and the old policy of a marriage with a French Princess, and peace with France, was revived. There was opposition, for the country patriotically hated the French, and the Duke of Gloucester, seeing his personal advantage on that side, was strongly against peace. Another objection was that the Princess Isabelle was but seven years old; and as hope of issue was the main motive in a royal marriage (in order to prevent a disputed succession), it was not unreasonable to ask that the King should marry a grown woman. But the objections were overridden and the King married the little Princess in November, 1396, at Calais, and a truce for twenty-eight years was made.

During the discussions over the proposed marriage and truce, our old friend, Jean Froissart, after an absence of twenty-eight years, paid a visit to England. He was now a canon in Chinay, Hainaut, and recalled the happy days of his youth, when King Edward, Queen Philippa and their children had been so kind to him. If his old friends were dead, he would see their children and he would also obtain more evidence for his history. So he procured letters of introduction and remembrance from various great personages, and also devised a gift for King Richard, who was a lover of the arts. He collected all the poems on love that he had written since he left England, had them handsomely copied and illuminated, and bound in a velvet cover, fastened with silver clasps. On July 12, 1395, he crossed from Calais to Dover, "but found [as he says] no one there with whom I had been acquainted in my former journeys, the inns were all kept by new people, and the children of my former acquaintances were become men and women." He stayed at Dover half a day and a night to rest himself and his horse, for he was near sixty years old, and, arriving early the next morning at Canterbury, visited the shrine of Saint Thomas, and the tomb of the Black

Prince. Hearing that the King was coming on a pilgrimage the following day, he went back to his inn to wait. The King, who had been in Ireland for nine months, arrived the next day, with a retinue of lords and ladies; but though Froissart went about among them he found no faces that he knew. He inquired after his old friend Sir Richard Stury; but Stury was at home in London. He then presented himself to Sir Thomas Percy (afterward Earl of Worcester), the Lord High Steward. Percy was gracious and agreeable, but advised Froissart to await a better opportunity to present his letters to the King, and in the meantime to follow the royal party to Ospringe and Leeds Castle, where he would find the Duke of York, whom he used to know when a youth. Froissart took Percy's advice. The Duke of York, gave him a hearty welcome and said: "Sir John, keep with us and our people. We will show you every courtesy and attention. We are bound to do so by remembrance of old days and by affection for the memory of our Lady Mother, to whom you were attached. We have not forgotten those days." All went well. The Duke presented him to the King, who received him graciously and said that since he had belonged to the household of his grandfather and grandmother, he must consider himself as still belonging to the royal household of England. Perhaps Froissart reminded the King that he had been at Bordeaux when his Majesty was born on Epiphany, 1367, but he withheld his present for a more convenient time, as the King was troubled by the news from Aquitaine, for the people there were complaining that they did not want the Duke of Lancaster, who had gone out to them as lord of the duchy. From Leeds Froissart proceeded to the Palace at Eltham, which had been under Chaucer's charge while he was clerk of the works, where the King was to hold a council. Here he met Sir Richard Stury who recollected him at once, and recalled the last time they had seen one another twenty-four years before. You remember that Chaucer had been associated with Sir Richard Stury as a commissioner for the Thames Conservancy in March, 1390.

After the council was over Froissart at last had his opportunity to give the King his gift, for all the courtiers had gone except the Duke of York, Sir Thomas Percy and Sir Richard Stury. He was admitted to the King's chamber, and laid the book on the King's bed. The crimson velvet, the ten silver gilt studs, with silver roses in the center, and the silver gilt clasps also worked with roses, made a gallant show. The King opened the book and asked what it treated of. Froissart replied, "Of love." The King was pleased, and opening the book here and there, read bits aloud, and made the poet many acknowledgments.

Froissart remained attached to the King's household, and went to various palaces. It would not, perhaps, be a violent guess—no more than guesses that Chaucer met Guillaume de Machaut, Petrarch, or Boccaccio—to hope that Chaucer and Froissart met somewhere, but there is no mention of it, and, if they had, it seems likely that Froissart would have learned more accurate details than his *Chronicles* record concerning Chaucer's former missions to France. But, let us return to King Richard and politics.

The King brought back his infant bride to England. The people were not pleased, they wanted an heir to the throne and they thought that in various respects too much had been conceded to France. Gloucester and Arundel seem to have encouraged this popular discontent. Both had long been at serious odds with the King. Gloucester, in addition to his general dislike of his nephew, was also angry for this reason: John of Gaunt immediately on his return to England from Aquitaine, had married his mistress, Katharine Swynford (January, 1396), and the King had conferred legiti-

macy upon their children. This, Gloucester thought, was
insulting to the royal family. Arundel and the King, like-
wise, had their personal quarrel. It is said that, when
Richard's beloved wife Anne died, Arundel had absented
himself from the funeral procession from Shene to Westminster, and that, during the funeral in the Abbey he had
come in late, and then merely to ask the King for permission to retire. True or false, the story went that the
irascible King seized a baton and struck the Earl bleeding
to the ground. Besides the King held fresh in an angry
heart how Gloucester and Arundel had bullied him in 1386,
and there was bitter hostility between him and these two.
It is said that Gloucester and Arundel were conspiring with
the Earl of Warwick to depose the King; certainly all three
were uneasy and put their heads together. Richard acted
with unwonted vigor. According to Froissart, who neglected archives and collected gossip, and thereby perhaps
brought inaccuracy near to truth, the King invited the three
magnates to dinner. Gloucester regretted to say that he was
ill, Arundel retired to his castle and dropped the portcullis,
but the simple-minded Warwick accepted and went. Warwick was arrested. At the King's instance Archbishop
Arundel persuaded his brother, the Earl, to give himself
up. Richard himself at the head of an armed troop marched
out into Essex to his uncle's manor at Pleshy, and arrested
him. "By Saint John the Baptist [there seems to have been
some grim humor in this oath], *bel oncle,*" he said, "all this
will turn out for the best for the both of us." Gloucester
was sent to Calais. The three prisoners were accused
of high treason (August 5, 1397). Parliament met on
September seventeenth. The King attended the session, accompanied by two thousand archers from Cheshire, and a
great body of "valets of the crown" wearing the badge of
the White Hart. The three prisoners were found guilty and

condemned to death. John of Gaunt, as high steward, pronounced judgment on Arundel: "Richard! I, John, Steward of England, judge thee to be a traitor, and I condemn thee to be drawn and hanged, to be beheaded and quartered, and thy lands, tailed [entailed] and not tailed, from thee and from heirs of thy body descending to be confiscate." The Earl of Arundel was immediately led to Tower Hill, and there beheaded. The Earl of Warwick was then arraigned. He made no bold defiance as Arundel had done, but "as hee had been some miserable old woman, confessed all things contayned in appeale [the accusation] weeping, wayling, and howling, to be done traitorously by him, and submitting himselfe to the King's grace in all things." He was condemned to perpetual imprisonment. As for the Duke of Gloucester, the captain of Calais reported that he was dead. Two others associated with Gloucester, Henry Bolingbroke, Earl of Derby, Gaunt's son, and Thomas Mowbray, Earl of Nottingham, were pronounced innocent of malice in whatever they had done, and were created respectively Duke of Hereford and Duke of Norfolk. Richard's *coup d'état* had removed three enemies, but it stirred up wide fear and anger.

Shakespeare now takes up the story. Bolingbroke, to make himself safer, accused Norfolk of high treason. You know how an appeal to battle was agreed on, how Richard threw his warder down and interrupted the combat, how he banished Bolingbroke for six years and Norfolk for life (September, 1398). The King, thus rid of his enemies, then assumed autocratic power; he declared that the laws of the realm were in his breast, and that he only could change them. And now Richard's fate rolled headlong down-hill. Old John of Gaunt, shaken by his son's banishment, died on February 3, 1399. Bolingbroke, who by his father's death became lawfully Duke of Lancaster, and had

had full assurance from the King that he should inherit his dukedom, was denied his rights. The foolish King, thinking himself secure, disported himself with Bushy, Bagot and Greene, of whom Stow says they were men "in whom no goodnesse at all could be found, but a natural covetousness, unsatiable ambition, intollerable pride, and hatred of the truth."

But the act that wrought his downfall was that, after refusing Henry Bolingbroke the right of succession to the immense inheritance of Lancaster, he departed with his army to complete the subjugation of Ireland (May 31, 1399). This was Bolingbroke's opportunity. The King was long without word from England owing to bad weather, and then, late in summer, came heavy news. Henry Bolingbroke had landed at Ravenspurgh on the Yorkshire coast, and had taken and beheaded William Scrope, Bushy and Green; and rumor added that he had a bull from Rome promising paradise to all who should aid him. On hearing this the King sent the Earl of Salisbury ahead to a place called Conway on the north coast of Wales, while he himself was to stay, gather his other ships together, and follow within six days. Salisbury, on landing, learned that most of England had gone over to Bolingbroke, but he hoisted the King's standard and from among friends in Cheshire and Wales collected seven thousand men. Day by day they watched the horizon expecting the King, but not a sail hove in sight, and on the fourteenth day the recruits stole away and went back to their homes. The King, following evil counsel, had waited eighteen days, and then landed not at Conway but far distant at Milford Haven; from Milford Haven, privily, dressed like a priest, and riding by night, he journeyed across Wales to Conway. He came too late. The curtain now rises upon high tragedy, and Shakespeare tells it best:

RICHARD: . . . of comfort no man speak:
        Let's talk of graves, of worms, and epitaphs;
        Make dust our paper, and with rainy eyes
        Write sorrow on the bosom of the earth.
        Let's choose executors and talk of wills:
        And yet not so, for what can we bequeath
        Save our deposed bodies to the ground?
        Our lands, our lives, and all are Bolingbroke's,
        And nothing can we call our own, but death,
        And that small model of the barren earth,
        Which serves as paste and cover to our bones.

The meeting between the King that had been and the King that was to be took place as Shakespeare says at Flint Castle in North Wales. Stow's narrative is this: "King Richard came down to meet the Duke, who as soon as he sawe the King, fell down on his knees, and coming neere unto him, he kneeled the second time with his hat in his hande, and the King then put off his hood, and spake first. 'Fayre Cousin of Lancaster, ye are right welcome—' The Duke bowing lowe to the grounde answered, 'My Lord, I am come before you sent for mee, the reason why I will show you. The common fame among your people is such, that ye have for the space of twenty or twenty-two yeeres, ruled them very rigorously, but if it please our Lord I will help you to govern better.' The King answered, 'Fayre Cousin of Lancaster, seth it pleaseth you, it pleaseth me well.' " In Shakespeare it runs thus:

RICHARD: Fair cousin, you debase your princely knee
        To make the base earth proud with kissing it:

           *   *   *   *   *

        Up, cousin, up; your heart is up, I know,
        Thus high at least, although your knee be low.

[313]

BOLINGBROKE: My gracious lord, I come but for mine own.
RICHARD: Your own is yours, and I am yours, and all.
BOLINGBROKE: So far be mine, my most redoubted lord,
        As my true service shall deserve your love.
RICHARD: Well you deserve; they well deserve to have,
        That know the strong'st and surest way to get.

So the King made ready to leave the castle and go with his captor. Froissart says: "I heard of a singular circumstance that happened, which I must mention. King Richard had a greyhound called Math, beautiful beyond measure, who would not notice or follow any one but the King. Whenever the King rode abroad, the greyhound was loosed by the person who had him in charge, and ran instantly to caress him, by placing his two forefeet on his shoulders. It fell out, that as the King and the Duke of Lancaster were conversing in the court of the castle, their horses being ready for them to mount, the greyhound was untied, but, instead of running as usual to the King, he left him, and leaped to the Duke of Lancaster's shoulders, paying him every court, and caressing him as he was formerly used to caress the King. The Duke, not acquainted with this greyhound, asked the King the meaning of this fondness, saying, 'What does this mean?' 'Cousin,' the King replied, 'it means a great deal for you, and very little for me.' 'How,' said the Duke, 'pray explain.' 'I understand by it,' the King answered, 'that this greyhound fondles and pays his court to you this day as King of England, which you will surely be, and I shall be deposed, for the natural instinct of the dog shows it to him. Keep him therefore by your side, for he will now leave me and follow you.' The Duke of Lancaster treasured up what the King said, and paid attention to the greyhound, who would never more follow Richard of Bordeaux, but kept by the side of the Duke of Lancaster, as was witnessed by thirty thousand men" (August 19, 1399).

The King, cruelly enough, was put in charge of the sons of Gloucester, Warwick and Arundel, and conducted by stages to London. The last scene or rather the last but one, was enacted in Westminster Hall, where parliament was assembled on the twenty-ninth day of September. The Archbishop of Canterbury read Richard's admission that he was not worthy to reign and would resign the crown. The Archbishop then asked whom they would choose for King. All declared they would have none other than the Duke of Lancaster. So, in this fashion, the shrewd and capable Bolingbroke became Henry IV of England. Still, one more happening was necessary to make that crown secure. On February 14, 1400, Richard died in prison at Pomfret Castle in Yorkshire. Stow says: "Fourteen days and nightes they vexed him with continual hunger, thirst and cold, and finally bereft him of his life, with suche a kinde of death as never before that time was known in England." Gower in his *Vox Clamantis* said in Latin verses, as translated by Stow:

Lo, God doth hate such rulers, as heere viciously doe live:
And none ought rule, that by their life, doe ill example give.
And this King Richard witnesseth well, his end this plaine
      doth shewe:
For God allotted him such ende and sent him so greate woe,
As such life deservd; as by the Chronicles thou mayst know.

It is the sort of thing that the moral Gower would write, but one is glad that Chaucer did not write it.

CHAPTER XXXV

Last Days

THERE has been a persistent belief that Chaucer was poor in worldly goods during the last years of his life in spite of temporary alleviation while he was clerk of the works and forester. It is difficult to tell how such traditions start, and whether their origins contain the whole truth, a little truth, or none. I will cite to you some of the evidence that seems to justify the theory, and leave it to you to decide whether any such justification lies therein or not. The most important evidence is a short poem entitled, *The Compleint of Chaucer to his Purse,* that, in its present form, must have been written in the last months of his life, very soon after the accession of King Henry IV:

To yow, my purse, and to noon other wight
Complayne I, for ye be my lady dere!
I am so sory, now that ye been lyght:
For certes, but ye make me hevy chere,
Me were as leef be layd upon my bere [bier];
For whiche unto your mercy thus I crye:
Beth [be] hevy ageyn, or elles mot [must] I dye!

Now voucheth sauf this day, or [before] yt be nyght,
That I of yow the blisful soun may here,
Or see your colour lyk the sonne bryght,
That of yelownesse hadde never pere.
Ye be my lyf, ye be myn hertes stere [guide],
Quene of comfort and of good compayne;
Beth hevy ageyn, or elles moote I dye!

[316]

Now purse, that ben to me my lyves light
And saveour, as doun in this world here,
Out of this toune helpe me thurgh your myght,
Syn that ye wole nat ben my tresorere;
For I am shave as nye as any frere.
But yet I pray unto your curtesye:
Beth hevy agen, or elles moote I dye!

O conquerour of Brutes Albyon,
Which that by lyne and free eleccion
Been verray [true] kyng, this song to yow I sende;
And ye, that mowen [can] alle our harmes amende,
Have mynde upon my supplicacion!

This is the pleasantest pinch of poverty that ever I read of. Where Poverty catches a man in her cruel claws his cry is very different. The verses on poverty by Rutebeuf are not like these; and there is far more pathos in Cervantes' dedication of the *Second Part of Don Quixote,* humorous though it is, to the Conde de Lemnos. At any rate, the verses or causes behind them, were effective. Stow says that Henry Bolingbroke was no sooner elected king than he forthwith appointed new officers: His second son Prince Thomas, steward of England; Henry Percy, Earl of Northumberland, constable of England; Ralph Neville, Earl of Westmoreland, marshal of England; Sir John Scerle, chancellor of England; Sir Richard Clifford, keeper of his privy seal; John Norbury, Esquire, treasurer; *Thomas Chaucer, constable of Wallingford Castle,* and other officers. Two weeks later, on the same day as the coronation, October thirteenth, the King granted Geoffrey Chaucer an annuity of forty marks (four thousand dollars), and confirmed the pension given by King Richard of twenty pounds a year (three thousand dollars), and five days later he confirmed the annual gift of a butt of wine. Taking all things together it is

[317]

hard to believe that this begging poem was really inspired by poverty. The accession of a new sovereign is not unlike that of a president; all those who think or hope, that they deserve, or may receive, political favors, ask for them. And Chaucer, knowing that rewards were going about, that his son Thomas was to be made constable of Wallingford Castle, naturally put in his petition. I can see no evidence of poverty here.

There is another diatribe against poverty in *The Prologue to the Man of Law's Tale:*

> O hateful harm, condicion of poverte!
> With thurst, with coold, with hunger so confoundid!
> To asken help thee shameth in thyn herte;
> If thou noon aske, with nede artow [art thou] so woundid
> That verray nede unwrappeth al thy wounde hid!
> Maugree thyn heed, thou most [must] for indigence
> Or stele, or begge, or borwe thy despence!

And so on. It appears, however, that *The Man of Law's Tale* was written about 1390, just at the time when Chaucer was translating a treatise by the great Pope Innocent III, *De Contemptu Mundi,* in which among other miseries of man the Pope dilates upon poverty. This apostrophe to poverty is without doubt purely literary and therefore irrelevant.

But there are records of sundry borrowings of money that may be more pertinent. Way back in 1385 when the Chaucers migrated from London into the country, on September twentieth Mrs. Chaucer anticipated nearly one-half her yearly pension, four pounds six shillings eight pence, between six and seven hundred dollars. And in 1387 Chaucer drew half his annual pension in advance. There may have been a dozen reasons other than poverty for taking these

[318]

moneys at those times; perhaps Mr. and Mrs. Chaucer made a payment upon their country property, or wished to repair the house, or to lay out a garden, perhaps their son Thomas was to be sent to the university or the inns of Court, perhaps Chaucer had an opportunity to make a good investment, who can say? In 1387, on December twenty-first, Chaucer borrowed twenty shillings from the Exchequer. As to this and other anticipations of his annuity, all one can say is that, in those days when there were no local banks, a countryman who had come up to London would be likely to draw some small sum on account of his pension, very much as he would from a deposit in his bank nowadays. On the other hand, when in 1388, on May first, Chaucer procured the transfer of his annuity (that for twenty marks given him by King Edward in 1367) to another man, a reasonable inference is that Chaucer felt that he could invest the money elsewhere more profitably; unless we may suppose that, as this is the time when the lords-appellant were beheading the King's friends, he apprehended that they also might put an end to his annuity. His other pension of ten pounds you remember came from the Duke of Lancaster.

In 1392, in July, Chaucer borrowed the sum of twenty-six shillings eight pence from a London merchant, less than two hundred dollars, and during the next few years (1395-1397) he drew from time to time small sums from the Exchequer against moneys due on account. As I say this was but like drawing moneys from his own bank. And during these years, one must remember, that from July 12, 1389, to June 17, 1391, he was getting a salary as clerk of the King's works; that as soon as that employment terminated he was receiving a salary as forester; that he was drawing a pension of ten pounds from the Duke of Lancaster; that in the beginning of 1393 the King gave him ten pounds as a reward for his good services; that in February,

1394, the King granted him a new annuity of twenty pounds, and that while clerk of the works he had been able to advance sixty-six pounds (near ten thousand dollars) which was repaid to him in 1393 or 1394, and that every year he received robes as a perquisite due him as an esquire of the King, and also a butt of wine, or, I presume, its equivalent in money. Ten pounds from Gaunt, twenty from the King, his salary as forester and his perquisites would seem to raise him above the need of borrowing little sums except as a matter of convenience, and be quite enough to overturn the theory of his poverty, except in so far as well-to-do people always complain of poverty when their income is diminished.

But there are two more items to be noted. In April, 1398, one Isabella Buckholt, administratrix of Walter Buckholt, brought an action of debt against him in the Court of Common Pleas to recover fourteen pounds one shilling eleven pence. One can be very sure that, when Chaucer consulted a lawyer, the first thing the lawyer did, before putting in a demurrer or a plea of denial, was to ask Chaucer what his occupation was, and on being told that he was a forester in the King's service, advised him to take out letters of protection on the ground that he was engaged on important public business for the King. It was the obvious first move, like that of the King's pawn, and Chaucer played it. There the matter lies; and no inference is to be drawn beyond such as the doctrine of probabilities offers on the point whether plaintiffs or defendants are more often in the right. It shows that there was a disagreement between Chaucer and Walter Buckholt, but not that Chaucer was poor. There is one more item and the list ends. In October of the same year, 1398, Chaucer petitioned King Richard, in language such as one has often heard from thirsty men, "For God's sake and as an act of charity," to give him a butt of wine every year. He had had such a gift from King Edward, and as Richard had the reputation of easy giving, he might expect a favorable answer. He asked and he received.

The theory that Chaucer suffered from poverty seems to me also to contradict likelihood in other respects. Chaucer's son it is said married early, about 1394-1395. He married the second daughter of Sir John Burghersh, whose great-uncle in his day was Bishop of London, and chancellor. The family was very rich; and this marriage brought Thomas Chaucer the manor of Ewelme, in Oxfordshire, although perhaps not until Sir John's death, as well as other large estates. He was chief butler to King Richard; early in 1399 he exchanged certain offices he held for an annuity of twenty marks a year; he was also receiving a pension of ten pounds a year from the Duke of Lancaster, his uncle by marriage. On the accession of Henry IV, he was not only made constable of Wallingford Castle, but also steward of the honors of Wallingford and of Saint Valery and of Chiltern Hundreds at forty pounds (six thousand dollars) a year and ten pounds for his deputy. It seemed clear that Thomas was rich and prosperous, even in Richard's reign.

And in January, 1396, Geoffrey Chaucer's sister-in-law, Katharine Sywnford, became Duchess of Lancaster. It can hardly be that the wife of the richest man in England would suffer her brother-in-law to remain in any real poverty; indeed, she would be likely to draw closer to him because she was snubbed at first by the great ladies of the court. The Duchess of Gloucester, the Countess of Arundel—this was before Richard's coup d'état—the Countess of Derby (Harry Bolingbroke's wife) and other ladies of royal descent "greatly disdained that she [Katharine] should be matched with the Duke of Lancaster, and by that means accounted second person in the realm and be preferred in roome afore them; and therefore they sayde they would not come where she should be present, for it should be a shame to them, that a woman of so base birth, that had been concubine to the Duke should goe and have place before them." But King Richard approved and legitimized the children, and when the King and his uncles, John of Gaunt and Thomas of Gloucester, went to France to celebrate the King's marriage with the little French Princess, the Duchess of Lancaster was present as the chief lady from England, with her son and two daughters, and they were well received by the Duchesses of Burgundy and of Brittany and the other great ladies of France. And, perhaps, these proud disdainful ladies would not have turned up their noses so high if they had been prophetically gifted to foresee that their descendants, for three hundred years and more, would bow down and do obeisance to the descendants of Katharine Swynford—Henry VII, Henry VIII, Queen Elizabeth, the Stuarts, the House of Hanover, Queen Victoria, and his present Majesty, George V. So, Chaucer's sister-in-law was a very great lady, and it is not likely that she or the Duke, her husband, suffered him to remain in any real poverty.

However all this may be, after the accession of Henry IV Chaucer's fortunes were on a firm foundation. That December he took a lease of a house in the garden of Saint Mary's Chapel, beside Westminster Abbey, the site where Henry VII's chapel now stands. But before a year was out his joyous pilgrimage through life came to an end. He died on October 25, 1400, and was buried in a corner of Westminster Abbey, not as a poet but because he lived hard by; and now near his lie other ashes, and that rich earth makes the sanctuary, vexed in other corners by records of worldly pomp, a holy place. John Stow in his *Annales* for the year 1400, says this of the poet: "The famous poet Geoffrey Chaucer Esquire, the first illuminator of our English language, deceased. This was a worshipfull gentleman,

[322]

and of faire possessions, whose abode was chiefly about Woodstocke (where he had a faire Mannor) and Newelme (in Oxfordshire) which also was his [Stow confounds Geoffrey with Thomas], with divers other Mannors: he was oft times imployed by King Edward III as embassador into Fraunce, and into other forraine lands: he had to wife the daughter of Paine Roete alias Guian [Guienne] King at arms, by whom he had issue Thomas Chaucer who married Maud daughter to Sir Bartholomew [John] Barwash [Burghersh], by whom hee had issue Alice Chaucer, first married to Sir John Philips Knight, after to the Earle of Salisbury, and thirdly to Wil. Duke of Suffolke, who at his wife's request founded an hospital called God's house, by the parish church of New-Elme, which Church he also builded, in this church lieth buried Tho. Chaucer the last heir male (1434)."

CHAPTER XXXVI

Down the Centuries

Miss Caroline F. E. Spurgeon, professor of English literature in the University of London, a lady of great intelligence and industry, has collected in her book, *Five Hundred Years of Chaucer Criticism and Allusion,* 1357-1900, an enormous multitude of references to Chaucer. It is extremely interesting, but (unless one were Macaulay on an ocean voyage) beyond the range of the reader, and so I quote—for it is impossible to find any criticism not included in her three massive volumes—a few, comparatively few, references that help one to understand Chaucer by the light of his reflection in many lettered minds.

John Gower, *Confessio Amantis* [1390]

> "And gret wel Chaucer whan ye mete,
> As mi disciple and my poete:
> For in the floures of his youthe
> In sondri wise, as he wel couthe,
> Of Ditees and of Songes glade,
> The whiche he for mi sake made,
> The lond fulfild is ouerall:
> Whereof to him in special
> Aboue alle othre I am most holde.
> For thi now in hise daies olde
> Thow schalt him telle this message,
> That he vpon his latere age,
> To sette an ende of alle his werk
> As he which is myn owne clerk
> Do make his testament of loue. . . ."

[324]

John Lydgate, *The Serpent of Deuision* (division) (year 1400): "ye flower of Poets in our English tung, and the first that euer elumined our language with flowers of rethorick eloquence: I mean famous and worthy Chaucer," and again in *The floure of curtesye* [1401]

"Chaucer is deed that had suche a name
Of fayre makyng that [was] without wene
Fayrest in our tonge, as the Laurer grene";

and from *The Life of Our Lady* [1409-11?]

"The noble rethor Poete of breteine
That worthy was the laurer to haue
Of peetrie and the palme atteine,
That made firste to distille and reyne
The golde dewe droppis of speche and eloquence
In-to oure tounge thourgh his excellence,
And founde the flourys first of rethoryk
Oure rude speche oonly to enlumyne. . . ."

Thomas Hoccleve, *The Regement of Princes* [1412]

"O, maister deere, and fadir reuerent!
Mi maister Chaucer, flour of eloquence,
Mirour of fructuous entendëment
O, vniuersel fadir in science!

. . . for vn-to Tullius
War neuer man so lyk a-mongës vs.

Also, who was hier in philosophie
To Aristotle, in our tonge, but thow?
The steppës of virgile in poesie
Thou filwedist eeke, men wot wel y-now."

[325]

James I, King of Scotland, *The Kingis Quair* [1423]:

> "Vnto [the] Impnis of my maisteris dere,
> Gowere and chaucere, that on the steppis satt
> Of rethorike, quhill thai were lyvand here,
> Superlatiue as poetis laureate
> In moralitee and eloquence ornate . . ."

John Shirley, *Verses* [c. 1450]:

> ". . . Geffrey Chaucier
> Whiche in oure volgare had neuere ys pere
> Of eloquencyale Retorryke
> In Englisshe was neuer noon him lyke."

Robert Henryson, *The Testament of Cresseid* [1475]:

> ". . . Worthie Chaucer glorious . . ."

William Caxton, Printer, *Epilogue to Boethius* [1479]:

> ". . . the worshipful fader & first foundeur & embel-
> issher of ornate eloquence in our englissh. I mene Maister
> Geffry Chaucer . . ."

William Dunbar, *The Goldyn Targe* [1503]:

> "O reverend Chaucere, rose of rethoris all,
> As in oure tong ane flour imperiall
> That raise in Britane ewir, quho redis rycht,
> Thou beris of makaris [poets] the tryumph riall."

Sir Brian Tuke in preface to Thynne's Edition of Chaucer's works, written in name of William Thynne [1532]:

[326]

". . . that noble & famous clerke Geffray Chaucer, in whose workes is so manyfest comprobacion of his excellent lernyng in al kyndes of doctrynes and sciences, suche frute-fulnesse in wordes, wel accordynge to the mater and pur-pose, so swete and plesaunt sentences, suche perfectyon in metre, the composycion so adapted, suche freshnesse of in-uencion, compendyousnesse in narration, suche sensyble and open style, lackyng neither maieste ne mediocrite couenable in disposycion, and suche sharpnesse or quycknesse in con-clusyon . . ."

(This is the best criticism, reckoning brevity as a merit, that I have come upon).

Raphael Holinshed, *Chronicles of England* [1577]:

"But nowe to rehearse what writers of oure English na-tion liued in the days of this Kyng, [Henry the Fourth]. That renowmed Poete Geffreye Chaucer is worthily named as principall, a man so exquisitely learned in all sciences, that hys matche was not lightly founde anye where in those dayes, and for reducing our Englishe tong to perfect con-formitie, hee hathe excelled therein all other."

Edmund Spenser, *The Shepheardes Calender* [1579]—he refers to Chaucer as Tityrus:

"The God of shepheards Tityrus is dead,
Who taught me homely, as I can, to make.
He, whilst he lived, was the soueraigne head
Of shepheards all, that bene with loue ytake:

* * * * *

And all hys passing skil with him is fledde,
The fame whereof doth dayly greater growe,
But if on me some little drops would flowe
Of that the spring was in his learned hedde
I soone would learne these woods, to wayle my woe
And teache the trees, their trickling teares to shedde."

Also *The Faerie Queene* (Book IV, Canto 2, XXXI) [1590-1596]:

". . . Dan Chaucer, well of Englishe vndefyled,
On Fames eternall beadroll worthie to be fyled."

Book VII, Canto 7, IX:

"That old Dan Geffrey (in whose gentle spright
The pure well head of Poesie did dwell)."

William Webbe [1586]:

"Chawcer, who for that excellent fame which hee obtayned in his Poetry, was always accounted the God of English Poets (such a tytle for honours sake hath been giuen him), . . ."

Thomas Nashe, *Strange Newes,* etc. [1592]:

"Chaucer, and Spencer the Homer and Virgil of England . . ."

Francis Beaumont, father of the poet, Letter to Thomas Speght, editor of Chaucer's works [1597]:

"Chaucer [may] bee rightly called, The pith and sinewes

[328]

of eloquence, and the verie life it selfe of all mirth and pleasant writing: besides one gifte hee hath aboue other Authours, and that is, by the excellencie of his descriptions to possesse his Readers with a stronger imagination of seeing that done before their eyes, which they reade, than any other that euer writ in any tongue."

Richard Hakluyt, *The Principal Nauigations,* etc. [1598] :

"And lastly, our old English father Ennius, I meane, the learned, wittie, and profound Geoffrey Chaucer, . . ."

Thomas Dekker, *A Knights Coniuring* [1607] :

". . . old Chaucer, reuerend for prioritie, blythe in cheare, buxsome in his speeches, and benigne in his hauiour . . ."

Henry Peacham, *The Compleat Gentleman* [1622] :

"Of English poets of our owne Nation, esteeme Sir Geoffrey Chaucer the father; although the stile for the antiquitie, may distast you, yet as vnder a bitter and rough rinde, there lyeth a delicate kernell of conceit and sweet inuention. What Examples, Similitudes, Times, Places, and aboue all, Persons, with their speeches, and attributes, doe as in *Canterburie*-tales (like those threds of gold, the rich Arras) beautifie his Worke quite thorough? And albeit diuers of his workes, are but meerely translations out of Latine and French, yet he hath handled them so artificially, that thereby he hath made them his owne, as his *Troilus* and *Cresseid*."

[329]

Michael Drayton, *To Henery Reynolds Esquire* [1627]:

> "That noble Chaucer, in those former times,
> The first inrich'd our *English* with his rimes,
> And was the first of ours, that euer brake,
> Into the Muses treasure, and first spake
> In weighty numbers, deluing in the Mine
> Of perfect knowledge, which he could refine,
> And coyne for currant, and asmuch as then
> The *English* language could expresse to men,
> He made it doe; and by his wondrous skill
> Gaue vs much light from his abundant quill."

Samuel Pepys Diary [June 14, 1663]:

". . . to Sir W. Pen's to visit him. . . . By and by in comes Sir J. Minnes, and Sir W. Batten, and so we sat talking. Among other things Sir J. Minnes brought many fine expressions of Chaucer, which he doats on mightily, and without doubt he is a very fine poet."

John Evelyn, *The Immortality of Poesie* [1685]:

> "Old Chaucer shall, for his facetious style,
> Be read and prais'd by warlike Britains, while
> The Sea enriches, and defends their Isle."

Joseph Addison, *An Account of the Greatest English Poets* [1694]:

> "Long had our dull Fore-Fathers slept Supine,
> Nor felt the Raptures of the Tuneful Nine;
> Till Chaucer first, a merry Bard, arose;
> And many a Story told in Rhime and Prose,
> But Age has Rusted what the Poet writ,
> Worn out his Language, and obscur'd his Wit:
> In vain he jests in his unpolish'd strain
> And tries to make his Readers laugh in vain."

John Dryden, *Fables Ancient and Modern* [1700]:

Dryden, comparing Chaucer with Ovid says: "Both of them understood the Manners; under which Name I comprehend the Passions, and, in a larger Sense, the Descriptions of Persons, and their very Habits: For an Example, I see *Baucis* and *Philemon* as perfectly before me, as if some ancient Painter had drawn them; and all the Pilgrims in the *Canterbury Tales,* their Humours, their Features, and the very Dress, as distinctly as if I had supp'd with them at the *Tabard* in *Southwark;* Yet even there, too, the Figures of Chaucer are much more lively, and set in a better Light. . . . It remains that I say somewhat of Chaucer in particular.

"In the first place, as he is the Father of *English* Poetry, so I hold him in the same Degree of Veneration as the *Grecians* held *Homer,* or the *Romans Virgil:* He is a perpetual Fountain of good Sense; learn'd in all Sciences; and, therefore speaks properly on all Subjects: As he knew what to say, so he knows also when to leave off; a Continence which is practis'd by few Writers, . . .

"Chaucer follow'd Nature every where, but was never so bold to go beyond her: . . . The Verse of *Chaucer,* I confess, is not Harmonious to us; . . . There is the rude Sweetness of a *Scotch* Tune in it, which is natural and pleasing, though not perfect. 'Tis true, I cannot go so far as he who publish'd the last Edition of him; for he would make us believe the Fault is in our Ears, and that there were really Ten Syllables in a Verse where we find but Nine: But this Opinion is not worth confuting; 'tis so gross and obvious an Errour . . . We can only say, that he liv'd in the Infancy of our Poetry, and that nothing is brought to Perfection at the first. . . . But enough of this: There is such a Variety of Game springing up before me, that I am distracted in my Choice, and know not which to follow. 'Tis sufficient to say according to the Proverb, that here is God's Plenty. . . . *Chaucer,* I confess, is a rough Diamond, and must first be polish'd e'er he shines."

Dryden, in modernizing some of Chaucer tales, says: "I have confined my Choice to such Tales of *Chaucer* as savour nothing of Immodesty. If I desir'd more to please than to instruct, the *Reve,* the *Miller,* the *Shipman,* the *Merchant,* the *Sumner,* and above all, the *Wife of Bathe,* in the Prologue to her Tale, would have procur'd me as many Friends and Readers, as there are *Beaux* and Ladies of Pleasure in the Town. But I will no more offend against Good Manners: I am sensible as I ought to be of the Scandal I have given by my loose Writings; and make what Reparation I am able, by this Public Acknowledgement. . . . *Chaucer* makes another manner of Apologie for his broad speaking, and *Boccace* makes the like; but I will follow neither of them. Our Country-man, in the end of his Characters, before the *Canterbury Tales,* thus excuses the Ribaldry, which is very gross in many of his Novels:

> But firste, I pray you of your courtesy,
> That ye ne arrete it nought my villany,
> Though that I plainly speak in this mattere, [etc.].

Yet if a Man should have enquir'd of *Boccace* or of *Chaucer,* what need they had of introducing such Characters, when obscene Words were proper in their Mouths, but very undecent to be heard; I know not what Answer they could have made: For that Reason, such Tales shall be left untold by me."

Alexander Pope, *Anecdotes of Books and Men* [1728-1730]:

"I read Chaucer still with as much pleasure as almost any of our poets. He is a master of manners, of description, and the first tale-teller in the true and enlivened natural way."

James Thomson, *The Seasons* [1744]:

> "Chaucer, whose native Manners-painting Verse
> Well-moraliz'd, shines thro' the Gothic cloud
> Of Time and Language o'er thy Genius thrown."

And the Abbé Yart [1749] says: "*Ses autres contes sont encores plus licencieux que ceux de nos poètes les plus obscènes; je les laisserai par la même raison dans l'obscurité de leur vieux langage.*"

Samuel Johnson, *Dictionary* [1755]:

> "Geoffry Chaucer . . . may perhaps, with great justice, be stiled the first of our versifiers who wrote poetically. He does not however appear to have deserved all the praise which he has received, or all the censure that he has suffered."

Oliver Goldsmith, *The Poetical Scale* [1758]:

> Reckoning 20 as perfection, his marking in the scale of Genius is as follows: Chaucer 16, Spenser 18, Shakespeare 19, Ben Jonson 16, Cowley 17, Otway 17, Milton 18, Dryden 18, Addison 16, Prior 16, Swift 18, Pope 18.

Edward Gibbon, *Outlines of the History of the World* [1760]:

> "If any barbarian on this side of the Alps deserves to be remembered [in connection with literature], it is our coun-

tryman Chaucer, whose Gothic dialect often conceals natural humour and poetical imagery."

William Cowper, *Anti-Thelyphthora* [1781]:

> "But what old Chaucer's merry page befits
> The chaster muse of modern days omits.
> Suffice it then in decent terms to say,
> She saw—and turn'd her rosy cheek away."

Dorothy Wordsworth, *Journal* (Dec. 26, 1801):

> "After tea we sate by the fire comfortably.
> I read aloud *The Miller's Tale*."

William Godwin, *Life of Geoffrey Chaucer* [1803]:

"The Canterbury Tales is certainly one of the most extraordinary monuments of human genius."

Lord Byron, *List of the different Poets* [1807]:

"Chaucer, notwithstanding the praises bestowed on him, I think obscene and contemptible:—he owes his celebrity merely to his antiquity."

John Keats, *Letter to Messrs. Taylor and Hessey* [May 16, 1817]:

"At Canterbury I hope the remembrance of Chaucer will set me forward like a Billiard Ball."

Henry Crabb Robinson, *Conversation* with Lamb [1810]:

(Speaking of Blake's drawing and description of the
Canterbury Pilgrims and comparing Stothard's picture with
Blake's) "Lamb preferred the latter greatly, and declared
that Blake's description was the finest criticism he had ever
read of Chaucer's poem."

Thomas Moore, *Diary* [April 14, 1819]:

"Chaucer, for instance, in what terms some speak of him!
while I confess I find him unreadable. Lord L. said he was
glad to hear me say so, as he had always in silence felt the
same."

Robert Southey, *Select Works of British Poets* [1831]:

"Chaucer is not merely the acknowledged father of English poetry, he is also one of our greatest poets. His proper
station is in the first class, with Spenser, Shakspeare, and
Milton; and Shakspeare alone has equalled him in variety
and versatility of genius."

Leigh Hunt, *Preface to his Own Poetical Works* [1832]:

"To return to double rhymes. They are as old in our
language as Chaucer, whose versification is as unlike the
crabbed and unintentional stuff it is supposed to be, as possible, and has never had justice done it. The sweet and
delicate gravity of its music is answerable to the sincerity
of the writer's heart."

Elizabeth Barrett (Browning), *The Book of the Poets*
[1842]:

"But it is in Chaucer we touch the true height, and look
abroad into the kingdoms and glories of our poetical litera-

[335]

ture, . . . And the genius of the poet shares the character of his position: he was made for an early poet, and the metaphors of dawn and spring doubly become him. A morning-star, a lark's exaltation, cannot usher in a glory better. The 'cheerful morning face' . . . 'the breezy call of incense-breathing morn' you recognize in his countenance and voice. . . . He is a king and inherits the earth, and expands his great soul smilingly to embrace his great heritage. . . . His senses are open and delicate, like a young child's—his sensibilities capacious of supersensual relations, like an experienced thinker's. . . ."

Henry David Thoreau, *Homer, Ossian, Chaucer* [1843]:

"We admire Chaucer for his sturdy English wit. . . . But though it [the Prologue] is full of good sense and humanity, it is not transcendent poetry. . . . The charm of his poetry consists often only in an exceeding naturalness, perfect sincerity, with the behaviour of a child rather than of a man. . . . Such pure and genuine and childlike love of Nature is hardly to be found in any poet."

Hartley Coleridge, *Notes on Shakespeare* [1848]:

"The 'Troilus and Cresseide' of Chaucer, the most beautiful diary of love ever written."

George Meredith, *Poems* [1851]:

"Gray with all honours of age! but fresh featured and ruddy
As dawn when the drowsy farm-yard has thrice heard
    Chaunticlere.
Tender to tearfulness—childlike, and manly, and motherly;
Here beats true English blood richest joyance on sweet English ground."

[336]

Bulwer-Lytton, *Letter to his Son* [1860]:

"I am amazed at his [Chaucer's] wonderful accuracy of rhythm; according to his own accentuation, there are as few lines with a defective foot as there are in Dryden."

William Morris, *The Earthly Paradise* [1868-1870]:

"O Master, O thou great of heart and tongue, . . ."

Matthew Arnold, *The Study of Poetry* [1880]:

"Chaucer is not one of the great classics. . . . He has not their accent. What is wanting to him is suggested by the mere mention of the name of the first great classic of Christendom, the immortal poet who died eighty years before Chaucer,—Dante. The accent of such verse as

'In la sua volontade è nostra pace . . .'

is altogether beyond Chaucer's reach; we praise him, but we feel that this accent is out of the question for him."

Algernon Charles Swinburne, *Short Notes on English Poets* [1880]:

"It is through no lack of love and reverence for the name of Chaucer that I must question his right, though the first narrative poet of England, to stand on that account beside her first dramatic, her first epic or her first lyric poet. But, being certainly unprepared to admit his equality with Shakespeare, with Milton, and with Shelley, I would reduce Mr. Rossetti's mystic four to the old sacred number of three. Pure or mere narrative is a form essentially and avowedly inferior to the lyrical or the dramatic form of poetry; and the finer line of distinction which marks it off from the epic marks it also thereby as inferior. . . . Chaucer was in the main a French or Italian poet, lined thoroughly and warmly throughout with the substance of an English humourist. And with this great gift of specially English humour he combined naturally as it were and inevitably, the inseparable twin-born gift of peculiarly English pathos. . . . Dante represents, at its best and highest, the upper class of the dark ages not less than he represents their Italy; Chaucer represents their middle class at its best and wisest, not less than he represents their England; Villon represents their lower class at its worst and best alike, even more than he represents their France. And of these three the English middle class, being incomparably the happiest and wisest, is indisputably, considering the common circumstances of their successive times, the least likely to have left us the highest example of all poetry then possible to men. And of their three legacies, precious and wonderful as it is, the Englishman's is accordingly the least wonderful and the least precious."

You see that with all this praise Chaucer has hardly ever had so much as he receives from the learned men living to-day. In Lydgate's time eulogy was like a grain of mustard seed, and now it is become as a tree, so that the birds of the air might lodge in it.

CHAPTER XXXVII

A Summary, Criticism

A reader, I am told, has his choice among three measures in making an estimate of Chaucer's greatness. He may adopt the historical measure, and praise Chaucer for excellencies that were never known in England before him, for his novel versification, for his return to Nature, for the new humanity he shows; he will call him the father of our English poetry, the morning star of our literature, and proclaim his verse as the foundation on which the greatest of subsequent English poets have built.

Or, the reader may adopt what I should call the objective estimate, but which the self-assured sometimes call the *real* or the *true* estimate; he will then not regard Chaucer primarily as a poet of the fourteenth century; he will push the historical measure aside, and also shut the door upon his own chance preferences—got in boyhood, perhaps, or in a period of adolescent fervor, or from some accidental circumstance that affected his life—and he will seek some larger, more general measure, such as a highly educated man, sensitive to delicate impressions, might be expected to feel; he will swell himself out to larger dimensions, drop his associations with the concrete, huddle up to the abstract, and talk of the absolute in poetry, of truth and beauty in themselves, and so construct a universal measure that shall serve for everybody. The danger here is that this is like painting a landscape as you think you would see it, if you were able to hoist yourself up by your boot-straps to the top of a church steeple; you forswear the testimony of your own senses for the finer standards of a more highly cultivated abstract personage; you renounce the right of private judgment and set up a compromise. If several persons, differing markedly among themselves, say Hamlet, Lady Macbeth, Iago and Cordelia, were each to judge Chaucer by the taste of a highly cultivated gentleman, or by some similar ideal standard, we should surely find as great discrepancies between their four judgments, as if each judge made an estimate according to his or her personal predilection. In order to agree, Hamlet must make concessions to Lady Macbeth's point of view, Iago to Cordelia's. This is the usual way that academic opinions are formed, by compromise. But sometimes critics of great prestige, men of strong character, impatient of uncertainty, impatient of inconstancy, men that like to behold definite and solid accomplishment, are able, of themselves, to establish what they think is, or should be, the opinion of the highly educated ideal gentleman. Whichever the way, by means of this objective standard the edifice of good taste is built, each new critic adding a congruous member, a pillar, a gable, a pinnacle—if there are errors, the error of one counterbalances the error of another—and you have a convenient edifice to which professors and teachers may betake themselves when they are preparing to instruct their classes. If you are going to have a science of criticism, if you mean to construct something that shall last, you must treat poetry in some such objective fashion. But the edifice remains an edifice of convention, and will depend upon polite acquiescence, until such time as all children, learning as they learn a language, shall accept it as a matter of course.

The third measure, one suited to dilettanti, to the whimsical, to the idle-minded, I here advocate: the personal standard. Let me hasten to say that I would not advocate this standard for all readers. I have in mind the egoist, who sets great store by his own private feelings, rather than a conventional person, who prefers the highroad to the by-path, who seeks the ready-made rather than the raw material. If you believe in a *mariage de convenance*, if you choose your club because ample windows look out on some famous avenue, where church-goers pass and repass of a Sunday, if you read books because other people read them, and pick a dog because of his points; why, follow the critics. But, if you marry for love, if you will join a club on a side-street because of good fellowship, if you read a book to please yourself, and take a mongrel because of the way he cocks his head at you, whines to be let in, and frantically frolics when you go for a walk; why, then, put your feet up on the fender and read Chaucer in good print. A plague on these editions that cram all his works into one cover! Good print should be a necessary form of respect for a great poet.

My personal standard then, for it comes down to that, I offer, not for a guide, but as an example, and, if I fall into the language of the objective or the historical standard, it will be merely from carelessness, or to avoid frequent repetition of the first personal pronoun. What does Chaucer mean to me? That, I take to be the important question; not what is his place between Cædmon and Spenser, not what he means to a highly cultivated graduate of Oxford or Harvard, but to me, who have no quick intelligence, no delicate sensitiveness, who am pestered with trivial matters, who have but little time of an evening to sit with my feet on the fender, and yet desire to be ushered into a larger, freer, more stimulating life.

What, then, are the qualities we ask for in the greatest poets? To this question I reply: Good sense, knowledge, learning, human sympathy, intensity, imagination, the grand manner, and melodious verse. To amuse, to entertain, to narrate, are in my judgment lesser qualities. And great poetry must be serious, it should treat human life, human pain, human happiness, as solemn, as sanctified, it should lead the reader to high and holy places, the top of Caucasus, the Mountain of Purgatory, Cordelia's tent.

Montaigne says: "It's a strange thing: we have many more poets than judges and interpreters of poetry: it is easier to write it than completely to comprehend it. In the lower ranges of criticism we can judge it by rules and theories; but true, supreme, divine poetry is above rules and reasons. . . . It does not come within the sphere of our understanding, it sweeps us away, it overwhelms us." I agree; and this very attempt to analyze Chaucer's qualities is in itself a criticism. With Shakespeare, with Milton, with passages in Shelley, Keats, Wordsworth, the poetry *me ravit et ravage;* but with Chaucer, however it may be with scholars, it is not so with me. And, for that reason, I attempt to analyze; and you will notice that, as I think *The Canterbury Tales* should be approached by way of prose, I have demanded various qualities that belong to prose as well as to poetry.

Good sense, then, is indeed a fundamental quality; we need it both in life, and in literature, which is a magic mirror reflecting life, but in its own wondrous way. Shakespeare has it, though his other qualities make us at times forget it, Walter Scott has it abundantly, Dryden has it, Fielding, Jane Austen, Defoe have it, Robert Herrick, and many another, but no one has it in more generous measure than Chaucer. It is the quality that enables him to catch both the outward look and the inward stuff of his characters. By *knowledge* I mean the gatherings of a curious mind, that has observed many people and many things, that has stored them in memory, and brooded over them, till the inert records are converted into energy and power. Chaucer knew a great deal. *Learning:* most of the great English poets were learned men, not perhaps in the sense in which scholars use the word, but as ordinary men employ it, Ben Jonson, Milton, Andrew Marvell, Sir Thomas Browne, Gray, Browning, Tennyson, Matthew Arnold, Swinburne, and so on; one might write a long discourse on the immense value of learning to English poetry. Chaucer was a scholar, a learned man, and found a great part of his materials as we have seen in French and Latin literature. His *human sympathy,* I need not dwell upon; *The Canterbury Tales* is its monument. *Intensity:* this quality I do not find in Chaucer, or but very seldom, one has but to think of Farinata, Ugolino, Shylock, Othello, Moloch, horrid king, Helen MacGregor, the Shropshire Lad, in order to assure oneself of this. *Imagination:* this is the poet's domination, half unconscious, half purposeful, over the the stores of experience that he holds in remembrance, a domination that quickens what memories it touches, impregnates them with fire and power, so that they all, like fairies at Titania's wand, leap from where they lie, join and unite to create new forms, never met before, in blackness, in chiaroscuro, in radiant light—until those old memories, as at a resurrection, in sharp outline and delicate modeling, become metamorphosed into "shapes more real than living man, nurslings of immortality." It is that quality I venture to think, that caused Chaucer—instead of casting his eyes about to find some living sergeant at law, or reeve, or prioress to copy—that caused him, I say, to gather together human traits that he had seen in a hundred different persons and put them together into Madame Eglantine and the others. A *melodious ear:* certainly Chaucer had that, for though the old forms of words, the odd spellings, the antiquated language are hindrances to us in our appreciation of

[343]

him, as they were to Dryden and to Pope, yet we must accept the testimony of those that know Chaucer's poetry by heart. And as for *amusement, entertainment, narration,* Chaucer stands in the front rank. With his wit, his humor, his irony, he is as amusing and entertaining as anybody, and as a story-teller he is admirable, though I should not call him nonpareil, as scholars do. Think of all the tellers of short stories since his time: Prosper Mérimée, Poe, Bret Harte, Maupassant, Paul Heyse, Turgenef, Verga, Mrs. Wharton, O. Henry, not to mention Walter Scott's story of *Wandering Willie,* Hardy's *The Three Strangers,* and a great company of others.

You see I humbly concur in almost all the qualities that scholars have assigned to him. But the *grand manner,* how about that? Matthew Arnold, you remember, denied it to him, and, as I think, justly. Great poets are *spiritual* men. Their imagination renders visible a light—I do not attempt to define what that light may be—that we common men do not see, they are sensitive to a tremulous something that we do not perceive, and thereby they are enabled to portray great characters, to say to us great words that dignify, comfort, encourage and console. The grand manner is a gift of the spirit, the expression of spiritual greatness. Take Shakespeare's characters Hamlet, Othello, Lear, Brutus, Shylock, Antony; take certain phrases of Shakespeare on woman's love:

> You are my true and honorable wife,
> As dear to me as are the ruddy drops
> That visit my sad heart.

Or, when Posthumus puts his arms round Imogen:

> Hang there like fruit, my soul,
> Till the tree die!

[344]

Or, to leave Shakespeare, take Milton's words:

> Farewell, happy fields,
> Where joy for ever dwells! Hail, horrors, hail,
> Infernal World! and thou, profoundest Hell,
> Receive thy new possessor—one who brings
> A mind not to be changed by place or time.

Or, Calderon:

> *Qué es la vida? Un frenesí:*
> *Qué es la vida? Una ilusion,*
> *Una sombra, una ficcion,*
> *Y el mayor bien es pequeño;*
> *Que toda la vida es sueño,*
> *Y los sueños sueños son.*

> What is life? Madness:
> What is life? An illusion,
> A shadow, an imagining,
> And the greatest good is small;
> For all life is a dream,
> And dreams are dreams.

Or the sad cry of Faust:

> *O das dem Menschen nichts Vollkommnes wird,*
> *Empfind' ich nun.*

> O, now I know that nothing Perfect
> Comes to man!

Chaucer does not have the grand manner because he does not deeply touch the soul. Of the ennobling passions, the love of God, or the love of a woman's soul, or the love of a

[345]

great cause, of humanity as a whole, he has nothing to say. I will not attempt to define what religious men mean by the word *God;*

Wer darf ihn nennen?
Und wer bekennen:
Ich glaub' ihn?
Wer empfinden
Und sich unterwinden,
Zu sagen: Ich glaub' ihn nicht?
Der Allumfasser,
Der Allerhalter,
Fasst und erhält er nicht
Dich, mich, sich selbst?
Wölbt sich der Himmel nicht dadroben?
Liegt die Erde nicht hierunten fest?
Und steigen, freundlich blickend,
Ewige Sterne nicht herauf?

Who can name Him?
Who can avow:
I believe in Him?
Who can feel,
And be so bold
As say, "I do not believe in Him"?
The All-encompasser,
The All-upholder,
Doth He not
Uphold and encompass,
You, me, Himself?
Is not the vault of heaven above?
Is not the solid earth below?
And are not those eternal stars
That twinkle kindly down?

Most men during their lives, in moments of exaltation or agony, concern themselves with the relation of the individual soul to the sum of things; but in Chaucer I see no religious emotions, nor do I forget his *A.B.C.*, his translation of St. Bernard's Prayer, or the stanzas at the end of *Troilus and Criseyde;* to me these last stanzas show the artist, the consummate artist, if you will, not the religious-minded man.

As to love of woman, his conception is akin to Boccaccio's, which is physical, but not merely physical, because love in Boccaccio is in great measure a worship of beauty. Even Troilus's love for Cressida, however deep, is of the same category. But there is another love of woman that we call spiritual; and though, in this exquisite plant, the flower no doubt depends upon the root, it is the flower that fills the soul:

> When in disgrace with fortune and men's eyes

> *   *   *   *   *

> Haply I think on thee, and then my state,
> Like to the lark at break of day arising
> From sullen earth, sings hymns at heaven's gate.

Such a lover thinks more of the flower than the root; but Chaucer was not such a one; whenever he appears to be, he is merely "exquisitely weaving reminiscences" gathered from other poets. And as to great causes, as to humanity, Chaucer never loses himself in any enrolment in companies that carry such banners; his irony, his love of the *comédie humaine,* his skeptical spirit, prevents.

Nor, when he recounts the sorrows of the black knight, or of Troilus, or of Arcite, or the grievous blows of misfortune, whether to great kings as in *The Monk's Tale,* or to forsaken ladies, as in *The Legend of Good Women,* is there any of that "high seriousness" that Matthew Arnold demanded, except for a line here or there, maybe. He is always the conscious artist, and the conscious artist does not lose himself in entangling emotions. Indeed, his admirers generally claim pathos and humor as his greatest endowments, and I think they are right. Pathos and humor he possesses in God's plenty, but they are not to me the highest gift. Poetry, as we know, should be "simple, sensuous and impassioned"; Chaucer has the quality of simplicity as his talents for narration prove, he is sensuous as many beautiful stanzas clearly show; but in all his poetry his favorite quality *irony* pops its head up, and you can not have real simplicity, nor real sensuousness, with irony. Irony is an intellectual quality, an alloy that will not blend with the fine gold of emotion. And for passion, as I have said, I think the Elizabethans and many a modern poet surpass him.

CHAPTER XXXVIII

A Summary, Praise

In my last chapter I enacted the disagreeable rôle of a carping critic, a sort of Benjamin Backbite. I denied to Chaucer, very likely on account of personal obtuseness, the qualities that mark the greatest poets. I asserted that Chaucer does not take us up to the high, holy regions that the greatest poets do. I thought that Nature had never said to him:

> Thine, too, these golden keys, immortal Boy!
> This can unlock the gates of Joy;
> Of Horrour that, and thrilling Fears,
> Or ope the sacred source of sympathetic Tears.

He has tender passages, very lovely, the prayer of Custance, when cast adrift, the grief of Troilus betrayed, the lament of the black knight in *The Book of the Duchess,* the murder of the little child that sang *Alma Redemptoris;* these are full of pathos, but one does not brood over them, they do not darken the day. Nor does Chaucer stir the deep chords of one's egoism by singing such joy or sorrow, as one has felt but of oneself can not put into adequate words; he has not the lyrical gift. His verses are not winged like Petrarch's; none of his shorter poems can be compared to Petrarch's *Canzone to the Virgin,* to Dante's *Donne ch'avete intelletto d'amore,* to Shakespeare's sonnets. No; Chaucer's great excellencies lie elsewhere, as you would expect from a man who had lived so much in the world.

[349]

Those excellencies are plain enough. He has an extraordinary fluency of verse; it flows like the River Tarn in its lovely, deep, sapphire-colored reaches, among the high hills of Languedoc. We are a little hindered, most of us, by our unfamiliarity with the form and spelling of many of his words; but if we resolutely disregard a complete apprehension of the meaning, and courageously force the syllables into the beat of the verse, we shall see that Chaucer possesses what the commentators are fond of calling virtuosity. He is a master of sweet sounds. His great poem, *Troilus and Criseyde,* is as melodious, or, should I say nearly, as *The Faerie Queene* or *The Eve of Saint Agnes,* or *Venus and Adonis.* Here his familiarity with Italian served him well, for after he had read Dante's *terza rima,* Petrarch's *canzoni,* and Boccaccio's stanzas, all liquid with soft Italian syllables, all voweled, all ll'd, and mm'd, and rr'd, like music, his ear could not bear such verse as he found in his English predecessors.

It is this sweetness of language, and also, it must be admitted, his fidelity to his French models, that make his descriptions of gardens so charming:

> Doun by a floury grene wente [path]
> Ful thikke of gras, ful softe and swete,
> With floures fele [many], faire under fete,
> And litel used, hyt seemed thus;
> For both Flora and Zephirus,
> They two that make floures growe,
> Had mad her [their] dwellynge ther, I trowe,
> For hit was, on to beholde,
> As thogh the erthe envye wolde
> To be gayer than the heven,
> To have moo floures, swiche seven,
> As in the welken sterres [stars] bee.
>   *Book of the Duchess.*

Or this:

> A gardyn saw I ful of blosmy bowes,
> Upon a ryver, in a grene mede,
> There as swetnesse evermore inow is,
> With floures white, blewe, yelwe, and rede,
> And colde welle-stremes, nothyng dede,
> That swymmen ful of smale fishes lighte,
> With fynnes rede and skales sylver bryghte.
> *The Parlement of Foules.*

And his charm is the same in his description of young
people, for instance, Virginia in *The Physician's Tale:*

> This mayde of age twelve yeer was and tweye,
> In which that Nature hadde swich delit.
> For right as she can peynte a lilie whit,
> And reed a rose, right with swich peynture
> She peynted hath this noble creature,
> Er she were born, upon her lymes [limbs] fre,
> Where as by right swiche colours sholde be;
> And Phebus dyed hath hire tresses grete
> Lyk to the stremes of his burned heete.
> And if that excellent was hire beautee,
> A thousand foold moore vertuous was she.

Or, in *The Knight's Tale* take the description of Emelye:

> . . . that fairer was to sene
> Than is the lylie upon his stalke grene,
> And fressher than the May with floures newe . . .

Or the gay delineations of hende Nicholas, or the parish
clerk Joly Absolon, and of Alison, the carpenter's wife,
all three in *The Miller's Tale*. And what is more charming,

more sparkling in its dewy glitter, than the Ballade in *The Prologue to The Legend of Good Women?*

> Hyd, Absolon, thy gilte tresses clere;
>   Ester, ley thou thy meknesse all adown;
> Hyd, Jonathas, al thy frendly manere;
> Penalopee and Marcia Catoun [Cato's Marcia],
> Make of youre wifhod no comparysoun;
> Hyde ye youre beautes, Ysoude and Eleyne:
> My lady cometh, that al this may disteyne [bedim].

How right it is to praise Chaucer for his sunshine ways, his love of the bright morning air! I think that *fresh* is his favorite adjective. How he enjoys the glint of Nature, the sheen that lies on mother earth, the glamour, as of Apollo's presence, in grove, in garden and on pictured walls. The beat of his verse, when the matter is joyous, resembles the trot of a greyhound, it moves with light, sure-footed ease, bounding through the heroic couplets, as if it followed its master's scent. Masefield states, unless I mistake, that the rhyme-royal is admirable for telling a story; yes, admirable for narration, but to express passion, no; the repeated rhyme holds back the quick rush of emotion, such as blank verse, or the heroic couplet, permits. But the stanza is at its best (perhaps, by aid of the cæsura, or by sounded final *e*'s) when the subject is sad, and the poet drops into his favorite mood of pathos—for though he loves the high noon of life, he loves the twilight even better. For instance, take this stanza from *Troilus and Criseyde:*

> The lettres ek that she of olde tyme
> Hadde him ysent, he wolde allone rede
> An hondred sithe atwixen noon and prime,
> Refiguryng hire shap, hire wommanhede,

Withinne his herte, and every word or dede
That passed was; and thus he drof [drove] t'an ende
The ferthe [fourth] day, and seyde he wolde wende.

Cheerfulness and pathos are, then, the moods that he best expresses. But still Chaucer's rarest gift is elsewhere. I do not mean his wit, which is delightful, nor his good sense which is not matched in any poet till we come to Walter Scott, nor his irony, which is as good or better than in any man from Lucian to Swift, or whoever the masters of irony are, I mean his dramatic portraitures: Harry Bailly, the Wife of Bath, the Miller, the Reeve, the Friar, the Prioress, and some of the personages in the Tales.

And now we come to an awkward point in judging Chaucer. We are, in this matter of portraiture, passing from poetry to prose, for Chaucer's dramatic presentation of personages is really a matter of prose, even as Falstaff is in prose, as Pistol, Bardolph, Justice Shallow are in prose, or Parson Adams, Squire Western, Square, Twackum, Robinson Crusoe, Meg Merrilies, Andrew Fairservice, Mr. Collins of *Pride and Prejudice,* Pecksniff, Sam Weller, Mrs. Proudie, and other familiar characters in English fiction, are in prose.

You will say that Chaucer's *dramatis personæ* are not in prose, but in verse. Yes, in verse, but not in poetry; for there is an intermediate region of meter and rhyme which is not prose, and yet not what we mean by poetry, at least not when we use the word in any strict sense. Verse, no doubt, is a better medium than prose for Chaucer's characters, but better because it brings them more smartly, more dramatically, to our minds, not because it makes them more poetic. One needs but run over the *dramatis personæ* of any one of Shakespeare's plays—*e.g., As You Like It,* Rosalind, Orlando, Touchstone, the melancholy Jacques—to

[353]

mark the difference between them and the Canterbury pilgrims. Shakespeare's characters are in the order of poetry, Chaucer's pilgrims are in the order of prose. Fielding might have drawn Harry Bailly and the Wife of Bath; Dickens, if he had not belonged to a Victorian age, could have drawn the Miller, the Reeve, the Summoner and the Friar; Walter Scott could have described the Knight; Jane Austen the Prioress; Hardy the Poor Parson, or, if you insist that Chaucer's dexterity of verse has added to the effectiveness of his descriptions, it is a difference of degree, not a difference of kind; his personages still remain in the order of prose, or of versification, not in the order of poetry.

Chaucer, then has a brilliant wit, good sense, a delightful many-hued irony, a power of showing us a beauty in familiar things, an unsurpassed skill in drawing characters of comedy in clear, definite, realistic exactitude—how much better they are than Sheridan's or Bernard Shaw's, it is this that makes Professor Manly and Professor Rickert sure that he is describing real people—a tender sense of pathos, an ability to suffuse his pictures with the light of rising suns, and he possesses a mastery of the craft of verse. But all these gifts are not enough to raise him into the class of the supreme poets—Shakespeare, Dante, Homer, Milton, Goethe. He lacks the power to make us feel the heroic elements in life, the dignity of the soul, the poignancy that grief may contain, or all the rapture of joy. I often ask myself, Why? and propose various answers. Circumstances certainly hindered him from listening to the deep solemn undertones that to a great poet's ear lift human life from the animal to the spiritual. His attendance at court, his studies in shallow French poetry, his employment in the custom-house, his allegiance to John of Gaunt, his embassies, all these were hindrances. The times, too, were unfavorable. England's glory was on the wane, and could not give an exaltation, such as the Elizabethans felt when their seamen were singeing the King of Spain's beard. The Catholic religion had lost its power to stir the heart, it was stained by avarice and political chicanery; the worship of the Virgin had become mere lip service. The spirit of realism was brushing away the mystical yearnings that had flooded the twelfth and thirteenth centuries; the Reformers, Wycliffe and his friends, had set their faces toward Protestantism, and concerned themselves with moral behavior, or metaphysical questions such as transubstantiation. A poet can not escape the limitations of his age, and Chaucer could not of himself break through the unspiritual limitations of his time. But more than these outer hindrances, there was a personal lack of sympathy in Chaucer himself with the deep possibilities of life; to me this seems perfectly clear from his relation to Dante. He knew the *Divina Commedia* and he knew it well, for he borrows metaphors and images from various cantos in the *Inferno,* the *Purgatorio* and the *Paradiso;* but he is like a pagan going into the cathedral at Chartres. The glory of it never makes him fall on his knees; his eyes stare but do not see, his ears are open but he does not hear. How different when he is in Boccaccio's company, a man in so many ways very like himself; he took to Boccaccio as a duck takes to water. If then, Chaucer does not stir our souls, it is because he was not interested in the soul; he was not a religious man, religious, I mean, in the sense of feeling— in the teeth of science, in the teeth of common sense—that the consciousness of an overarching holiness is the greatest attainment of the supreme poet. In Shakespeare you feel, as you feel in the New Testament, that the characters are spiritual beings, not animals, and you judge them by spiritual standards; but you never think of Chaucer's pilgrims in that manner.

As to the coarse stories in *The Canterbury Tales,* it is

easy to affect a purity of mind that is disgusted with such stories. Lord Byron, I assume, delicately refrained from reading them, and that is what we all can do. Would any man expunge Rabelais, Boccaccio, the dramatists of the Restoration, Fielding and many another, because they depicted human nature as they saw it? Nonsense.

Chaucer took his materials for story-telling as he found them, and the medieval material had a large streak of Oriental nastiness; and possibly friend Strode pestered him too much with scholastic philosophy or friend Gower bored him with conservative morality, until he felt an imperious need of rolling in something gross. However this may be, Chaucer certainly had "a roast-beef stomach"; he enjoyed Grylle's humor, and perhaps he counted, rightly or wrongly, on finding most readers in sympathy with him. Churls amused and interested him, and he painted them to the life. A man's taste in drollery is his own affair. That does not affect his place in literature. Peace to that matter.

Of the scholars that deal with Chaucer whom I have read, Mr. Legouis, the Frenchman, is to me the most sympathetic. He finds in Chaucer neither the highest passion, nor the highest imagination; he believes that he has read other poetry which is more noble, more essentially poetical, more exquisite, more refined, "but where shall we find [he says] except in Chaucer, a work where the principal aim has been to portray men truthfully, without exalting or disparaging them, and to present an exact picture of average humanity? Chaucer sees things as they are, and paints them as he sees them."

True, but is that the task of great poetry? Many of us, in times of sorrow, of tedium, of vexation, when the lamp of life burns low, when the vulgarity of the world sickens the heart, or the nonsense of human existence dogs us like Mephistopheles, many of us, I say, desire to behold things as they are not, to behold them painted in colors that never were on land or sea—desire to behold a brave world as Homer, as Turner, as Walter Scott, saw it, or better still, to be lifted into such regions of the mind as Shakespeare imagined, or Dante. Chaucer is not (I repeat), in my judgment, among the greatest, but immensely clever, immensely shrewd, kindly and generous, a consummate master of meter, and a jolly good fellow.

But I must terminate. Let us say good-bye to him as he sits, surrounded by his books, in a chamber within his newly hired house in the garden of the Chapel of Saint Mary, Westminster, brimming over with broad humanity, with kindliness, good temper, generous sympathies, tender pity, love of beauty and love of innocence. Perhaps a service may be going on in the Abbey, and if it is evening, the storied windows may be lit up, and the sound of an organ and the voices of choristers mount to his ears; perhaps they sing Thomas Aquinas's great hymn, *Pange lingua,* in passionate protest against Wycliffe's attempt to apply common sense to that which common sense does not subtend:

Verbum caro, panem verum
Verbo carnem efficit.

And, though Chaucer believes but little, very little, of tenets and dogmas, nothing perhaps, the sound may draw his attention from what he is reading and send his thoughts back to the early days of his red and black breeches, of his crossing the Channel with men at arms and archers in the train of Edward III, of his first sight of Philippa in all the radiance of sixteen years, of meeting Froissart and reading the *Roman de la Rose,* of the applause that greeted *The Book of the Duchess,* of his visit to Italy, of olives and oranges, of Giotto and Orcagna, of Boccaccio's poems, of the custom-house, of Jack Straw's men tramping through Aldgate, and all the brilliant procession of his life. Perhaps he looks out the window up at the stars, wondering, not whether there are spiritual powers there, but whether, as they twinkled on from generation to generation, they would see men reading *Troilus and Criseyde* and *The Canterbury Tales,* and whether those readers would realize that he, Geoffrey Chaucer, was not only a great poet, but in the person of Harry Bailly had drawn the truest typical Englishman that has ever been delineated, would realize that he had done more than any other man to make English men Englishmen. And with an ironical smile at the notion that he cared what future generations might think, he leaves the window.

But perhaps the fresh autumnal air has chilled his old bones and warned him that the hour was at hand when he should say good-bye to this dear world and all its drollery, to England, to poetry, to all the gladness and all the sadness of poor humanity, and blending with those thoughts, perhaps, came again the strains of the noble hymn:

> *Genitori Genitoque*
> *Laus et jubilatio,*
> *Salus, honor, virtus quoque*
> *Sit et benedictio:*
> *Procedenti ab utroque*
> *Compar sit laudatio.*

Was there, then, some truth in it? Could there be a God the Father, and a God the Son, and a God the Holy Ghost? Could there be a life hereafter, and a Day of Judgment? Would he appear before the throne of the Lamb and have to answer for every idle word? Was the whole Christian scheme of right and wrong, of free will, of reward and punishment, a wild Patmian dream of bigoted ascetics, or was there something in it? What had Harry Bailly thought of it all? What had the Knight? Why had the Wife of Bath made all her pilgrimages?

He shut the window. It was very chill. The manuscript of *The Canterbury Tales* lay on his table; he had not been able to arrange their order to his liking. What should he do about it? He felt very old; it was too late to make any material alterations, besides many copies were abroad. *The Parson's Tale,* of course, must come last. He picked it up. Why had he written all this stuff? He read a few pages and smiled. Another strain from the organ reached his ears, and the smile died out. He took his pen, and wrote fast; "Now preye I to hem alle that herkne this litel tretys or rede . . ." He wrote and paused, wrote again, "Wherefore I biseke yow mekely, for the mercy of God, that ye preye for me and foryeve me my giltes; and namely of my translacions and enditynges of worldly vanitees, the whiche I revoke in my [what word should he use?] retracciouns; as is the book of Troilus; the book also of Fame; the book of the XIX Ladies; the book of the Duchesse; the book of Seint Valentynes day of the Parlement of Briddes; the tales of Caunterbury, thilke [those] that sownen into [tend toward] synne; . . . and many another book, if they were in my remembrance, and many a song and many a leccherous lay; that Christ for his grete mercy foryeve me the synne." But, as he remembered, some of his writings had been pious and moral. Thank Christ and his Mother and all the saints for that! and he continued: "Bisekynge hem that they from hennes forth unto my lyve's ende send me grace to biwayle my giltes, and to study to the salvacioun of my soul, and graunte me grace of verray penitance, confessioun and satisfaccioun to doon in this present lyf, thurgh the benigne grace of him that is Kyng of Kynges. . . . Qui cum patre

[359]

et Spiritu Sancto vivit et regnat Deus per omnia secula. Amen."

There it is, at the end of *The Poor Parson's Tale,* this prayer of repentance for vain, idle or sinful books. My thinking is that he has been enough blamed in this world for his churls' tales, and that in any other judgment he will be forgiven. If it will do good, it would be well for us to pray for him, and still better if he will pray for us.

God rest his soul.

THE END

APPENDIX

I

CONFIDENTIAL ADVICE

I ventured, in my first chapter, to suggest that scholars, with their learning, with the enthusiasm and bias bred of learning, are not safe guides for us common folk. Our little steps can not keep pace with their great strides. Their relish is caviar to us. And so I make bold, not to counsel, but rather to suggest, that in your first acquaintance with Chaucer you should not read all that they admire, but that you should skip certain parts and only read a portion. What I should do is this:

Read

The Book of the Duchess
Troilus and Criseyde
Prologue to The Legend of Good Women
The Prologue and all connecting matter
    that joins *The Canterbury Tales* together
The Knight's Tale
The Wife of Bath's Prologue and Tale
The Pardoner's Tale
The Prioress's Tale
The Nun's Priest's Tale

Skip

The House of Fame
The Parlement of Foules
The Tales in *The Legend of Good Women*
The Franklin's Tale
The Physician's Tale
The Shipman's Tale

The Man of Law's Tale
The Clerk's Tale
The Second Nun's Tale
The Squire's Tale
The Tale of Sir Thopas
The Tale of Melibee
The Monk's Tale
The Canon's Yeoman's Tale
The Manciple's Tale
The Parson's Tale
Boece
Treatise on the Astrolabe

All these I skip, in spite of some brilliant passages in *The House of Fame* and *The Parlement of Foules,* because they bore me. As to the tales that Petrarch, Dryden, Matthew Brown, l'Abbé Yart and Lord Byron disapprove of, those told by the Miller, the Reeve, the Friar, the Summoner and the Merchant, all spiced and redolent of elementary ale-house humor, I leave them to the reader's discretion.

As to the short poems, please yourselves, I should only read a few:

The Former Age

A blisful lyf, a paisible and a swete,
Ledden the peples in the former age.
They helde hem payed of the fruites that they ete,
Which that the feldes yave hem [them] by usage.

Personally, I prefer Don Quixote's apostrophe to the Golden Age, but that may be because his eloquence gains so much by the setting: "*D_ _ _ _ edad, y siglos dichosos aquellos á quien los antiguos pusieron nombre _ _ rados . . . porque entonces los que en ella vivian, ignoraban estas dos palabras de tuyo y mio*—Happy Age! Happy Centuries which the ancients called Golden . . . because the people that lived then did not know those two words *Thine* and *Mine*."

Truth

Balade de bon Conseyl

Flee fro the prees, and dwelle with sothfastnesse,
Suffyce unto thy good, though it be smal;
For hord hath hate, and climbing tikelnesse,
Prees hath envye, and wele blent overal;
Savour no more than thee bihove shal;
Reule wel thyself, that other folk canst rede;
And trouthe thee shal delivere, it is no drede.

This praise of truth, these good counsels of Polonius-like character, are dear to schoolmasters on graduation days; and the poem has a personal interest because it seems to be addressed to Sir Philip de la Vache, notable as son-in-law to Chaucer's friend, Sir Lewis Clifford, and as possessor of an interesting crest; *a cow's leg ermine, bent toward the dexter, the hoof upward, or.*

Gentilesse and *Lak of Stedfastnesse*, moral ballades that seem to come from Chaucer's heart, and *Lenvoy to Scogan*, *Lenvoy to Bukton*, *The Complaint of Chaucer to his Purse* and the *Lines to Adam Scriveyn*, are all interesting for the personal element in them.

There, then, is the canon that I commend to readers.

II

CHRONOLOGY

Taken for the most part from the Life Records of Chaucer

1340   Sea-fight off Sluys.

1342?   Birth of Chaucer.

1346   Battle of Crécy.

1348–1349   Black Death.

1350   Sea Fight of Espagnols-sur-mer.

1356   Battle of Poitiers.

1357   April 4, Geoffrey Chaucer, page to the Countess of Ulster, wife of Prince Lionel, receives a paltok, or short cloak, costing 4s; a pair of red and black breeches, 3s.

            May 20, Chaucer receives 2s.

            Dec. 20. Chaucer receives 2s-6d for necessaries against the feast of the Nativity, Christmas.

1359   John of Gaunt marries Blanche, daughter to Henry, Duke of Lancaster.

            Oct. King Edward's campaign in France.

1360	March 1. King gave £16 in aid of Chaucer's ransom, *in subsidium redempcionis sue.*
	Peace of Brétigny.
	Oct. Payment to Chaucer by order of Prince Lionel of 9s for carrying letters from Calais to England.
1366	Death of Chaucer's father. Remarriage of his mother. His own marriage to Philippa Roet now or earlier.
	Sept. 12. Grant to Philippa Chaucer, *una domicellarum camere* of Queen Philippa, of 10 marks per annum to be paid for life, at Michaelmas and Easter.
1367	Dilectus Vallectus (yeoman) noster Geoffrey Chaucer to receive an annuity of 20 marks for life payable at Michaelmas and Easter.
	Victory of Black Prince at Navarete in Spain.
1368	Prince Lionel, a widower, goes to Milan to marry Violante Visconti.
	Dec. A schedule of the names of the Household of Edward III includes Chaucer among the Esquires and Philippa among the Damoiselles.
1369	Charles V of France summons the Black Prince to appear before him.
	April. War with France renewed.
	Summer. John of Gaunt makes raid in northern France.
	Return of Plague.

Aug. 15. Death of Queen Philippa.

Sept. 12. Death of Blanche, Duchess of Lancaster, wife of John of Gaunt.

1370   June 20. Chaucer, going to parts beyond the seas, receives letters of protection till Michaelmas.

1371   John of Gaunt marries his second wife, Constance, daughter of Don Pedro, late King of Castile.

1372   May 1. Gift to Katharine Swynford from John of Gaunt, £10.

Aug. 30. The Duke of Lancaster grants a pension of £10 yearly to Philippa *pur le bon et agreable service que nostre bien ame Damoysele ad fait et ferra en temps avenir a nostre treschere et tresame compaigne la Reine* [Constance].

Nov. 12. Commission appointing James Provan, John de Mari and Geoffrey Chaucer, as envoys to treat with the Doge, Citizens and Merchants of Genoa.

Dec. 1. Payment to Chaucer of £66-13s-4d for his expenses in his mission to foreign parts on the King's secret affairs. The first Italian journey.

1373   May 1. Gift of a "buttoner" and six silver gilt buttons to Philippa from John of Gaunt through his Wardrobe Keeper.

May 23. Chaucer's account of receipts and expenses for his journey to Genoa and Florence from Dec. 1, 1372, to May 23, 1373. First Italian journey.

1374   Feb. 4. Payment to Geoffrey Chaucer, Esquire, *(armiger Regis)* of £25-6s-8d for his wages and expenses in going to Genoa and Florence.

April 23. King Edward grants Chaucer a pitcher of wine daily, to be received in the Port of London.

May 10. Mayor of London grants lease of "mansion" above Aldgate to Chaucer for life.

June 8. Chaucer is appointed comptroller of the custom and subsidy of wools, hides and wool-fells in the Port of London.

June 8, 12. Chaucer is also appointed comptroller of the petty customs of wines, etc., in the Port of London.

June 13. John of Gaunt grants £10 for life to Chaucer for Chaucer's services to him, and also for the services of Philippa Chaucer to Queen Philippa, and to John of Gaunt's wife.

1375   Nov. 8. Chaucer appointed guardian of lands and person of Edmund Staplegate, of Kent, aged 18, for which he was subsequently paid £104.

Dec. 28. Chaucer granted the wardship of the heir of John Solys of Kent.

1376   April-July. Session of Good Parliament.

June 8. Death of the Black Prince.

July 12. Chaucer receives grant of the price of wool forfeited by John Kent of London for evading customs.

Dec. 23. Chaucer receives £6-13s-4d (equal to ten marks) for going on the King's secret affairs in company of Sir John de Burley.

1377   Jan. 27. Session of Bad Parliament.

Feb. 12. Letters of protection to Chaucer till September 29, he being about to go abroad in King's service.

Feb. 17. Payment of £10 to Chaucer, who is to go to Flanders with Sir Thomas Percy, on the King's secret affairs.

Feb. 19. Trial of Wycliffe before convocation of Bishops.

April 11. Chaucer receives £20 as a reward for his services in several voyages abroad.

April 28. Letters of protection to Chaucer till August 1, who is about to go abroad in the King's service.

April 30. Payment of £26-13s-4d on account, to Chaucer, sent to France on the King's secret affairs; probably to treat of peace, or a truce.

June 2. Death of Edward III, accession of Richard II.

June 22. King Richard II confirms Chaucer in office of comptroller of the customs.

1378   March 23. Richard II confirms Chaucer's annuity of 20 marks.

March 26. Richard II confirms Philippa's annuity of 10 marks.

April 18. Chaucer's daily pitcher of wine commuted for 20 marks a year.

May 10. Letters of protection to Chaucer, going abroad on the King's service, until Christmas.

May 21. Letters of attorney to John Gower and Richard Forester during his absence abroad.

May 28. Payments to Edward de Berkeley, £133-6s-8d, and to Geoffrey Chaucer £66-13s-4d, sent to the Lord of Milan and to John Hawkwood, on certain matters concerning the King's wars.

Sept. 19. Chaucer's accounts for his journey from May 28 to date.

1380   Jan. 2. New Year's gift from John of Gaunt to Philippa Chaucer of a silver-gilt cup with cover.

May 1. Deed of Release from Cecily Chaumpaigne to Chaucer in respect to her "raptus," (usually interpreted to be a forcible elopement).

1381   March 6. Payment to John of Gaunt for another New Year's gift to Philippa of a silver-gilt cup with cover.

March 6. Gift of £22 from King to Chaucer as compensation for his wages and expenses in going to France in the time of Edward III to treat of peace and again to negotiate a marriage between the King and a French Princess.

June 7-15. Wat Tyler's Rebellion.

June 19. Chaucer releases his rights to his father's old house on Thames Street next Walbrook.

Nov. 28. Payment to Nicholas Brembre and to John Philipot, Collectors of Customs in the Port of London of £20 each, and to Geoffrey Chaucer, 10 marks, for their assiduous labor and diligence in their offices for the collections of moneys from customs during the last year.

[371]

1382	Jan. Marriage of King Richard and Anne of Bohemia.

1382   Jan. Marriage of King Richard and Anne of Bohemia.

April 20. Grant to Chaucer of the office of comptroller of the petty customs in the Port of London.

May 6. Payment by John of Gaunt for another silver-gilt cup with cover, given as New Year's present to Philippa.

1384   Feb. 11. Again a gift of £20 each to Brembre and Philipot, and of 10 marks to Geoffrey Chaucer, as on November 28, 1381.

Nov. 25. License to Chaucer to be absent from his office for one month, provided he appoint a proper deputy.

Dec. 9. A gift to Brembre, Organ (successor to Philipot deceased) and Chaucer, for their assiduous labor and diligence in office during the past year with respect to collection of moneys from customs, as well as for their costs and expenses during that year, £46-13s-4d (the same as before).

1385   Feb. Chaucer petitions for leave to appoint a permanent deputy at the wool-quay in London (comptrollership of customs) : Granted.

Oct. 12. Association of Chaucer with Simon Burley Warden of the Cinque Ports, John de Cobham, and fourteen others, as justices of the peace for the County of Kent.

Dec. 11. Rewards to Brembre, Organ and Chaucer as before.

1386 Feb. 19. Philippa Chaucer admitted together with Henry Bolingbroke, Sir Thomas Swynford and others as Sister and Brethren of Lincoln Cathedral Church.

June 28. Commission of the Peace to Simon Burley, Warden of the Cinque Ports, John de Cobham, Robert Tresilian, thirteen others, and to Chaucer, for the County of Kent.

Aug. 8. Geoffrey Chaucer, and William Betenham, elected Knights of the Shire to Parliament, sitting on October 1.

Oct.-Nov. Session of parliament.

Oct. 5. The dwelling at Aldgate, formerly occupied by Chaucer, let to Richard Forster (one of Chaucer's attorneys in 1378).

Oct. 15. Chaucer testifies in the refectory of Westminster Abbey, Westminster, in *Scrope v. Grosvenor*, concerning the right to bear arms *dazure ove une bende dor.*

Nov. 28. Payment to Chaucer and his colleague as knights of the shire, for 61 days' service, £24-9s.

Nov. 28. Rewards to Brembre, Organ and Chaucer as on Dec. 11, 1385.

Dec. 4 and 14. Appointment of Adam Yerdele in place of Chaucer as comptroller of the customs of wools, etc., and of Henry Gisors as comptroller of the petty custom.

1387 May 16. Commission to William Rikhill, Geoffrey Chaucer and others to inquire as to the abduction of Isabella, daughter and heir of William atte Halle at Chiselhurst, Kent.

Dec. 20. Threat of civil war. Defeat of De Vere by the Magnates at Radcot Bridge.

1388   Feb. 3. The Merciless Parliament meets and impeaches King's friends. Execution of Brembre and others.

May 1. Chaucer surrenders his annuity of 40 marks, which is granted to John Scalby.

1389   May 3. King Richard resumes Royal authority.

July 12. Chaucer appointed clerk of the works at Westminster Palace, the Tower of London and elsewhere.

Aug. 15. Truce with France.

Nov. Return of John of Gaunt.

1390   March 12. Commission to Sir Richard Stury, Geoffrey Chaucer and others to survey the walls, ditches, sewers, bridges, etc., along the Thames from Greenwich to Woolwich.

July 12. Chaucer appointed to repair St. George's Chapel, Windsor, etc.

1390–1400? Chaucer sub-forester of the Forest of North Petherton, Somerset, appointed by Peter Courtenay.

1390   Sept. Chaucer robbed two or three times.

1391   April 6. Loan from Chaucer to the Exchequer of £66-13s-4d.

June 17. Chaucer surrenders his office as clerk of the works to John Gedney, his successor.

July 8. He resigns, also, his job at St. George's Chapel, to Gedney.

1393   Jan. 9. Gift of £10 by the King to Chaucer, as a reward for his good service during the present year.

May 22. Repayment to Chaucer of the £66-13s-4d lent to Exchequer.

1394   Feb. 28. King grants Chaucer annuity of £20.

March 24. Death of Constance, wife of Gaunt.

May 24. Truce with France renewed for four years.

June 7. Death of Queen Anne.

Sept. Gaunt goes to Guienne.

1395   July. Froissart revisits England.

Dec. (?) Gaunt recalled to England.

1396   Jan. Gaunt marries Katharine Swynford.

March 9. Marriage between King Richard and Princess Isabelle arranged, and truce with France extended.

April 6. Gregory Ballard appoints Chaucer and others his attorneys to take seisin of certain lands in Kent.

Nov. 4. Richard marries Princess Isabelle at Calais.

1397	Feb. King legitimizes Gaunt's children by Katharine Swynford, the Beauforts.
	July. Richard's *coup d'état;* he arrests Gloucester Warwick and Arundel.
	Sept. Parliament meets. The three lords condemned, Arundel is beheaded, Gloucester dies at Calais.
1398	April-May. Renewal of truce with France.
	April 24-May 20. Action of debt in the Court of Common Pleas by Isabella, widow and administratrix of Walter Bukholt, Esquire, against Chaucer for £14-1s-11d.
	May 4. Royal protection granted to Chaucer because he is busy on urgent affairs of the King.
	Sept. Henry Bolingbroke and Thomas Mowbray, Duke of Norfolk, banished.
	Oct. 13. Chaucer petitions King for butt of wine yearly. Granted.
1399	Feb. 3. Death of Gaunt.
	March 18. Richard deprives Henry Bolingbroke of his Lancastrian inheritance.
	May. Richard goes to Ireland.
	July. Bolingbroke lands in Yorkshire.
	Aug. 19. Richard submits to Bolingbroke.
	Sept. 29. Richard resigns the crown, Bolingbroke elected King Henry IV.
	Oct. 13. Henry IV grants to Geoffrey Chaucer an annuity of 40 marks in addition to £20 given by King Richard.

Oct. 16. Henry IV appoints Thomas Chaucer constable of Wallingford Castle.

Oct. 23. Henry IV grants Thomas Chaucer 20 marks yearly, also the office of steward of the honor of Wallingford, etc.

Dec. 24. Warden of St. Mary's Chapel in Westminster Abbey, leases to Geoffrey Chaucer a tenement in the garden of the Chapel for 53 years at a rent of 53s-4d a year.

1400   Feb. 14. Death of King Richard.

Oct. 25. Death of Chaucer.

III

BOOKS FOR BEGINNERS

The Complete Works of Geoffrey Chaucer, edited by W. W. Skeat, in six volumes, Oxford, 1894.

The Complete Works of Geoffrey Chaucer, edited by F. N. Robinson, Students Cambridge Edition, 1933.

Life-Records of Chaucer, published by the Chaucer Society, 1875-1900.

Chaucer, a Bibliographical Manual, E. P. Hammond, 1908.

A Bibliography of Chaucer, D. D. Griffith, 1908-1924.

Chaucer's Official Life, J. R. Hulbert, 1912.

Chaucer, Essays and Studies. O. F. Emerson, 1929.

Geoffrey Chaucer, E. Legouis, Paris, 1910, translated by L. Lailavoix.

Some New Light on Chaucer, J. M. Manly, 1926.

Five Hundred Years of Chaucer Criticism and Allusion, 1357-1900, C. F. E. Spurgeon, 1925.

A Chaucer Handbook, R. D. French, 1927.

Chaucer, George H. Cowling, 1927.

Chaucer and His Poetry, lectures, G. L. Kittredge, 1915.

Geoffrey Chaucer, lectures, John Livingston Lowes 1934.

Three Chaucer Studies, Krauss, Braddy, Kase, 1932.

Froissart's Chronicles.

John of Gaunt, Armitage-Smith, 1904.

The Great Revolt of 1381, C. W. C. Omen, 1906.

The Bibliography in the back of Professor French's *A Chaucer Handbook,* gives a full list of references to special and general studies. For those who care to look at Chaucer's models I mention:

Œuvres de Guillaume de Machaut, Société des Anciens Textes
Français, 1908.

Guillaume de Machaut, edited by V. Chicmaref, 1909.

Œuvres de Froissart, Poésies, edited by Auguste Scheler,
1870.

Œuvres Complètes de Eustache Deschamps, edited by le Mar-
quis de Queux de Saint-Hilaire, 1880.

Il Filostrato, Boccaccio, for *Troilus and Criseyde.*

La Teseide, Boccaccio, for *The Knight's Tale.*

And for literary criticism see:

Fables, Ancient and Modern, John Dryden, 1699.

Chaucer, James Russell Lowell, 1870.

The Study of Poetry, Matthew Arnold, 1880.

IV

INDEX

[380]

Chaucer, Lewis, 221
Chaucer, Richard, 28
Chaucer, Robert (father of John
  Chaucer), 28
Chaucer Society, 18, 58
Chaucer, Thomas, 86, 213, 221,
  222, 223, 319
  appointed constable of Walling-
    ford Castle, 317, 318, 321
  marriage to daughter of Sir
    John Burghersh, 321
Cheshire, 210, 310, 312
Child, Professor F. J., 18
Chiltern Langley (manor), 298,
  299
Chipping Norton, 210
Cicero
  Dream of Scipio, The, 159
Clarendon (manor), 298, 299
Clifford, Sir Richard
  appointed keeper of privy seal,
    317
Cobham, John de, 32, 206, 208, 212
Coblenz, 28
Coleridge, Hartley
  Notes on Shakespeare
    quoted on Chaucer, 336
Coleridge, Samuel Taylor, ix, 53,
  64, 66, 168, 228
  quoted on Chaucer, xiii
  quoted on Chaucer's meter, 66
  Rime of the Ancient Mariner,
    The
    quoted, 173
Collins, William
  Ode to Evening, 64
Cologne, 28, 137, 157
Colonne, Guido delle, 96
  Historia Trojana, 180
Constance (daughter of King of
  Castile), 87
  death of, 374
  marriage to John of Gaunt, 83
Conway, Lord, 312
  quoted, 225
Copton, Hamo de, 28
Cornwall, 84
Coruña, 83
Cotswolds, 210
Coucy, Lord de, 133
Courtenay, Sir Peter, 305
Cowper, William
  Anti-Thelyphthora
    quoted on Chaucer, 334

Crécy, battle of, 23, 24, 28, 32, 50,
  134, 135, 242
Cripplegate, 26

Dante, 66, 91-100, 109, 116, 117,
  212, 226, 354, 357
  Divine Comedy, 91, 355
  influence on *The House of*
    Fame, 93
  quoted, 97-98, 169
  spiritual difference between
    Chaucer and, 92
Dartford, 29, 142, 234
Dartmouth, 22
D'Aubrechicourt, Sir Eustace, 35
David, King of Scotland, 27, 30
Deguilleville, Guillaume de, 62
  Pèlerinage de l' Ame, 232
Dekker, Thomas
  Knights Coniuring, A
    quoted on Chaucer, 329
Delaware, Lord, 32
Deptford, 234
Derby, Earl of
  see Henry Bolingbroke
Deschamps, Eustache, 48, 91, 96,
  117, 232
  quoted, 51-52
Despenser, Sir Edward, 32, 44
Devon, 84
Donato, 114, 115, 116
Doncaster, castle of, 30
Don Pedro, King of Castile, 72,
  82, 83
Dover, 22, 32, 43, 46, 72, 82, 133,
  158
Drayton, Michael
  To Henery Reynolds Esquire
    quoted, 330
Dryden, John, 18, 112, 244, 333,
  342, 344
  Absalom and Achitophel
    quoted, 172
  Fables Ancient and Modern
    quoted on Chaucer, 331-32
Du Guesclin, 73, 83
Dunbar, William
  Golden Targe, The
    quoted on Chaucer, 326
Durham, Bishop of, 32, 207

East Midlands, 25
Edinburgh, 145
Edmund, Prince, 32, 86

Edward I, 26
Edward II, 207
Edward III, 17, 21, 22, 24, 28, 73, 84, 88, 152, 199, 204, 319, 357
  campaign in France, 32-37, 366
  grants Chaucer pitcher of wine daily, 369
Elizabeth, Countess of Ulster
  see under Ulster
Ellis, F. R., 60
Ellis, William, 130
Eltham (manor), 207, 298, 299, 308
Emerson, Ralph Waldo
  quoted, 55
England, 25, 26, 29, 32, 33, 37, 38, 43, 52, 55, 72, 73, 74, 83, 84, 85, 102, 106, 112, 124, 133, 134, 135, 136, 137, 138, 141, 142, 143, 145, 149, 152, 153, 155, 157, 158, 165, 195, 208, 209, 210, 215, 237, 254, 299, 302, 305, 308, 309, 312, 321, 322, 337, 339, 354, 358
  at time of Chaucer's birth, 21-24
  pride in, shown in Chaucer's poetry, x
Espagnols-sur-mer, 199, 366
Essex, 22, 145, 310
Europe, 109, 135, 225
Evelyn, John
  Immortality of Poesie, The
  quoted on Chaucer, 330
Ewelme, 222, 321
Exeter, Bishop of, 303

Fabliaux, 60
Faringdon, 210
Feckenham (manor), 298
Fielding, Henry, xiii, 231, 342, 356
  Joseph Andrews
  quoted, 229-30
Fiesole, 231
Flanders, 22, 25, 26, 84, 124, 130, 225
Fleet River, 26
Florence, 88, 89, 91, 101, 102, 109, 110, 111, 112, 113, 114, 136, 231
Florus, L. Annæus, 199

France, 22, 23, 24, 26, 32, 36, 37, 43, 47, 71, 72, 73, 84, 85, 132, 133, 134, 135, 136 137, 142, 152, 225, 233, 242, 248, 299, 307, 309, 322, 338
France, Marie de, 49
Francesco (Petrarch's son-in-law), 113, 115, 116
Froissart, Jean, 25, 27, 35, 42, 47, 48, 54, 80, 91, 96, 117, 143, 159, 208, 209, 232, 300, 307, 308, 357
  Chronicles, 309
  Paradys d'Amour, Le, 49, 75
  quoted, 133, 142, 149, 314
Fry, Roger, 225
Furnivall, Doctor, 18, 43

Galeasius, John, 135, 136
Gascoigne, Thomas
  quoted, 222
Gascony, 26, 27, 28
Gaunt, John of, x, 38, 39, 43, 73, 78, 82, 136, 155, 158, 204, 206, 212, 213, 215, 216, 222, 223, 309, 311, 320, 322, 354
  becomes Duke of Lancaster, 74
  death of, 311, 376
  death of Constance, wife of, 375
  grant to Chaucer, 369
  marriage to Blanche, Duchess of Lancaster, 31
  marriage to Constance, daughter of King of Castile, 83
  marriage to Katharine Swynford, 321-22, 375
  see also Duke of Lancaster
Genoa, 21, 84, 85, 86, 88, 89, 135, 137
Gentile, Marco, 84
Germany, 51, 299
Ghent, 25, 124, 158
Gibbon, Edward
  Outlines of the History of the World
  quoted on Chaucer, 333-34
Gilchrist, Alexander
  Life of William Blake, xiv
  quoted, 266-73
Gisers, John, 27
Gloucester, Duke of, 86, 206, 207, 208, 210, 211, 212, 303, 307, 309, 310, 311, 322
  see also Thomas of Woodstock

[387]

[389]

Scrope, William, 312
Serico, Lombardo da, 106
Séry, 34
Settignano, 231
Seville, 21, 83
Shakespeare, x-xi, xiii, 53, 56, 66,
    78, 91, 185, 199, 202, 225, 263,
    285, 304, 311, 333, 335, 337,
    342, 344, 354, 355, 357
  Antony and Cleopatra, 237
  As You Like It, 354
  characteristics of poetry of,
    ix-x
  Hamlet, 237
    quoted, 170-71
  Henry IV, 259
    quoted, 205-6
  Midsummer-Night's Dream, A,
    274
  Richard II
    quoted, 313, 314
  Romeo and Juliet
    quoted, 260-62
  Venus and Adonis, 350
Shelley, Mary, 18
Shelley, Percy Bysshe, ix, xii, 22,
    53, 89, 228, 342
  Adonais, 75, 80
  Ode to the West Wind
    quoted, 174
Shene (manor), 298, 299, 310
Shirley, John
  Verses
    quoted on Chaucer, 326
Sittingbourne, 235
Skeat, Reverend W. W., 18, 250,
    289
Sluter, Claas, 225, 226, 236
Sluys, 23, 207
Smithfield, 146, 147, 299, 300, 301,
    302
Solys, John, 234
Somerset, Forests of, 223
Somersetshire, 305, 306
Southampton, 28
Southey, Robert
  Select Works of British Poets
    quoted on Chaucer, 335
Southwark, 25, 29, 144, 234, 235,
    237
Spain, 47, 124
Speght, Thomas, 41
Spencer, Theodore
    quoted, 100

Spenser, Edmund, 53, 161, 285,
    333, 335, 341
  characteristics of poetry of, ix
  Faerie Queene
    quoted, 170, 328, 350
  Shepheardes Calender, The
    quoted on Chaucer, 327-28
Spurgeon, Caroline F. E., xiv
  Five Hundred Years of Chau-
    cer Criticism and Allusion
    quoted, 324-38
Staffordshire, 40
Stamford, Earl of, 32
Staplegate, Edmund, 234
Statute of Laborers, 140
Stendhal
  De l'amour
    quoted, 188
Stevenson, Robert Louis, xiii
Stow, John, 135, 154, 207, 210, 312,
    317
    quoted, 133-34, 141, 144, 146-47,
      148, 156, 313, 315, 322-23
Stratford, ix
Straw, Jack, 144, 145, 149, 234,
    358
Stury, Sir Richard, 82, 130, 132,
    133, 150, 303, 308, 309
Sudbury, Archbishop, 145
Suffolk, Earl of, 32, 206
Surrey, 22, 304
Sussex, 194
Swinburne, Algernon Charles, ix
  Short Notes on English Poets
    quoted on Chaucer, 337-38
Swynford, Sir Hugh, 45, 87
Swynford, Katharine, 47, 87, 128,
    204, 215, 220, 222, 309
  becomes Duchess of Lancaster,
    321
  descendants of, 322
  marries John of Gaunt, 321-22,
    375
Swynford, Sir Thomas de, 216
Syria, 84

Tabard Inn, 234-39
Tennyson, Alfred Lord, ix, 215,
    228, 343
  Choric Song
    quoted, 175
  Tears, idle tears, 64
Thames River, 26, 27, 303
Thibaut-le-Grand, 49, 50

[390]

Thomas, Prince (son of Henry Bolingbroke)
appointed steward of England, 317
Thompson, Francis, 194
Daisy
quoted, 176-77
Thomson, James
quoted on Chaucer, 333
Thoreau, Henry David
Homer, Ossian, Chaucer
quoted, 336
Trastamare, Enrique of, 72, 83
Tresilian, Sir Robert, 205, 210, 211
Trevelyan, G. M., 128, 129, 205
Troyes, Chrétien de, 49
Le Roman de la Charette, 49
Tuke, Sir Brian
quoted on Chaucer, 326-27
Tuscany, 110, 111
Tyburn Hill, 214
Tylar, John, 142
Tyler, Wat, 144, 147, 148, 154, 156, 205, 294
rebellion of, 139-49, 371
Tyrwhitt, Thomas, 17, 45, 231, 287, 289, 296

Uccello, Paolo, 137
Ulster, Elizabeth, Countess of, 29, 30, 82
Chaucer a page in household of, 30-31
Uske, Thomas, 211

Valenciennes, 42
Valois, Philippe of, 22
Venice, 102, 113, 114, 116, 135
Vere, Robert de (Earl of Oxford), 205, 206, 208, 211
defeat of, by Magnates at Radcot Bridge, 210
made Duke of Ireland, 207
Verona, 138
Gaspar of, 106
Versification, 64-70
Victoria, Queen, 60
Visconti, Bernabò, 137, 138, 158
Visconti, Violante, 47, 135

Wales, 210, 312
Prince of, 72, 73, 130
Princess of, 154

Wall Brook, 26, 28
Walton, Isaac, xiii
Walworth, William de, 125, 145, 148
Warwick, Earl of, 32, 73, 206, 210, 211, 212, 303, 310, 311
Watergate, 123
Webbe, William
quoted on Chaucer, 328
Wenceslaus (son of Charles IV), 157
Wessex, 22, 25
West Midlands, 25
Westminster, 25, 27, 39, 85, 103, 123, 127, 154, 207, 210, 212, 213, 223, 226, 298, 304, 310, 315, 357
Winchester, 212
Bishop of
see William of Wykeham
Windsor, castle of, 28, 29, 30, 56, 159, 208, 209, 299, 302, 305
Woodstock, 223
castle of, 30, 56
Woodstock, Thomas of, 86, 134, 145, 158, 206
see also Duke of Gloucester
Woolwich, 303
Worde, Wynkyn de, 18
Wordsworth, Dorothy
Journal
quoted on Chaucer, 334
Wordsworth, William, 215, 342
characteristics of poetry of, x
Sonnet Composed upon Westminster Bridge, 174
Wycliffe, John, x, 150-55
characteristics of, 152
opposition to existing ecclesiastical system, 153
Wykeham, William of (Bishop of Winchester), 208, 212, 303, 306

Yart, Abbé
quoted on Chaucer, 333
York, Archbishop of
see Thomas Arundel
and Alexander Neville
York, Edmund, Duke of, 206, 208, 222, 308, 309
Yorkshire, 30, 315
Ypres, 25, 124

[391]